Writer

OTHER BOOKS BY GRAEME KINROSS-SMITH

Mankind's Spies: How Writers Work
with G. V. Lawrence, *The Book of the Murray*
with Jamie Grant, *Turn Left at Any Time with Care*
Australia's Writers: An Illustrated Guide to their Lives and their Work
The Sweet Spot
with Joyce Evans, *Window to Australia*

ASSOCIATE EDITOR OF

The Oxford Literary Guide to Australia
Australian Sporting Anecdotes

Writer

A Working Guide for New Writers

Graeme Kinross-Smith

Melbourne

OXFORD UNIVERSITY PRESS

Oxford   Auckland   New York

OXFORD UNIVERSITY PRESS AUSTRALIA

Oxford New York
Athens Auckland Bangkok Bogota
Buenos Aires Calcutta Cape Town
Dar es Salaam Delhi Florence Hong Kong
Istanbul Karachi Kuala Lumpur Madrid
Melbourne Mexico City Mumbai Nairobi Paris
Port Moresby São Paulo Singapore Taipei
Tokyo Toronto

and associated companies in Berlin Ibadan

OXFORD is a trade mark of Oxford University Press

National Library of Australia
Cataloguing-in-Publication data:

Kinross-Smith, Graeme, 1936—

      Writer. A working guide for new writers.
      Bibliography.
      Includes index.
      ISBN 0 19 553231 7

      1. Authorship — handbooks, manuals etc. I.
      Title.

808.02

Edited by Nan McNab
Designed by Sarn Potter
Typeset by Syarikat Seng Teik Sdn. Bhd.
Printed through Bookpac Production Services, Singapore
Published by Oxford University Press,
253 Normanby Road, South Melbourne, Australia

Contents

For Judith,
who loves books, but
knows that a book in the writing is
a monster in the house.

*I do not doubt but the majesty and beauty of the world are
latent in any iota of the world . .*

*I do not doubt there is far more in trivialities, insects,
vulgar persons, slaves, dwarfs, weeds, rejected refuse, than
I have supposed . . .*

*I do not doubt interiors have their interiors, and exteriors
have their exteriors—and that the eye-sight has another eye-
sight, and the hearing another hearing, and the voice
another voice.*

Walt Whitman

*Learning music by reading about it is like making love by
mail . . .*

Isaac Stern

Acknowledgements

Many people, wittingly or unwittingly, have contributed to this book. My gratitude to them is heartfelt, remembering shared experience in the telling of stories in words. Of those named below, most are writers, but not all. Nevertheless, with nearly all these people I have sat down to talk about writing, art and life, and I have corresponded also with many of them.

First, there are those I interviewed and photographed while writing *Australia's Writers* during the 1970s and while continuing interviews during the 1980s with more recent writers whose stories might make a sequel to that book. Some of the earlier group—Alan Marshall, Christina Stead, Vin Buckley, R. D. FitzGerald, Hal Porter, Jack Johnston, Leonard Mann, Xavier Herbert, Judah Waten, Martin Johnston, Patrick White, Stephen Murray-Smith, James McAuley, Kylie Tennant and David Campbell among them—have died since then. Others continue to contribute richly to the tapestry of Australian writing—Peter Cowan, John Morrison, Dorothy Hewett, Frank Moorhouse, Bruce Dawe, Peter Carey, Peter Mathers, Murray Bail, John Blight, Roger MacDonald, David Malouf, Randolph Stow, Les Murray, Tom Hungerford, Mary Durack, Geoffrey Dutton, Thea Astley, Bruce Beaver, Ron Simpson, Axel Clark, Judith Wright, Maree Davison, Ruth Park, Thomas Keneally, Frank Hardy, David Williamson, David Rowbotham, and Dal Stivens.

There are those who have been colleagues and collaborators in writing, editing, photography and the teaching of writing—Vern Lawrence, Paul Carter, Philip Edmonds, William Mayne, Bob Burns, Rob Davies, Ian Reid, Brian Kiernan, Anna Rutherford, Bob Sessions, Peter Barclay, Matthew Kelly, Gerald Murnane, Gerry Tickell, John Forbes, Tony Delves, Bill Clydesdale, Beverley Farmer, Damien Broderick, Zoe Fairbairns, Peter Wilson, John Wallace, Clive Malseed, Ken Gray, Chris Fleming, Peter Lane, Sally Dugan, John Curtain, John Avieson, Peter Barclay, Murray Masterton, John Hurst, Sally White, Helene Chung, Graeme Coddington, Russell Grigg, Les Smith, Glen Tomasetti, Allan Johnston, John Barnes, Brian Thompson, Peter Pierce, Don Anderson, Henry Schoenheimer, Mark Johnston, Joyce Evans, Julie Brown-Rrap, Max Dupain, Gregory Corso, William Stafford, John O'Hara, Gordon Long, Mike Page, Patrick Tennison, Ian Wynd, Al Knight, Lyle Tucker, Frank Maloney, Jim Ellis, Rodney Hall, Barry Breen, Jenna Mead, Stan Lowe, Howard Bellin, Geoff Mauger, Tibor Selvay, Jack Clancy, Andrew Taylor, Alison Richards and others.

Over the years there have been many students and participants in workshops, principal among them Brian Cole, Isobel Carmody, Chris Fleming, Josephine Hoare, Andre Csauzov, and George Kubiak. And there are writers with whom I have shared public readings, seminars, conferences and writers' tours, many of whom have also offered honest second opinions of my work over the years—people such as Ron Simpson, Ania Walwicz, Lauris Edmond, Tom Shapcott, Robert Bly, Simon Hughes, Jennifer McKenzie, Jennifer Strauss, Alan Wearne, Jamie Grant, Judith Rodriguez, Π 0, Rod Usher, Philip Martin, Kevin Hart, Barry Hill, Rhyll McMaster, Michael Dugan, Philip Mead, Barry Dickins, Geoff Page, Barbara Giles, Myron Lysenko, Bev Roberts, Patrick Morgan, Mary Lord, William Dick, Dinny O'Hearn, Keith Harrison, Geoff D'Ombrain, Jenny Abella, Tom the Poet and John McLaren.

All these friends have provided influence, insight and example. I offer my special thanks also to the following friends and colleagues who have helped with specific advice, information and illustration, or who have checked sections of the text of *Writer*: Chris Fleming and Ken Gray of Clemenger; Peter Lane, Les Smith, Russell Grigg, John Avieson and Andrew Taylor of Deakin University; Lynne Ellis; Clive Malseed; Gary Wong; Howard Bellin; Colin Tyrus; Brett McLeod; Alison Richards; Isobel Carmody; Ruth Saunders; and Barry Dickins.

Finally, without the institutional understanding and flexibility of Deakin University in making it possible for me to devote meaningful time to the research for *Writer*; the book and its usefulness would be much the poorer.

The author and publisher wish to thank copyright holders for granting permission to reproduce copyright material. Sources are as follows:

Roger McGough: Extract from poem 'Why patriots are a bit nuts in the head' used with permission of Peters Fraser & Dunlop. William Stafford: Extract from poem 'Travelling through the dark' used with permission of William Stafford. Francis Webb: Poem 'Five days old' from *Selected poems* by Francis Webb used with permission of Collins Angus & Robertson. Denise Levertov: Extract from poem 'and as you read' by Denise Levertov, New Directions, New York. Paul Goodman: Haiku 'With your fists ablaze' from *Collected poems* by Paul Goodman used with permission of Sally Goodman. Basho: Haiku 'Breaking the silence . . .' and 'At sunrise I saw . . .' from *The narrow road to the deep north*, translated by Nobuyuki Yuasa, used with permission of Lemon Unna & Durbridge. Charles Reznikoff: Haiku 'This smoky winter morning' from *By the waters of Manhattan*, New Directions, New York. Ogden Nash: Extract from poem 'Kind of an ode to duty' used with permission of Curtis Brown Ltd. Retta Hemensley: Poem 'Egoism' used with permission of Retta Hemensley. Dorothy Hewett: Quote from the film 'Rapunzel in suburbia', directed by Patricia L'Huede and produced with assistance from the Women's Film Fund, the Australian Film Commission and the Literature Board and Archival Film Program of the Australia Council, used with permission of Patricia L'Huede. David Campbell: Poem 'Night sowing' from *Collected poems* by David Campbell used with permission of Collins Angus & Robertson. R. A. Simpson: Poem 'Diver' used with permission of R. A. Simpson. William Carlos Williams: Extract from poem 'Hunters in the snow' from *Pictures from Breughel and other poems* by William Carlos Williams, New Directions, New York. W. H. Auden: Poem 'Musee des beaux arts' from *The English Auden* used with permission of Faber and Faber Ltd. Craig Raine: Extracts from poem 'A Martian sends a postcard home' from *A Martian sends a postcard home* by Craig Raine used with permission of Oxford University Press. William Stafford: Poem 'The woman at Banff' from *Travelling through the dark* by William Stafford used with permission of William Stafford. John Morrison: Extract from 'Morning glory' from *The best stories of John Morrison* by John Morrison used with permission of Penguin Books Australia. Patrick White: Extract from *The aunt's story* by Patrick White used with permission of Penguin Books Australia. Thomas Keneally: Extracts from *Schindler's ark* by Thomas Keneally used with permission of T. Sayle Agency. AFTRS: Material from the 'Writers on writing' video series used with permission of the Australian Film, Television and Radio School. Cadbury: Paraphrasing of Cadbury Dairy Milk Chocolate television commercial. Esso Australia: Advertising slogan 'Put a tiger in your tank' used with permission of Esso Australia Ltd. PR Model: Public Relations Practitioner model from *The Australian public relations manual* by Candy Tymson and Bill Sherman, developed by Carol Clark, Gavin Anderson & Company, used with permission of Carol Clark. Ira Gershwin: Lyric 'I got rhythm' from *Lyrics on several occasions* by Ira Gershwin used with permission of Hamish Hamilton Ltd. Billy Joel: Lyric 'Baby grand' by Billy Joel, © 1986 Joel Songs, for Australasia EMI Songs Australia Pty Ltd, P O Box C156, Cremorne Junction, NSW 2090.

Every effort has been made to trace the source of all copyright material contained in this book. Where the attempt has been unsuccessful, the publisher would be pleased to hear from the author/publisher concerned, to rectify any omission.

Preface

Writing—and the teaching of writing—are of paramount importance to me. They are inextricably tied into my life, my way of thinking, my work. Writing, and to a lesser extent the photography that sometimes accompanies it, allow me to make sense of the world, to explain it to myself, to tell others what I see in it, whether I'm writing 'factual' material, fiction or poetry. Each piece I write is a story to be told. *Writer* is for those people for whom telling stories is as important, ultimately more important, than hearing or reading them. It is not a handbook—it covers more areas of writing than almost any other book in the field—it is a personal, idiosyncratic, hands-on introduction to writing as a craft and an art.

Writing can't be taught in any direct sense, but it can be learned, as the development of any professional writer attests. The writing course, writers' workshop, or this book—which is something of a workshop in print—in fact anything that helps you learn to write, is valuable. Books like this should provide an environment in which writing will happen, in which the professional writer's experience allows new writers to understand strengths and weaknesses in writing technique earlier than they would otherwise. In short, this book can provide a more efficient means of learning to write and gaining expertise. It cannot provide the personal spark that produces good writing, but it will uncover a spark that otherwise might have been smothered by lack of confidence, lack of opportunity, or by the sheer demands of daily living. Work with this book can provide confidence and fulfilment in ways that may surprise you. It can take writing from its high pedestal and present it instead as an activity that everyone can practise at some level to make sense of their experience.

Professional writing requires a great deal of time and application to achieve excellence, but in any endeavour the first step, and perhaps the most important, is to have a go. This book encourages you to hazard yourself in story-telling, and to develop your potential as a writer.

You yourself will bring to this book some understanding and skill in the art or craft of writing. Perhaps the most important factor in developing these skills is reading, for an attentive and discriminating reader has already encountered the best writing tutor—good prose or poetry. Other skills will come gradually. Often this happens when you are faced with a working problem in your current writing. The problem becomes acute and meaningful forcing you to learn ways to solve it.

Writer starts from the premise that your raw material in story-telling is *your* experience expressed in *your* words. It will be primarily direct experience, but writers are also readers and thinkers, and other people's ideas and experience are available to them. It's a matter of making connections. Writers are often inspired by what they read or hear or see.

Similarly, as you work through this book, you will become a student of what people have written. You don't need to enrol in a tertiary course in literature to gain ideas from these pieces of writing and to learn from other writers' techniques. The writer needs to be artistically and culturally aware, so this book is something of a cultural reference list, dealing with the arts that influence writing and which in turn are influenced by writing. The arts need each other, support each other, draw fire and spirit and hope from each other.

Writer invites you to combine experience and words, to experiment with them in telling your stories. The emphasis is on getting started, brainstorming, putting words on paper, going through the creative mess that enables you to see what your story will be. You will concentrate on making statements, on writing, without being particularly concerned about whether it is poetry or prose. You will be encouraged to think about telling stories from experience, and about the use of words and rhythm.

As you move towards poetry, and later begin writing it more consciously, you will encounter the words of the English language used to their full potential. Of all forms, poetry is the guardian of the language, using words specifically, drawing meaning from them, drawing power from their variety and fine distinctions. *Writer* is organized not only according to the depth of word use in writing, but also on you and your progress. A graded writing guide and introduction to writing forms, it introduces elements of the writing process when they become pertinent to you. For example, sections on manuscript presentation, or research, or the use of photography are not held over for an appendix: they appear in the sections of the book where they are most applicable. You can also use the Contents to refer to them wherever you may be in your reading.

Even if your main interest is in writing for radio or television, or journalism or public relations, it is important to follow the book's programme and not skip to later chapters. The skills you learn early on in the areas of poetry and prose fiction will be important in your later writing; the sensibility you develop will affect your work in those applied writing areas. All of the writing specializations dealt with in the second half of the book draw on the sophistication of language in the more 'pure' forms, but in ways specific to their character. Finally and most importantly, beginning as we do with 'creative' writing (and all writing is creative in some sense) means that new writers have a greater chance to experiment and express their individuality in a variety of forms and that is a natural starting point, since your writing will spring from *your* ideas and no one else's.

In Parts One to Three, you will do much of the basic training, and receive necessary advice about writing in general. By the time you reach the later and more applied sections, your skill in word use, in structuring stories, and your knowledge of how the writing world works will have been well established, and your writing can develop into something more practical, or market-specific, or professional. The book moves from 'deep' word use through analysis and practice of language and story-telling in poetry and in prose fiction in Part Two and Three, and then in Part Four to the forms that bridge the gap between fiction and fact—memoirs, life histories, autobiographies, and biographies. Part Five tackles the demands of writing for forms where vision and sound, rather than print, are paramount: first, story-telling for stage performance, followed by the application of those dramatic skills in film and radio scripts. *Writer* next introduces you to writing that is more closely linked to a market and market forces—areas that are also generally more lucrative for the writer. Certain skills are by this stage taken for granted, and you will be involved in writing advertising copy in Part Six, in writing for the media in other ways, in hard news journalism, feature journalism, radio and television journalism in Part Seven, in public relations for all media in Part Eight, and in song-writing for the popular music market in Part Nine.

In *Writer* story-telling comes first. The writer must often be able to tap spontaneous feeling. Writers' passions, loves, enthusiasms, and their concomitants and opposites, provide much of their power to affect readers. These in turn must be put into words. Writers, engaged in creating a piece of writing, often have to speak almost inarticulately about the work in progress in terms of whether the piece 'works' or not. In fact writers often know instinctively, when they are in the midst of a work, that it is dangerous to say anything about a passage of writing that is proving difficult or about an idea for a novel or poem. The inner fire that keeps them imagining it, and focussing on it, and writing it, may smoulder and go out if they do. Gulley Jimson, the painter in Joyce Cary's novel, *The horse's mouth*, mutters under his breath: 'Dangerous to talk too much about your work. It fixes it. It nails it down. And then it bleeds. It begins to die'.

However, at a later stage writers must begin to assess the quality of their own work. They begin to think about 'pace' and 'balance', 'contrast' and 'point of view', 'handling of time', 'tone of voice' and 'person'. This self-assessment can be a daunting, lonely and salutary task. It is important to distinguish between writing and writers' assessment of their own work on the one hand and criticism on the other. Writing and reading are natural bedfellows; writing and 'Literature' are not. There is a crucial disjunction of time and of imagination between them. Yes, writers are readers and have critical faculties, but basic story-telling, which provides the meat for criticism and literary appreciation, is crucial. Yes, the structures of literary criticism can usefully illuminate and expand our view of what writers create, but in the final analysis writers, as distinct from students of literature or practitioners of literary theory, do not need criticism, which can, at worst, distract them from their art. Even though writers as readers are influenced and invigorated by the techniques and ideas of other writers, writing, that basic act of creation, must come first.

In *Writer* the writer's story, the writer's point of view, are always of primary importance; it is the writer's voice that is heard. Anton Chekhov, the Russian writer of short stories and plays, speaks for many writers when he says disarmingly, humbly, and with a touch of irony:

I have often been reproached, even Tolstoy has reproached me, for writing about trifles . . . I haven't acquired a political, philosophical outlook on life. I keep changing it every month, and I therefore have to confine myself to descriptions of how my characters love, get married, beget children, and talk and die . . .

Graeme Kinross-Smith
1992

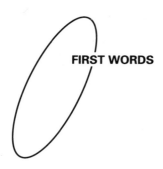

FIRST WORDS

'How do I know what I think until I see what I say?'

A writer is not so much someone who has something to say as he is someone who has found a process that will bring about new things he would not have thought of if he had not started to say them.

William Stafford

Get struck by the bolt of obsession . . .

Tony Morphett

Getting started

Writing does not take place unless pen touches paper, unless a keyboard is struck on a typewriter or word processor, unless you are prepared to commit your ideas to words. I have used all three ways of putting words down so that they can communicate their story and be assessed. I once wrote everything with a reliable ball-point pen—plans; jottings; first, second, third and subsequent drafts—and then typed up a final manuscript. Now I still plan and jot and take notes with the pen, but as my typing improved, I learned to type a first draft using my planning notes as a guide. Then, with the advent of the word processor, it was easy to move from handwritten notes and planning to a first draft tapped into the word processor. Depending on the material I am writing, I now find myself taking notes and planning on the word processor, and then tapping a first draft into the hard disk.

The word processor is a marvellous device for writing fiction, articles or poetry; it enables the writer to put slabs of words on to a screen so that they can be read, listened to with the inner ear, shaped more tenderly, and printed out on paper.

Whatever you use to write, it is important to overcome the major problem of new writers—the difficulty of 'making a mark'! Train yourself not to delay the act of putting pen to paper when you sit down to write. When you rough out a draft it does not matter too much where you start. Start *somewhere*, and eventually you will discover the ideal starting-point.

Do your thinking on paper. Plan on paper. Don't be afraid to waste paper! That does not necessarily mean wasting trees—in this early and rough stage of production you can use the clean backs of photostats or used computer paper. Be prepared to muck about on paper: ideas often begin to germinate in that free-wheeling way. As even the most experienced writer will tell you, the first thoughts, the first notes, leading to any piece of polished writing often appear messy and gauche, decipherable only by the writer, of little use to anyone else, but invaluable to their creator.

Experience and ideas: telling about them

I grew up in Brooklyn, not Chicago, but the atmosphere had the same flatness of effect. Until then I had never considered my life or the life of the people around me as even remotely worthy of—well, I didn't believe they could be treated as subjects for fiction. It had never occurred to me. Suddenly I realised you could write about your own life.

Norman Mailer

First, there is experience; any experience; not necessarily cataclysmic experience. All experience is valuable, relevant for the artist. As Samuel Taylor Coleridge said, 'There is nothing dissonant that tells of life.' Meaningful and moving stories come from experience and detail, used skilfully.

Let's try something straight away. It is the ploy that the Australian writer Alan Marshall used when he was approaching his autobiographical trilogy that starts with *I can jump puddles*. Life, he maintained, was a landscape of relatively featureless plains interspersed with peaks of experience, moments of much greater import and interest that changed one's outlook. He decided to plot those peaks and structure his story around them. He made a list of some eighty such peaks, simply summarized on the page—'learning to swim', 'the day I fought the boy with sticks'.

Write

Follow Marshall's example. List all the peaks in your own life up to the present. You'll notice that some of the more recent ones are less clear-cut in your mind, simply because you are not yet able to assess their ultimate significance in your life. But what you put down now, and the other peaks that you are sure to add to your list as they come to you later, will be a basic resource for everything you do in this book.

Now look at your brief summary of experience. Choose one event to write about at greater length. It will be an occasion that is still vivid, luminous, memorable. It probably involves you in a change of heart, or a revelation, or what might be called a 'life-step'. And yet, your fascination may stem from not quite knowing what it means. You may want to write about it to find out what, at its deepest level, it means to you. Notice that I am talking about it in the present tense: write about it in the present tense, as if it is happening before you in all its detail. Write quickly. Don't think about how to say what you want to get down. Start *somewhere* rather than wait for the ideal opening. Try to capture the event in no more than an A4 page of writing, as if you were telling the essence of it to another person. Write it, round it off, then stop.

What have you caught in your net? Read what you have written and weigh its importance. This is a draft of some of your experience. You may have already overcome the fear common to new writers that their experience is not 'deep' or significant enough to write about. That is nonsense. What is important about the experience you have written about is that it is yours, unique, and no one else can write about it as you can. You have the material from which to write—it is sacrosanct, it is yours, and, as we shall see later, if you go too far beyond it, you may strike trouble in convincing the reader.

Think again about what you have written. Did you realize until you had written it what you had to say? Did you have any idea that you would say it that way? Did you find detail surrounding the story that came, as it were, from nowhere: detail that you thought was lost? Does the piece you have written suggest other ideas, other stories you might follow up? If you are answering yes to any or all of these questions then perhaps there are common elements in all of this. To introduce them, I have some propositions to make.

• You are possessed of a marvellous computer. It is quite likely that you do not appreciate fully what it can do for you. It sits on your shoulders, surrounded by its sensory inputs, and unless you are very tired, or your blood sugar is low, it is eager to work for you.

• Your computer craves material, problems, and memory tests to work on. Given them, it begins work immediately, even though your attention might be distracted from the problems or questions you have thrown to it. It can work well in the subconscious mode and it has a memory capacity that will astound you at times.

• Your computer, although eager to solve problems, test its memory, organize the material that might become a story, *cannot* do any of these things until you prompt it with some initial planning. In my experience this is best done on paper. The earlier you sit down to that brainstorming, to writing lists, phrases, telegraphic ideas, arrowed instructions or crass initial lines of text, the better. Then the problem is registered in your conscious and subconscious and you will find your 'computer' working on it at the strangest times and coming up with suggestions and answers.

We can draw some conclusions from this.

• Writers, like other artists, are often arch-procrastinators, easily distracted workers. You may be no exception!

• This small detail can often be solved by trusting your 'computer', trusting yourself, and being prepared to risk putting your thoughts quickly on paper in jottings that become a plan of attack. Don't worry about writing things that later appear foolish. These 'mistakes' are necessary to bring out what you need.

• This plan begins to refine itself in your mind; you start to select what you *want* to say from the wealth of material you *could* say. As Archibald Macleish, the American poet, put it: 'The acts of selection are the actions of art'.

• This initial stage of writing is invariably messy, and yet the disorder is creative. No writer, no artist, is exempt from the uncertainty and creative floundering involved in this stage of making something new.

Despite these common elements, it is difficult to generalize about writing. Each writer is different and uses different strategies to produce her work. Each article, short story, poem, or novel presents itself in a different way and demands a different approach, poses a different set of problems. Not all writers need to do their early thinking with pen and paper; some will delay starting a draft by making notes and writing 'scenes' to get the feel of the work. Usually these are the practices of experienced and professional writers. I have a writer friend who for twenty years has had over sixty titles in print. He is so skilled at selecting a milieu, devising characters, imagining the twists of his stories, that he sometimes comes to a first draft with nothing but some skeletal notes. He taps it straight into his word processor, prints it out and mails the draft to his agent, who on some occasions has sold the book to a publisher before the author has begun his fine corrections! But all that is the product of years of experience and hardly a realistic method for a new writer!

Sometimes even experienced writers find it hard to say where or when a particular piece of work began. Some pieces of writing may have been gestating in the mind for months or years, and require a particular catalyst to bring them out. Others, unfortunately very few, seem to spring ready-crafted from the mind and on to the page. This generally means that your 'computer' has been working on them in its subconscious mode. Such 'given' pieces of writing probably result from a great deal of decision-making and thought that you never dreamt would express itself in that form. They are part of your accumulated life-wisdom and subconscious thought.

PART ONE

Seeking poetry

Keep the language of the tribe pure; remind people of their

humanity; make the rulers uncomfortable; corrupt the

young; ask what it means to be; make images inexhaustible

to nature . . .

Charles Simic

I think poetry is written mainly for pleasure, by which I

mean the pleasure of pain, horror, anguish and awe, as

well as the pleasure of beauty, music and the act of living.

Kenneth Slessor

Poetry and the scale of word-use

Let us assume for the moment that any statement that is made with words is a story. We know that many stories are told in other ways—through vision, touch, sound and, arguably, through taste and smell. But for now we are interested in *written* words.

Consider the following list of forms that writing can take:
business memo
business letter
private note or letter
instruction manual
'hard' news story (for print, radio, TV)
job advertisement
general or 'for sale' advertisement
factual feature article
book, record or film review
academic article (scientific, literary, etc.)
copywriting or commercial advertising
factual radio or TV script
interpretive, investigative journalism
biography
human interest story
'colour' piece or feature
autobiography
copywriting fiction or video-clip
radio, TV or film drama script
play
novel
novella
'*recit*' (a short novel that is strongly autobiographical)
short prose fiction
short story
prose poem
poem
This is not an exhaustive list, and the range of forms within some of these general descriptions can be considerable—there are so many different forms of short fiction, for example, or feature articles, or poems. We will make some of these finer distinctions later.

For now consider how this list of writing forms is arranged and what points it has to make. I see in it a general logical progression. What governs it?

If English is your first language, you have at your command a greater range of words, phrases, subtle shades of meaning and distinction than in any other language. At which end of the scale of story-telling is that language used most deeply and richly in terms of sophisticated vocabularies, refined meanings, even multiple meanings?

Just to underline the point, listen to the openings of two pieces of writing. First, a business letter from a publisher, with its direct and practical 'story'.

Dear Graeme

You may recall that when the first series of Paperback Poets concluded we published *The first paperback poets anthology* edited by Roger MacDonald. This anthology sold well and now, with the conclusion of the second series, Tom Shapcott, UQP's current poetry editor, has put together *Consolidation: the second paperback poets anthology.* I'm attaching a copy of the Contents so that you can see what of yours have been included . . .

It is a pleasant, relaxed, well-worded and informative business communication, and not an example of the more extreme and soulless business letter that runs 'Yours of the 17th Ult. received. We will expedite the goods as soon as available . . .' Nevertheless, compare these two missives with a Roger McGough poem, which arrests the reader from the first words of its title, a title which introduces the opening line of McGough's story.

>*Why patriots are a bit nuts in the head*
>Patriots are a bit nuts in the head
>because they wear
>red, white and blue-
>tinted spectacles
>(red for blood
>white for glory
>and blue . . .
>for a boy)
>and are in effervescent danger
>of losing their lives . . .

Listen to the opening of one of William Stafford's poems, speaking from the American west-coast country around Oregon and into the mountain chains through which he often travels.

>*Travelling through the dark*
>Travelling through the dark I found a deer
>dead on the edge of the Wilson River road.
>It is usually best to roll them into the canyon:
>that road is narrow; to swerve might make more dead.

The poem's narrator, in this case William Stafford himself, drags the deer off the road, but discovers that it is a doe, that its side is big and still warm with an unborn fawn.

> The car aimed ahead its lowered parking lights;
> under the hood purred the steady engine.
> I stood in the glare of the warm exhaust turning red;
> around our group I could hear the wilderness listen.
>
> I thought hard for us all—my only swerving—
> then pushed her over the edge into the river.

Immediately questions hang in the air. We are aware that both poets have a personally observed, emotionally felt story to tell. We want further human details. Given even these few lines it seems that Stafford's experience is something he will probably carry with him to the end of his life. And yet neither story-teller uses complex words or difficult language structures. So what is going on? How is this power achieved?

Let's look at another poet's story, and then make comparisons and draw conclusions. This is the opening of a poem by the Australian poet, Francis Webb. He is telling us what it felt like to be offered a five-day-old baby to hold—a new experience for him.

> *Five days old*
> Christmas is in the air.
> You are given into my hands
> Out of quietest, loneliest lands.
> My trembling is all my prayer.
> To blown straw was given
> All the fullness of Heaven . . .

The language, the words, are under a stress that gives them beauty and meaning. They are being asked to carry clues about things that are not directly stated. You can hear the story of Christianity and the Bible in them. You can detect the idea of a gift. You can feel the fervency of prayer. Blown straw is contrasted with the fullness of Heaven. Rising out of this is the unstated, the moving, impression of Webb's humility in the presence of the baby. Later, he describes himself as being 'wonderingly engrossed' in the baby's 'fearless delicacies'. Look back and see how far we have come from the way words are used in the business letter. Think of a baby, its face, hands, limbs, movement. Fearless delicacies! Webb goes on to study the baby's face. Again in the words he chooses there is the suggestion of how humble, how privileged, he feels.

Too pure for my tongue to praise,
That sober, exquisite yawn
Or the gradual, generous dawn
At an eyelid, maker of days . . .

A baby's 'sober, exquisite yawn' and the 'gradual, generous dawn at an eyelid': these lines do not use words in their usual or literal context, but as images and metaphors to sharpen the impression of the baby, to deepen its essence.

The first thing to say about poetry, and sometimes other forms of imaginative writing, is that its story is frequently told in imagery. Forget rhyme and rhythm and the other attributes usually used to distinguish poetry from prose, and consider the way poetry makes its points through images. It is often a matter of the poet looking at one thing, but seeing something else, of saying not only that something is *like* this, but that it *is* this. The American poet Denise Levertov finishes one of her short poems:

—and as you read
the sea is turning its dark pages
turning
its dark pages

We not only accept the metaphor, the image of the waves as pages turning, but the line arrangement and the rhythm of the words and syllables allows us almost to *hear* the waves breaking on the shore.

All this is to make the basic point that the language of poetry and other imaginative writing is a far cry from the plainer and more unequivocal language in most of the early forms of writing in the table above—the business letter, the 'hard' news story, the business memo, the instruction manual, the job advertisement. That's not surprising: different sorts of writing serve different purposes. In writing such as the business letter or technical brochure the aim is to use words well to convey clear information. Intelligence is involved in the word-use: emotion and powerful feeling seldom are. In poetry, however, words can dart round a corner and bite you, so novel is the way in which they are used, to stun, humble and move you with the emotion they transmit.

Look back at the lines of Francis Webb to see how else he gains his power over us. Look at his line endings, plot them as matching rhymes; this is poetry that offers us beautiful echoes. If the sound at the first line ending is nominated 'a' and the second 'b' and so on, we discover a rhyme scheme that runs a-b-b-a-c-c for the stanza. It is another way in which the language and its sounds are employed at a deep level that has much in common with music. If we listen more closely to the rhythm of the lines we find that each line has two main beats in it, so that even in this short extract our breathing rhythm chimes with the words. It throws our attention back to groups of words, parts of sentences, and the role of the sentence itself. Robert Frost, the American poet, says: 'I give you a new definition of a sentence: A sentence is a sound in itself, on which other sounds called words may be strung.'

Our emphasis here is on words, word-use, the resources of the language, the many ways in which the language can be used. This book is arranged on that basis. The language consists of and can create single-beat sounds or syllables; words; phrases; sentences; paragraphs; verses or stanzas; sections; chapters; short stories; longer stories; novellas; novels; shorter poems; longer poems. Even pauses can be vital, represented by blanks on white paper, between words, line ends, sentences, verses, chapters, sections, parts of a work. There are equivalents of all these in other arts—in painting, film, music, photography and theatre.

Roger McGough and William Stafford use the language to give power to their pieces—perhaps unwittingly or unconsciously, or intuitively, with the skill born of experiencing, listening, looking, and writing stories with words.

What is arresting about McGough's title and opening? Patriots, he tells us, are 'a bit nuts in the head', and then he repeats the notion in his first line. He goes on to imagine them wearing tinted spectacles modelled on the colours of the British (or for that matter the Australian or American) flag. But the tone of voice is set by those slightly slangy words, '. . . a bit nuts in the head', which are at once childish and direct. It is a tone of voice that continues to underlie what the poem is naively yet wisely demonstrating to us. In 'effervescent danger of losing their lives' we can hear the threat fizzing away, ready to explode, in that word effervescent. Again it is language used under stress, a word twisted out of its normal context, used in an unexpected situation and therefore given sharpness and power. We don't stop to think that it is also an image, a metaphor, coming to us through an adjective. Poetry is primarily metaphor.

William Stafford's way of reaching us through language is very different. Look at the opening of his poem again. He tells his story very simply, in practical language using plain words couched in uncomplicated sentences. It is what he chooses to describe that has so much power. He enables us to feel the event with him. He hardly ever resorts to direct metaphor—'the steady engine'—but the poem has elements in it that are basic to human experience. There is travelling and darkness, elemental life, death, wilderness and a terrible decision. Stafford's dilemma becomes ours.

The other source of power in Stafford's poem, although it is written in 'free verse' with no regular rhyme, is its rhythm. Compare the opening

11

two lines with the opening sentence of the business letter and the
inexorable tread in Stafford's lines will come to you through his words.
Most of the lines have a basic five beats to them, but they are not slavish-
ly regular. If you look at Webb's poem you will find a different but
equally powerful rhythm. Webb's lines have varying beats—sometimes
two basic beats, sometimes three—but he has carefully controlled the
rhythm so that no sudden paroxysms trouble its steady flow.

Write

Somewhere in your knowledge of the world there are plain statements
that you want to utter. That's what we are going to do.

You are only allowed a sentence. Note, by the way, that all the poetry
above is couched in proper sentences. Novice writers sometimes believe
that poetry is chopped-up prose, not written in sentences, divided by
slashes or dots, or that it is a series of phrases that end with '-ing' —
searing, flying cascading, undulating, etc. Nonsense. Beware the present
participle! Plain statements in pure sentences are what we want, for the
moment, at least, but plain does not mean uninteresting. Robert Frost
tells us: 'Somebody has said that poetry among other things is the marrow of wit. That's probably way back somewhere—marrow of wit.
There's got to be wit. And that's very, very much left out of a lot of this
laboured stuff. It doesn't sparkle at all.'

Write a sentence or two, with something intriguing to say, something
with an edge to it, a laugh in it, a surprise. Try to write with the utter
simplicity, brevity and depth that poets use in haiku, the Japanese poetic
form of seventeen syllables arranged in three lines (5–7–5). We'll return
to the haiku later. You need not count syllables in your sentence—I
mention haiku only as a form that emphasizes compression and yet has
depth, wit, point, revelation, surprise.

Begin each line at the left margin of your paper, but don't carry it to
the right margin; break it where rhythm seems to dictate a new line.
Give it a title, maybe when you have written and rewritten your sentence,
arranged its lines and rearranged them, repeated them to your inner ear
(or aloud) to test them. A final requirement: your poem is to be an
apology to someone or some thing, not unlike a recent piece of mine:

To my father
I am sorry
all those years ago
to have mistaken
your sister for a witch.

It was just that
stumbling out of sleep

after you had driven us
to Sydney
I came on her
from behind
in her black dressing-gown
her hair hanging
over the porridge
she was stirring . . .

When I spoke
she turned
to look at me.
She did not have
her teeth in.
You must remember
I was only seven
and had not seen her
for three years.

You can extend your individual and idiosyncratic apology beyond the one sentence if you have to, but not beyond three! All we want is a minimalist apology, but not necessarily in the tone of voice that mine adopts. Write!

When you have finished, cast an eye over what you have written. What happened as you sought for the subject of your apology? What about the person or thing it was addressed to? Was it to someone close to you? your lover? sister? brother? child? Was it to a car? Was it a deeply felt apology or was it flippant? If so, have you thought why? Was it an apology to the wilderness? to the sea? to an African child? to a fellow worker? to a relative now dead? to your guitar? your new gold chain? your surfboard? your old school? your books? your armchair?

Did this request for an apology touch you in a way that you didn't expect? Did it bring up things from the past, or unacknowledged things from the present? Did it impel you to use words in a certain way? Did it bring its own imagery with it? Was it a discovery as you wrote?

Several of these questions relate to your depth of feeling about the apology, the object or person for whom it is intended, and the effect of this on the words you need to express it honestly. This line of thought will recur at a number of levels as we explore different forms of the written word and its messages. You will have discovered in this and your earlier piece of writing that at this end of the writing or word-use scale you often have to admit your feelings, your emotions, to write convincingly. Despite this, you will soon discover that a simple spill of emotion does not make art. Art is worked over, is drafted and redrafted, and makes a new truth that does not lose sight of its original strength of feeling.

Drafting: how to say it best

How many drafts did you make of this short piece before you judged that it was as good as you could make it? Look at the finished version. Have you been too easily satisfied with it? Writers often go back to try other words and arrangements, drafting again and again. Drafts multiply: paper is consumed. Mozart, who composed almost entirely in his head and then transcribed his music with hardly a mistake or alteration is the exception: it is rare for a writer to be completely satisfied with a first draft.

During what one might call the stage of creative exploration, ideas and ways of saying things are discovered. It is an argument for putting pen to paper quickly, so that there is something *written* and visible to build on, although some experienced writers would argue for long thought before writing a word. Whichever way you choose, every writer goes through this process in some way at the beginning of a new work, and often at the beginning of each new section, new chapter, or new scene within the work.

Haiku

Five syllables in your first line, seven in your second, five again in your third—that is the Japanese form of haiku. Some novelists write haiku when they come to the desk in the morning to tone up their verbal muscles which can become slack unless exercised. The writer plays with words, discovers her distinctive voice, feels at home again, and proceeds.

Haiku, as Saul Bass says in his film *Why man creates*, is the art of looking at one thing and seeing something else. Here is a sample.

> With your fists ablaze
> with letters and coloured stamps
> beautiful mailman.
> Paul Goodman

Two of my Fishing Haiku:

> Painting this I'd have
> sky with trees trusting the cliff—
> the sea applauding.

> It's as if my eyes
> distil these wheeling ibis
> sun's milk in their wings.

The seventeenth century Japanese writer, Basho, recorded in haiku his experiences of travelling about Japan. They are beautifully crafted snap-shots of what he saw and felt centuries ago, but richer than snapshots because they touch deeper emotions in a tradition where the features of the natural world—reeds, lakes, water-birds, moonlight, mountain peaks, trees—have a mythic and religious significance beyond their physical presence. The seventeen Japanese syllables often result in a greater number in English translation. Basho's translator, Nobuyuki Yuasa, explains that the conversational tone of haiku lends itself to a four-line stanza or poem in English rhythm. As you read more deeply in haiku you realize you are entering not only an art, but a philosophy. This is Basho:

> Breaking the silence
> Of an ancient pond,
> A frog jumped into water—
> A deep resonance.

> At sunrise I saw
> Tanned faces of fishermen
> Among the flowers
> Of white poppy.

Write

Try writing some haiku. Walk, take a ride on a tram or bus, watch people, the passing parade, and describe it with utmost economy; look at one thing and see another. Write urban haiku, perhaps, in the style of the Manhattan poet, Charles Reznikoff; his haiku is very much of the late twentieth century, and yet he shares with Basho a particular way of seeing the world.

> *This smoky winter morning*
> This smoky winter morning—
> do not despise the green jewel shining among the twigs
> because it is a traffic light.

This piece has Frost's 'marrow of wit'. Look at the way the picture balances on the word 'despise' and the way the experience changes after the image of 'the green jewel' is revealed, at the last moment, as a traffic light. The power of this story is largely in the telling; so is the power of a joke, a legend, a ballad, a mystery, a feature article, a TV ad, a video-clip . . .

Poem titles: beginnings

Look at this list.

- Man about to enter sea
- A perfectly ordinary rainbow
- Tadpoles in the Grampians
- Nu plastik fanfare red
- Five days late
- Tourists in love
- Bricking a camel
- Sleeping in
- Nude descending a staircase
- Anthem for doomed youth
- In a station of the metro
- Noonday axeman
- Loving Hitler
- On the school bus
- Kissing
- Cock crow
- A book of Arnold Newman's portraits
- Credo
- Night sowing
- Woman to man
- Enter without so much as knocking
- Phallus
- The fury of aerial bombardment
- The door
- Suburban sonnet
- Into the forest
- Tibooburra cricket
- Travelling through the dark
- A child's essay about the sea
- Words with a black orpington
- On stopping by woods on a snowy evening

These are titles of poems; the ways a number of writers chose to open poems. Sometimes the title serves also as the first line, and some of them have also served as titles for books or collections of poetry.

Let the titles run through your mind; think of the range of experience they suggest. If you are hoping to go into advertising copywriting this is the sort of economy and intrigue you will often be seeking in your work. Could you write a poem for any of them? If so, try.

Write

Now make a list of poem titles from your life. Give them this mixture of irony, wit, this meditative quality, brevity, naivety, humour. List six perhaps. You could write under any one of them, perhaps repeating it as a first line. But pick the one that most immediately interests you, one you can see a way of writing about now. You might already hear words and ideas flowing from it, perhaps even a structure forming. Write the poem. Allow yourself *wide* margins: this is a first draft, and you will probably need to alter and annotate it. Leave room for that. It is not quite what you want yet. Your lines will be governed by what you hear in your head as you write. They will seldom, if ever, extend to the right-hand margin.

Keep to an *upper* limit of, say, twenty lines to tell your story. Say exactly what the experience was like; use imagery to do it, and write in complete sentences, breaking them where your inner ear tells you that a new line is apt. Remember that your story will not be prosaic. You can set your imagination free at this stage, so that you don't merely describe, but make something new from your experience.

As you write a first draft, the words of Ted Hughes, the English poet, will accompany you.

Imagine what you are writing about. See it and live it. Do not think it up laboriously as if you were doing mental arithmetic. Just look at it, touch it, smell it, listen to it, turn yourself into it. When you do this, the words look after themselves, like magic. If you do this you do not have to bother about commas or full stops or that sort of thing. You do not look at the words either. You keep your eyes, your ears, your nose, your taste, your touch, your whole being on the thing you are turning into words. The minute you flinch, and take your mind off this thing, and begin to look at the words and worry about them . . . then your worry goes into them and they set about killing each other. So you keep going as long as you can, then look back and see what you have written. After a bit of practice, and after telling yourself a few times that you do not care how other people have written about this thing, this is the way you find it; and after telling yourself you are going to use any old word that comes into your head so long as it seems right at the moment of writing it down, you will surprise yourself. You will read back through what you have written and you will get a shock. You will have captured a spirit, a creature.

Redrafting

Now you have the first draft of a poem. It is longer than a haiku. Even as you read it over again, there are parts of it you want to change, and others you are proud of, where the words you have spent are 'right', have an almost musical quality, rhythm and justness to them.

What next? Find another sheet of paper. Rewrite sections of the poem,

change line endings and arrangement where necessary. Try out particular stanzas, sections, individual lines that are proving troublesome.
Many poets find that their poems—except the 'given' poems that seem
to come from nowhere—go through, say, a dozen drafts. Even when
they have been submitted to a literary magazine or newspapers or when
they are requested for a book or anthology, poems sometimes still cry
out for a word to be changed here or there, or for a more rhythmically
comfortable or logical line arrangement. W. H. Auden continued to alter
his poems even at galley-proof stage, sometimes changing their shape
and sense. Les Murray, in his recent *Collected poems*, reworked and
retitled some of his poems. Some short story writers do the same thing
with their work. There is a sense in which a piece of creation is never
finished, and yet at other times the piece will 'tell' you when it is
complete.

There are some useful tricks to this drafting business. They work for
me: they may well work for you. Yes, commit material to paper, and
allow some space around your drafts for rewriting.

Tone of voice

You may discover that each poem has its own organizing genius, an
indefinable tone of voice that determines the direction of the changes
you make as you redraft. You may be able to discern it from the outset:
it may be in the content of the poem, or in the parts of the poem that
you are sure of, where the words seem 'right' from the outset. Or you
may have to write through several versions before the tone of voice
becomes apparent and then necessitates further drafts.

Reading aloud

You will find yourself reading in your head from the draft to see how
it sounds, to hear what rhythms govern it. You should also try to be
alone and to read it aloud. The sounds of your voice reveal things that
aren't so readily apparent reading it under your breath.

Fair copy

Another trick—and you will develop your own judgement about when
it is time to do this—is to convert the hand-written version of your poem
to a typed version. It becomes a different animal, and infelicities, unintended repetitions, passages of awkward rhythm, poor line arrangements, spring out at you. As Ernest Hemingway explained, we welcome
these chances to see our work as if anew, as if through someone else's
eyes—at the stage when we convert it to a typed version, and again at
the stage when it returns to us in galley or page proofs on its way to
publication.

In this era of word processing, you must make your own judgement
about when to advance from that handwritten, messy, but human draft

to the perfection of a print out. The more you work with electric typewriter or word processor, the more comfortable you will be drafting the typed versions of your poems. Even so, sometimes scribbling on another sheet of paper will help to get words down or rearrange a line here and there, before typing them into the word processor. 'It's like trying to catch a lizard without its tail falling off,' said Lawrence Durrell, the English novelist and poet, speaking of writing poems. Some people find the typewriter or word processor too formal and structured for this casting around. Other writers find they can work more easily on a typed draft. The print out sometimes seems to have an authority that can be dangerous until a piece is further advanced. It sometimes seems to say: this is now in print and not to be changed without special permission. It may blind writers to changes they ought to make. Much of this is a matter of personal judgement and experience.

The gift of time

The other vital ingredient in all this is time—the most blessed thing that can be offered to a writer or artist—time and solitude. 'To be completely alone in a room, to know that there'll be no interruptions and I've got eight hours is just exactly what I want—yeah, just paradise,' said William Burroughs, the American novelist who writes by 'cut-ups'. Time and solitude can allow the writer to go into another world, as it were. Elizabeth Bowen, one of the greatest short-story writers, described how she felt when, as a twenty-year-old, she began writing her first stories in the attic of her aunt's house.

The room, the position of the window, the convulsive and anxious grating of my chair on the board floor were hyper-significant to me: here were the sensuous witnesses to my crossing the margin of a hallucinatory world ... for me reality meant the books I had read—and I turned around, as I was writing, from time to time, to stare at them, unassailable in the shelves behind me.

Elizabeth Bowen's sense of excitement, romance, fascination with discovery, other-worldly experience, conviction that what one is pursuing is important and will reach other people, is vital. How else do writers sustain their days, weeks, months, or years pursuing a single work, the like of which no one has written before? When we come to talk of longer works, we will return to this.

Let's consider time and solitude more pragmatically. For the writer there is both *conscious* and *subconscious* working time. Many writers have developed similar techniques to make effective use of time, although they do not work for everyone. Mine are listed below.

• Put something on paper about your ideas for writing as soon as possible, even a note to remind yourself if you are too busy to do more. Your 'computer' will register the idea and begin work on it in spite of your other preoccupations. One piece of writing can be the avenue, albeit a 'failed' avenue, to that other piece of writing you most urgently want to do but cannot discern just yet. The path to completed and published works is littered with the bones of failed pieces, snippets that helped writers find their way to what they really wanted to say. Some of those 'failures', once sown in your mind, are only temporary failures because their time is yet to come. Over a writing life you'll be surprised how many of these the subconscious brings to the surface again, partially worked-on and ready for further and more successful work. A. D. Hope, the Australian poet, says:

I am usually writing—or failing to write—perhaps a dozen or so poems at any one time. Some of them trail along for a long time. I work at one until it comes to a stop. Then I transfer to another. They come about in different ways. Sometimes reading starts a poem, but then has nothing to do with what emerges. It links with something else in the mind, gives you an idea that shoots off in another direction.

• Allow time to put away your work for a day or two after you have developed it as far as you can—you may like to leave it even longer. Then take it out and reread it. You will find that you are more objective now; earlier you were too engrossed with it, too close to it. Now you can work on it with greater conviction.

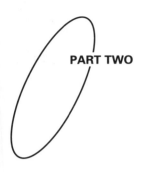

PART TWO

From poetry towards prose

You may have said it to see whether you believed it or

not . . .

Ernest Hemingway

Since feeling is first

who pays any attention

to the syntax of things

will never wholly kiss you . . .

e. e. cummings

What is poetry?

We are in little doubt about what prose is. This is prose:

One of my difficulties is the one felt by almost everyone, of having to do things that are necessary for survival or out of a sense of duty or of what is right and proper—things that if left to my own inclinations I would not spend my living time upon for one moment . . .

And this, we are probably in no doubt, is poetry, a poetic version of the same sentiments:

Oh Duty,
Why hast thou not the visage of a sweetie or a cutie?
Why displayest thou the countenance of the kind of conscientious
   organizing spinster
That the minute you see her you are aginster?
Why glitter thy spectacles so ominously?
Why art thou clad so abominously?
Why art thou so different from Venus?
And why do thou and I have so few interests
mutually in common between us?

That's how Ogden Nash puts it for us. It has rhyme. It has rhythm. It has wit. It is more memorable than the prose version, more likely to be taken to heart, both for its play on words and for its rhyme and rhythm, but also for the pictures, the images it uses to personify Duty, that stern mistress.

So what is poetry? By poetry I mean something more than verse, but here we have to hedge our bets. Poetry in English through the centuries has been, in the main, regularly rhymed and quite strongly rhythmic verse, largely because of its oral origins in the days before verse was committed to print. Rhyme, rhythm, and other poetic devices allowed the oral poet to remember a story more easily.

These strong elements of rhyme and rhythm were modified by experimentation. 'Blank verse' rhythmically followed the iambic line (a line with alternating short and long syllables) but discarded formal and regular rhyme. Shakespeare in his plays, and John Milton in his epic poem 'Paradise Lost' stand out among lesser lights who used blank verse.

Then came 'free verse', practised by writers who began using it in the late nineteenth and early twentieth century, as well as poets like Walt Whitman, the great American poet of the Civil War period, or T. S. Eliot, Wallace Stevens, D. H. Lawrence, Ezra Pound and later many others in the remarkably strong period of American poetry that has lasted from the 1940s until the present—William Carlos Williams, Sylvia Plath, Robert

Lowell, Anne Sexton, Theodore Roethke, Denise Levertov, John Berryman, Elizabeth Bishop, Robert Bly, Adrienne Rich, and many more. Free verse goes further still in breaking down the regularity of rhyme and rhythm. Often it discards not only rhyme but also metrical regularity. It still controls rhythm, but its rhythm is generally based on more organic things—the rhythm of a heartbeat, the rhythm of a person's breathing or reading, rhythm that arises from the poem's subject matter, rhythm dictated by the listing of things and events, or by repetition, and so on. Free verse, as Paul Fussell says in his useful book, *Poetic meter and poetic form*, is 'free, sort of'.

The upshot of all this is that although formal verse, which is enjoying something of a revival, still coexists with blank verse and free verse, when we seek a definition of poetry we are reduced, as someone has suggested, to a holdall definition that runs something like this: 'Poetry is writing in which the length of line does not depend on the position of the right-hand margin.'

That is probably the most mechanical and pragmatic distinction; others are more important. Generally poetry uses the language differently, uses its possibilities more deeply; operates at the level of metaphor, of imagery, looking at one thing, seeing another. Poetry often twists the language beyond our day-to-day use of words and phrases, so that it becomes something else, suggests other things. As one poet put it: 'poetry says what otherwise must remain unsaid'. The Sydney poet, Kenneth Slessor, used to say that poetry points to something beyond itself: the rest of literature points towards poetry.

Poetry is often intensely individual and subjective. Judith Wright says: 'You write a poem because you don't know something. When you've finished, you do know it.' And what concerns the poet most, she maintains, is not the question, 'Why did it happen?' nor 'How did it happen?' but rather, 'What does it mean to me that it happened?'

Write

Let's stick with the notion of poetry—pieces of writing in which (as we have seen when we searched for a minimal definition of poetry) the length of line is not determined by the position of the right-hand margin —and explore some of the infinite possibilities in structuring stories.

• Write a poem describing a street. In the first section it will be devoid of life. In the second it will include a short human drama. In your third and final section, it will empty again, except for some reminders of human interaction. This final section will draw the piece to a close.

• Now write a piece that will be titled 'Decade'. It will portray the same person at intervals of ten years, each section headed by a date—1936? 1946? 1956? Write a brief portrait (12 lines) of the person at the turn of three decades, depicting the changes wrought by experience and time.

Several photographers, notably the American Nicholas Nixon, have done this exercise, rephotographing the same subjects at distinct intervals of time.

• Become an 'imagist' poet. Write about daybreak in terms of imagery, treating the sun as a person addressed as 'you'. Read the small book, *Imagist Poetry*, edited by Peter Jones.

• Write a 'concrete poem', in which the physical shaping of words, the arrangement of lines, the disposition of sections on the page, all suggest the subject-matter visually. Here is Retta Hemensley's 'Egoism', an Australian example of concrete poetry.

Egoism
egoism
ego is m
m is ego
(go esi m)
ME IS GO
GO
GO
eGOism

Your poem may play with only one phrase, or even with certain letters, making a pattern which is painterly and visual in one sense, and yet also tells a simple story via the meanings or suggestions of words. A concrete poem by the Australian Alan Riddell, for instance, is composed of a block of single letters. All are either i's or u's, the i's surrounding the u's. It is entitled 'The Affair'! You will find other examples of concrete poems, or poems using some of the visual elements of concrete poetry, in Thomas Shapcott's anthology of the 1970s, *Australian poetry now*.

• Write a poem in two columns, each of which is composed of single or at most double words, the columns running beside each other down the page. Each column of words should tell its own story and yet the two stories should have some link with each other. Each column may function as a story in itself, and yet the two stories must be clearly related.

• Write a poem that keeps echoing a particular consonant (ppp?) or vowel (eee?). Listen to the repetitive vowel sounds in this piece:

Provincial Matters
I keep seeing
the valley's bowl
below us in the dusk
and hear her saying:
Ah, yes, he has a lady love
down there. She's been on heat

for a week. He won't even
eat his tea. Can't keep
him home . . .
            and the dog careering
past the black dam
rilled with water beetles, leaning
against the momentum
of his lust, scattering
twigs and leaves, hell bent
on that scent from the dim
line of trees that cuts
across vine rows
to the creek's dark.

- Write a poem that depends on repetition of a sentence or phrase.
- Write a poem in ballad form, taking the aabb rhyme scheme and four-line verse of Essex Evans' 'The Women of the West' as a model:

    They left the vine-wreathed cottage and the mansion on the hill,
    The houses in the busy streets where life is never still,
    The pleasures of the city, and the friends they cherished best:
    For love they faced the wilderness—the Women of the West . . .

You will probably find that poetic form and possibility begin to intrigue you. In studying the possibilities in poetic form we employ scansion (the sounding of lines of poetry to count the number of stresses or main beats per line) and analyse rhyme schemes, simply allotting a to the sound at the first line's end, b for a different sound at the end of a second, c if the third line is different again from first and second line-endings and so on.

Pursuit of poetic form carries with it some of the challenge and fascination of a mathematical problem. As David Campbell said of the writing of Shakespearian sonnets: 'It's like working through a theorem in geometry. Twelve lines of argument, then the couplet like a QED at the end'.

Possibilities in poetic form

Poetry moves us with its combination of feeling and philosophy. Poetry relies heavily on imagery, rhythm and rhyme for its power. It is often melodious meditation.

If we make a deeper study of the elements of rhyme and rhythm, and others that flow from them, we find there is nothing particularly complex about any of them. Many experienced poets find that there is great satisfaction in employing the more formal elements of poetry. So it is good to know how they work. Some, including W. H. Auden and Peter Porter, have set out to write at least one poem in every traditional form.

Nevertheless, a warning. For most new writers the most natural and expeditious path towards the writing of good poetry is to proceed *first* via the sorts of exercises you have been doing above. They have the advantage of starting from the idea of story and words first, rather than from the imposition of formal verse forms. They appeal, at this important early stage of writing, to *your* sense of story, statement, imagery, rhythm and rhyme in that order—a natural dog-paddling motion towards poetry, as William Stafford would say. It is better to come to consciousness of form, when you feel the need for it, by proceeding from your own freedom to invent and narrate, rather than plunging into the regularities of English verse structure initially and then working back to the practice of 'free verse'. *Freedom* is important in finding your own poetic voice and rhythm. It is all too easy to become the early slave of form and to produce formally perfect but arid poetry in which the need for rhyme and rhythm produce inane, even dishonest sentiments, and in which you never develop your own voice or integrity. At a later stage of your writing experience, however, you may feel the need for the greater power that form and poetic technique will bring to your work and for the possibilities they offer.

What follows, therefore, is a general introduction to poetic form. Treat it as you might an appendix, experimenting as much as you want with the writing suggestions it offers. Then leave suggestions of further formality in poetry to lie for a time, until you have explored word-use, statement, imagery and rhythm much further.

When you do feel the need for further form and structure in your poetry, you can consult some excellent books on the subject: John Hollander's *Rhyme's reason*; Paul Fussell's *Poetic meter and poetic form*; G. S. Fraser's *Metre, rhyme and free verse*; and James McAuley's *A primer of English versification*. You will find others in the Bibliography.

The poetic line and its metre

What can be done with the poetic line, whose length is not determined by the position of the right-hand margin? Here we begin to explore the fascinating subjects of metre (rhythm within the line) and rhyme (echoing of sounds from line to line).

As we shall see when we discuss rhythm in prose and in speech, everything that is said or written has a rhythm of some sort, whether it be a weaker phrase following a stronger one, or a short, stark statement following something long and mellifluous. We apply normal stress to certain syllables in words as we speak according to the pronunciation of the word—persuade, kangaroo. We might also stress a word for emphasis—'He can go'; 'Take the other one'. But in poetry, rhythm can be more closely governed in each line, and this is done by control of metre. Metre and rhythm in English poetry depend on where stressed syllables or strong beats occur in the line and how they interact with unstressed syllables. The possible types of metre in poetry are many. Here are some of them:

• Plain four beat line—four strong beats to the line, with varying numbers of off-beats (perhaps one separates the beats, perhaps two, or sometimes one and sometimes two) in a stanza of four lines. The number of off-beats between the beats are what makes for variety of effect in the stanza (when the consistent sections of a poem are more than four lines long they are termed stanzas rather than verses). This metre is common in popular poetry (and hence is often called 'popular' metre) and in some limericks, hymns and ballads.

• Tetrameter—four beats again to the line, but with four unstressed syllables or off-beats, giving eight syllables to the line.

• Pentameter—five beats to the line with five accompanying off-beats, to make ten syllables to the line. This is a rhythmically more supple line. It allows in its greater length for more variation as well as less insistent and more subtle rhythm.

In each of these lines, it is possible to tread with a different sound and rhythm, depending on what sort of metrical 'foot' the line is composed of. A metrical foot is made up of two or three syllables, only one of which carries a strong beat, the other one or two being off-beats.

• The most common foot is an iambic foot—an off-beat followed by a strong beat. In English poetry it is more commonly combined with a pentameter line than with any other, thus:

Let Hearts be trumps, she said, and frumps they were . . .

• The trochee is a foot in which the strong beat comes first, followed by its off-beat, thus:

There they are my nifty men and women . . .

If we move from two-syllable (disyllabic) feet to three-syllable (trisyllabic) feet, we open up further possibilities.

• We can arrange lines as a series of anapaests—two off-beats followed by a strong beat, thus:

From the pig in a poke, from the hair of the dog . . .

• Or we can write a series of amphibrachs—off-beat/strong beat/off-beat, thus:

He pushed it down harder and burst its thin flanges . . .

- Or, finally, we could write a line of dactyls—strong beat, then off-beat and off-beat, thus:

Knock your head skilfully
Pass the jam wilfully . . .

Write

- Try the unusual dactylic rhythm, creating a sequence of instructions to a harassed mother confronted by a mountain of domestic work. Let the instructions begin with great *élan* and optimism—'Make the beds gleefully . . .'—but become more and more despondent and weary. Or perhaps begin with conscientious and responsible instructions, but then allow them to become bitter and subversive. Don't neglect to vary the sentence structure so that it sometimes becomes other than the verb/definite article/noun/adverb pattern above.
- Take some quizzical, ironic or amusing situation and write a limerick about it, using this model, with its strong beats and off-beats:

The Limerick packs laughs anatomical
Into space that is quite economical.
  But the good ones I've seen
  So seldom are clean
And the clean ones so seldom are comical.

(Anon)

- Write a short 'nature' poem in the form of iambic pentameters, and with six-line stanzas, as in this example from Wordsworth's 'Prelude':

The leafless trees and every icy crag
Tinkled like iron; while far distant hills
Into the tumult sent an alien sound
Of melancholy not unnoticed and the stars . . .
Eastward were sparkling clear, and in the West
The orange sky of evening died away . . .

Note that Wordsworth's five-beat lines are not always regular: he rings changes on the general beat of the poetry. That is the art of poetic metre—to establish an expectation in the reader by announcing the metre that governs the poem, and then making subtle, interesting and moving departures from it when mood and subject matter allow.

Poetic form

As we have seen already, there are various types of poem—the concrete poem, the imagist poem, the syllabic poem (in which each line has a predetermined number of syllables and of which the haiku is one terse example). We no sooner begin to consider these types of poem, however, than we are forced to look at the form of the whole poem, how many lines it has, how many verses or stanzas, whether it has a regular number of 'beats' to the line, whether it has regular rhyme, whether it is telling its story in free verse, how its lines are arranged and differ from each other, and so on.

Stanzas

A poem can be composed of stanzas—similar and regularly structured sections of three or more lines, as well as regular groupings of lines that have no rhyme or metre.

It can be composed of couplets—groups of two lines.

It can be composed of tercets or triplets, both terms for stanzas of three lines.

It can be composed of quatrains—stanzas of four lines.

These segments of poetic organization can be written with different types of stanza rhyme schemes. Here are some of them:

• Terza Rima—in this Italian form each verse consists of three iambic pentameter lines with rhymes that interlock—aba bcb cdc and so forth.

• Ottava Rima—an eight-line stanza of iambic pentameter lines, with a rhyme scheme abababcc. Lord Byron showed his genius in suiting this stanza form to his bawdy, humorous and ironic subject-matter in his long poem 'Don Juan'.

• Rhyme Royal—a stanza form used by Chaucer in his 'Troilus and Criseyde' and Shakespeare in his 'Rape of Lucrece', and consisting of seven pentameter lines rhyming ababbcc.

• Spenserian stanza—a nine-line poem or stanza of eight iambic pentameter lines rhyming ababbcbc and a final alexandrine line (a six-beat iambic hexameter line, providing a relief from the pattern of the shorter iambic pentameter) that rhymes c. You can find examples in Spenser's 'The Faerie Queene' and in Keats' 'The Eve of St. Agnes'.

• Skeltonics—poetry of no fixed length, written in short, two-beat lines and perpetuating the *same* rhyme as long as practicable, sometimes for six lines or more. This rhyme scheme lends itself to comic verse.

Given these and other stanza forms, the types of poems that can be written are numerous. Some of the more intriguing are:

• The Syllabic poem—in which the length of line is governed by a predetermined number of syllables—five, then seven, then five in a haiku: or an unvarying number of syllables per line in other forms.

• The Sonnet—this can be Italian, English (including Shakespearian) or Spenserian in form, but each of these variations is a fourteen-line, rhyming poem. In the English form it consists of three quatrains (sets of four lines) and then a rhyming couplet. Shakespeare's sonnets are radiant models.

• Blank Verse poems—these are written in unrhymed lines, each consisting of five beats per line. It is the insistent rhythm that is compelling in blank verse. The speeches of Shakespeare's plays are written in it.

• Free Verse poems—these consist of lines with no regular metre and of irregular length. But in 'Free' verse repetitions and patterns other than syllabic and metrical ones become important—repetition of patterns of word use, phrasing, rhythmic patterns or cadence, individual words, sounds, half-rhymes that come as nothing more than an echo. Also important is enjambment—where the sense of the poems spills over in words from one line to the next in the middle of a phrase. Look at the example below, read it aloud and accent the line endings to test the enjambent (strangers/found; loneliness/and love; obscene/than yesterday):

Our feckless Mowglis tumble in,
just for a moment strangers
found in forests of past loneliness
and love.
The sunrise fumbles red,
more northerly and more obscene
than yesterday
across our bed . . .

Free verse may still carry a consistent rhythm of sorts, determined perhaps by the length of the human breath, or a heart-beat, or the surge of waves. The long lines of the 1611 Authorized Version of the Bible are examples, as are Walt Whitman's writing in *The leaves of grass.*

• The Villanelle—this Provencal form and the French Sestina both rely on repetition for their unusual reflective power. The villanelle is written in tercets of iambic pentameters, with the first and third lines rhyming a and the middle line b. This rhyme scheme that repeats like a two-sound refrain persists until the poem's final stanza, when the two refrain sounds are brought together in a quatrain that rhymes abaa.

• The Sestina—here the poem consists of six stanzas, each of six lines, usually iambic pentameters. The repetition is unusual, taking each of the final words of the first sextet and repeating them in a different order in subsequent stanzas, although the first line of each new stanza ends with the final word of the previous stanza. The poem concludes in a three-line stanza or *envoi* which uses all six words in either a middle or end position.

- The Acrostic poem—in this the first letters of each of the lines, when read down the page, spell out a secret message.
- The Ballade—this form consists of three stanzas of eight lines, each rhyming ababcdcd with a final quatrain rhyming cdcd. It adheres to the same rhymes in all stanzas.
- The Rondeau—this consists of ten or thirteen lines, with the first stanza carrying an aabba rhyme scheme and subsequent stanzas using the same rhymes. The feature of the rondeau is that its opening word or phrase is repeated twice as a refrain that does not rhyme with anything but itself in the poem.
- A Blues—arising from negro work songs, this stands at the junction of poetry and song. Blues can come in a number of forms, but all have the common elements of repetition, simple message (sometimes a lament, sometimes a wry observation of life, sometimes a celebration of it), variation on a refrain, slow and relaxed delivery, a casual vernacular tone and a sense of being pondered as they are created.

Write

As you complete this section with voices and rhythms in your head, try writing a simple three-verse blues, using the model below. It will be something of a preparation for the song-writing you will attempt in Part Ten. Note the repetition of the refrain in each verse and the advancement of the story in each final line:

Empty pockets blues
Got me a strong brown shoulder, and I want to work it hard.
Got me a willing shoulder and an itch to work it hard.
But old boss-man won't have me, he just waves me from the yard.

I know the length of timber and a saw that keeps it just.
I can feel the feet in timber and saw it so it's just.
Sweat in my face all of the day, wading in the dust.

The boss he think he need me, so I quit the river line.
The boss he says he need me, I look back to that bright line.
Now he put mountains all around me, and not a dollar's mine.

Now you can sense the range of possibilities in poetry in English, where fewer words offer themselves as rhymes than in some other languages, thus forcing poets to seek consonantal and vowel echoes in place of formal rhyme. Consult books on poetic metre and structure, where you will find examples of these forms, and others. Experiment with them yourself.

Writer's antennae

Who writes the great books? It isn't we who sign our names. What is an artist? He is a man who has antennae, who knows how to hook up to the currents which are in the atmosphere, in the cosmos; he merely has the facility for hooking on, as it were.

Henry Miller

The Australian poet and playwright, Dorothy Hewett confesses:

I think it isn't so much, perhaps, that people tell you bizarre things as that you have your ear tuned to bizarre things. It's like a tuning fork. You go about the world with a tuning fork in your head. And all these things are coming in at a rate of knots. You're picking up and discarding and choosing—even writing little notes to yourself—throughout the whole of your life. So that you become this terrible person who, when the most dreadful things are happening to you—no matter what they are—and you are going through the horrors of the damned, there's a little small still voice somewhere in the back saying, 'What good material this would make!'. And this terrifies me. Because it makes you in a sense a very inhuman person.

As you write, you might also hear the message of David Malouf, Australian novelist and poet, reflecting on the relationship between reality and fiction: 'As soon as we start "remembering" things that happened to us, we change their shape. We re-work them each time in the telling. We shape them differently . . .'

Detail and repetition

You will be discovering by now that effective writing, immediate story-telling, needs detail: not detail for its own sake, because that becomes boring or covers up the point you are making, but detail used to put the reader beside you as you tell your story. If you know a street name, use it, or the name of the district or region. If you know the bird is a rufous fantail, name it. The word 'bird' is impenetrable. If you know the tree, name it; if you don't know it, seek it, or use something plausible. The word vegetation is impenetrable: the words lemon-scented gum or silver birch are luminous. Invent place names. The childhood town of John Updike, the American novelist, short-story writer and poet, was Shillington, Pennsylvania, and it was part of the geography of his stories. It becomes Olinger in his fiction, which beckons the reader to enter the spirit of his story much more than the flat description, 'the town'. Olinger is specific: the reader comes to know it, to visualize it. There are other occasions where the nature of the story-telling, its concentration on what is happening to characters, or perhaps its dealing with 'town' and 'country' as elemental facts in nature, make the simple concept, 'the town', exactly what is wanted.

There are other words that have been so devalued they can seldom be used well. They are impenetrable; we cannot get behind them to find out just what shade of feeling or meaning they represent. 'Serenity' is a virtually meaningless word because it can mean too many things to too many people. The word 'peace' is similar: so are 'love', 'bliss', 'happiness', 'good', 'holy', 'nice', 'tranquil', 'horror', 'sadness', 'noise', etc. Phrases like 'she felt an aura of contentment' or 'the experience went beyond description' or 'he was very supportive' are vague and flabby. This does not mean that these words and phrases do not at some time have their uses, but in most cases there are words that are plainer or stronger or more individual.

Write

Describe the room of a person you know, so that you reveal their personality and interests purely through detail of what their room contains and how it is arranged. Give it a title.

Practise finding the detail, and the exact words to bring colour and light alive. In one of his novels, for instance, Patrick White writes of '. . . the dented light of milk cans'. Detail can tell us precisely what a sound was like, or a smell, or a movement. Again Patrick White sees truly— through his character Arthur Brown, who is riding in a buggy behind a bay mare, not simply called a mare, but called Treasure—as she 'clumped and snorted down the empty roads, her rear opening curiously like a passion fruit. The yellow dung went plop, plop . . .' Find the words for the touch of gnarled wood or lace, or oranges or grease; for the taste of mango, or Brussel sprouts. And how do you describe the essence of new sensations? A boy of five tastes soda water for the first time and says, 'It tastes like my foot's asleep'. Use detail, but don't overload it.

Repetition, if it reinforces or adds a rhythmic insistence, is a powerful thing in writing or in song, writing's precursor; not only repetition of sounds, or particular words, but of thought patterns, constructions, concepts. This applies whether what you are producing is poetry or prose.

Try writing single sentences, each taking a new line, in which you carry a word from the first line and repeat it in the second, taking another from the second and finding a place for it in the third, and so on for four or five statements. Then see what you have made and give it a title.

The reading writer

Writing draws its material not only direct from life, but also from vicarious sources—the products of other arts, painting, sculpture, photography, music, and from even the slenderest evidence of other people's thinking. Reading is a natural accompaniment to writing at many points in the process, but not necessarily at all. Reading is a catalyst; it makes connections; it reminds us of the classical structures of story-telling. Reading is a touchstone for your own work-in-progress when you are in doubt about its tone or quality: sometimes it is good to be reminded how other people do it.

Reading can also be an initiator. Xavier Herbert, author of *Capricornia* and *Poor fellow my country*, was sometimes unable to strike the right mood and tone for a new section of his big novel, *Poor fellow*. So he used to walk or read the novels of others in his bush writing camp on the mountain above Redlynch in North Queensland. 'I read most of Patrick White that way,' he explained. 'I admire his work a lot. After reading other people's work I'd get this feeling of delinquency. That meant I'd worked out my problem. Then I could get back to the writing.'

Viewing or looking can be another sort of reading. Writers 'read' music, films, paintings and photographs—it is a way of raising or preserving a sensibility, and of touching another sensibility that is civilizing and valuable in many ways to the artist who uses words. Reading, viewing and listening have much in common. A. D. Hope, for example, has been nourished by music and painting. 'Almost always, when writing a poem,' he explained in an interview, 'I have the sense of music that matches it, that sets a tone of feeling at which the poem aims.' And his poem 'The double looking glass' springs from pieces of art as apparently disparate as Tintoretto's painting of *Susanna and the elders*, parts of the thirteenth chapter of the book of Daniel in the Bible, and has echoes of Mallarmé's 'L' Après-midi d'un faune'. Hope admits quietly:

When I go abroad, one of my main objects is to go to the great galleries. For instance, I think I've been three times to Washington under various pretences, but knowing that the real reason was to visit a little private gallery there full of Impressionists, to see one particular picture—the Renoir picture of lunch on the river, you know.

Reading, viewing, listening, thinking, asking unobtrusive questions are all writers' resources, but in writing, and in the multiplicity of choices a writer must make, other factors come into play: self-analysis and criticism. Ted Hughes again puts it succinctly:

In writing, you have to be able to distinguish between those things about which you are merely curious—things you heard about last week or read about yesterday—and things which are a deep part of your life. The difference between a fairly interesting writer and a fascinating writer is that the fascinating writer has a better nose for what genuinely excites him, he is hotter on the trail, he has a better instinct for what is truly alive in him. The worse writer may seem to be more sensible in many ways, but he is less sensible in this vital matter: he cannot quite distinguish what is full of life from what is only half full or empty of it. And so his writing is less alive, and as a writer he is less alive, and in writing, as in everything else, nothing matters but life . . .

A resource list of writing exercises

These workshop ideas build on what we have already done. They are arranged in a progression. Some suggest writing that you might do to make yourself more comfortable with the essence of poetry, others begin to cross the divide between poetry and prose which we are now approaching. You will be invited to write freely in both poetry and prose.

You can return to this list, pick exercises when it suits you, or when a particular approach excites you. You may decide to try them in the sequence in which they are arranged: you may not. But use them to write. Don't worry too much whether you are writing poetry or prose. You will be telling stories, and they will find their own form, but don't forget, at this stage, to continue to write in complete sentences, whatever the line arrangement you choose. Some poets begin poems by writing a prose version of the moment they want to unravel and celebrate: then they reduce the prose statement, condensing it to poetic form. Be flexible about form!

It would perhaps be helpful to use each of the exercises as a focal point for a meeting where you write, read and discuss your work in a group. Whatever way the exercises take you, hook on to your experience in writing these stories, as Henry Miller advises, but retain your freedom to invent.

1 Single sentences

In a single sentence make a statement about the sea that no one has ever heard or seen before—a statement that is your view of the ocean and its significance, at least for this moment. Read it to someone, not for criticism, but simply to hear it stand up for itself as you read it. Try other drafts, keeping all your versions. Don't be satisfied with any phrase, statement, or word combination if you have the faintest suspicion you might have heard or seen it before. Read it aloud again, weigh it up, commit it to the typewriter or word processor when you are satisfied with it. Then, maybe, rework it again if you see flaws in it. Its title is 'Ocean'.

On a later occasion, not necessarily now, do the same for such unlikely subjects as:
- Library
- City
- Service station

- Chapel
- Rock group
- Weir
- Hayshed

2 The colour green

Say four or five things from your experience about the colour green, each as a single sentence, each beginning on a new line, each containing the word green. Green your writing until the word green becomes something other than its usual self.

3 The object—still life and sensory input

This idea is best for a self-motivated writing workshop of three or more people. One member of the group should bring a well-packaged secret object. When the group is ready, it should be revealed to them and placed on a table for them so that they can write about it. Some advice about the type of object: it should be something that is intriguing, that is perhaps foreign to the situation you set it in, that has some sort of patina about it—perhaps of age, or another culture, or repeated use. I have used a sculptured ebony head from Nigeria; an old nineteenth-century tobacco jar with koala and gumtip and wattle motifs let into its squat wooden bowl; a pre-war stamp collection; a crystal set; a dramatic severed log's end from the paddocks, weathered grey; my Scots ancestors' china-handled dinner bell.

All members of the group use all their senses on the object—look at it, smell it, go to it and feel its weight, touch its surfaces, listen to the dinner bell's ring, even taste the log's dusty-smoky fissures. And then they write about it, in two paragraphs or stanzas. The first is pure sensuous description of the object, as if describing it for someone without senses. Nevertheless, the description may need imagery or comparison to give an immediate awareness of its nature. The second paragraph or stanza concentrates on what the object seems to be saying about its period or milieu or culture or accustomed place and how human life went on around it. Only fifteen minutes should be allowed for the writing of each paragraph or stanza, so that the effect is not ponderous and cerebral. Then the raw pieces should be read aloud around the group, more as a basis for discussion and comparison than for criticism. Redrafting should be done later, away from the group.

4 Second-guessing the poet

Some writing courses rely almost completely on emulating the work of gifted writers. This exercise is not quite that. It invites you to look over the shoulder of the poet, to steep yourself in the subject-matter, imagery, tone of voice, rhythm and rhyme structure of the piece, but leaves you to supply words in the poem that have been blanked out. You will develop a better knowledge of the challenge poets face in finding the most telling word or phrase to convey their story in poetry. You will end up feeling something of a kinship with the poem and the poet. Here is David Campbell's poem, redolent of his days farming the upland country north of Canberra.

Night sowing
O gentle, (two syllable) land
Where the green ear shall grow.
Now you are (one syllable) with light:
The moon has (one syllable) the fallow,
The furrows run with (one syllable).

This is the season's hour:
While (two syllables) are in bed,
I sow the (two syllables) late,
Scatter like sparks the seed
And see the dark (two syllables).

O gentle land, I (one syllable)
The heart's (two syllables) (one syllable).
Stars draw their (two syllables) over,
Dews send their (two syllables) rain:
I meet you as a (two syllables).

Enter the world, the way of telling, of R. A. Simpson's poem.

Diver
Alone on the tower
I'm not (three syllables).
The water is black
And (two syllables).

I think of style
And raise my arms and (one syllable),
Holding back the (one syllable).
It's mostly a game

That touches (two syllables),
Then (two syllables) goes—
I view my fingers,
My (one syllable).

'Defiance, (one syllable) and (two syllables)
Make the diver dive
And prove, through dying,

> He's (two syllables),'
> A voice preaches in my head . . .
>
> And so I dive.
>
> Water (one syllable) me down,
> Chilling me with its (one syllable),
> Then arms pine up and up
> Like (two syllables).

When you have finished and thought again about how well your chosen words have kept faith with the poet's tone and preoccupations, you can turn to page 52 and read the original, like a moment of artistic truth. You'll be surprised in some instances how close you have come to the words of the original poet. In other cases you will conclude that you haven't dug as deep among the language's store of words and suggestions as you might have.

5 *Two days*

Write, simply, about two days you recall when you felt a rare stillness. Get as deep inside the experience as you can, not necessarily in poetry, but in two, perhaps related, short bursts of writing, numbering them I and II. Give each a title.

6 *Opposites*

Much of the interest of our lives comes from opposites. Make yourself a list of them. They may be external to you (ocean and shore, miner and greenie, body and soul, winter and summer); oppositions within yourself (the need for company and for solitude, the demands of children and the demands of the self, your instinctual way of behaving and society's prescriptions); they may appear in almost mythical or allegorical terms when you think about them. Try writing about one or two sets of opposites. You may find yourself returning in some form to the list later in your writing.

7 *Question and answer*

There is probably no more potent dramatic starter than a question of depth, wit, irony or burlesque, asked about the human situation. You could begin this exercise by writing an elongated, interesting question that conjures up its own context as a poem does:

> *Tourists in love*
> Will they kiss there at the plain-wood
> table provided by the Shire under
> the suitable pines beside the
> swinging rubbish bin and
> picnic fire place?

And then, having established the world of your question, answer it from within the same world, but with perhaps different possibilities, or with an unexpected change in tone:

> Unlikely. As they lean towards
> each other over the Thermos
> flask a bull ant every
> color of the rain-
> bow has entered
> the recess
> between
> his
> straining
> belt and the
> sweaty small of
> his back while their
> can of Aerogard left far
> too close to the hearty blaze
> of the barbecue is about to explode.

8 The definition

We are all aware of the literal definitions we use every day—define a road, a bridge, a teapot, an easel, a book, a microwave. Ah yes, but what about the definition of a cat, a cello, a ball, a spade, that no one has ever heard before—because it is so ironic, idiosyncratic, subjective or personal, so loaded, biased, one-sided or bitter? Try writing such definitions, of objects only for now, in complete sentences and with the formal structure of a dictionary definition suggested in them. Make them from three to twenty lines long. You might arrange them as poetic lines, or as prose. You might be interested to see where this takes you: the definitions may organize themselves as products of a particular type of person or world view.

9 Paintings

American poet X. J. Kennedy did it for Marcel Duchamp's painting, 'Nude descending a staircase'. William Carlos Williams did it for Breughel's painting, 'Hunters in the snow' and also for the Dutch painter's beautiful, 'The fall of Icarus', which also fascinated the English poet W. H. Auden, in his poem 'Musée des Beaux Arts'. These poets wrote poems about specific works of art. If you can find a good reproduction of Breughel's 'Hunters in the snow' look long at it. William Carlos Williams's poem, based on it, is deceptively simple in its tone, almost like verbal naive painting:

> The over-all picture is winter
> icy mountains
> in the background the return
>
> from the hunt it is toward evening
> from the left
> sturdy hunters lead in
>
> their pack the inn-sign
> hanging from
> a broken hinge is a stag a crucifix . . .

Part of the poem's simple power is its rejection of normal punctuation and the way ideas run on from one line or one stanza to the next. That, and its unblinking observation, its hint of drama, of stage direction.

Breughel's pictures are apt because they depict multifarious human activity against the landscape. It's as W. H. Auden says, before he goes on to talk about 'The fall of Icarus':

> About suffering they were never wrong,
> The Old Masters: how well they understood
> Its human position; how it takes place
> While someone else is eating or opening a window or just
> walking dully along . . .

Choose a painting that has a particular resonance for you. Think of Arthur Boyd, Sidney Nolan, Van Gogh, Matisse, Bonnard, Marc Chagall, Brett Whiteley, Picasso, Noel Counihan, Jeffery Smart, Roger Bacon, Constable, Delacroix, David Hockney, Larry Rivers, Monet, Seurat, Emile Bernard, Stanley Spencer, Willem de Kooning, Spencer Gore, Henry Moore or countless others, and also, if you know the context sufficiently, the art of the Arnhem Land or Central Australian Aborigines. Look at your painting, inhabit it, then write about it. Whatever form it takes, it will be a very subjective rendering of the painting. You will in a sense be making the painting your own narrative.

10 Move over author: two experiments in displacement

Authors often do not speak directly from their own position or beliefs, although these most probably determine the narrative devices they use to affect and move the reader. The very choice of a fictional narrator is such a 'displacement' of the author. The following suggestions have implications for prose fiction, but are also fascinating to consider in writing poetry.

First, try putting yourself into the persona of a famous historical figure and write his or her latter-day first-person account of the event with which she or he is generally associated in people's minds—Mary giving birth to Jesus; Martin Luther pinning the Theses on the door of the Wittenberg church; Christabel Pankhurst leading a women's suffrage demonstration in London; Neville Chamberlain after Munich; Boadicea and the sacking of Colchester; Carboni Raffaello hiding from troopers' bullets in the chimney of his goldfields tent at the Eureka Stockade; King Charles I on the way to his execution; Joan of Arc after she raised the English siege of Orléans and conducted the future Charles VII to his coronation; Truganinni accompanying George Augustus Robinson to Port Phillip after helping him contact the Tasmanian tribes.

You will probably begin reading and gathering information about the subject of your piece, but even though historians tell you certain things about your subject, your personification will be idiosyncratic and partly imaginative. Your view of the figure may affect your tone of voice as much as an official historical view of the character. The important thing is what *you* imagine the person to have been like.

What you write will be a drastic distillation from all the material that *could* be included. Concentrate on the sort of compression and image-making that is endemic to poetry, whether you are writing poetry or prose. The piece should be short—twenty lines of poetry or thirty lines of prose, so think about the point at which you want to enter the story. Assume your reader knows the basic story, but you may ring the changes on that fact. If you have the opportunity, share your piece in a group, in exchange for the pieces written by others. Put together, they will reflect quite a range of interests, voices, points of view, events.

The second suggestion for an experiment in 'displacement' has to do with authorial displacement in favour of a narrator, but also with another sort of displacement. You may know the slim books of poetry of Craig Raine, the English poet—*The onion, memory, Rich*, and *A martian sends a postcard home*. The title poem of that last collection is written with the innocence conferred by lack of knowledge: its narrator is a Martian and she is (he is?) writing a postcard to send home from planet Earth. For Craig Raine, of course, this device allows a rich opportunity to observe human life in an unprejudiced, unvarnished way, touching its strangeness, its contradictions, its irony and humour. It allows us to look at ourselves in a new way. For instance, the Martian has seen telephones:

In homes, a haunted apparatus sleeps,
that snores when you pick it up.

If the ghost cries, they carry it
to their lips and soothe it to sleep
with sounds. And yet, they wake it up
deliberately, by tickling it with a finger.

And he has observed the toilet habits of small children and adults:

> Only the young are allowed to suffer
> openly. Adults go to a punishment room
>
> with water but nothing to eat.
> They lock the door and suffer the noises
>
> alone. No-one is exempt
> and everyone's pain has a different smell.

Try setting yourself aside via a narrator in the Craig Raine way. Hold up the familiar as the unfamiliar. You might choose as subject a service station, an airport lounge, a video shop, a church, a milking shed, an auction, a kindergarten, a concert, parliament, a university, a dinner-party, a barbecue, an op shop, etc. You might emulate Raine's tone, continue his poem, as it were, proliferating examples and adopting his two-line stanza. You might employ a denser, prose-like short stanza of your own.

As you reorient yourself and your way of seeing, think of other examples of 'displacement' such as Jonathan Swift's classic, *Gulliver's travels*. Swift organizes his narrative so that humankind is viewed from the standpoint of Gulliver, who first finds himself far larger than his fellow humans in Lilliput, then far smaller. Later he sees his fellows as repulsive Yahoos, while the epitome of dignity and compassion are the Houhnhnms—the horse-like beings who succour him and impart great wisdom. When Gulliver returns to England and his family, he is drawn more to the horses in his stable than his fellow human beings.

Think of Cervantes' *Don Quixote* and the devices the author uses in his narrative. His third-person narrator tells the story of a sadly deluded Spanish knight who sees everything in terms of medieval courtly chivalry, so that the book's view of the 'real' world skates constantly along the edge of madness, with the phlegmatic squire, Sancho Panza, anchoring us to fact and 'reality'. By playing off one world-view against the other Cervantes created in Don Quixote's adventures across the Spanish landscape one of the most richly humorous stories ever written.

Both Swift and Cervantes had other axes to grind, and these determined what devices, what 'displacements', they adopted to tell their stories so as to hold up human affairs to the scrutiny of their readers in a new way. Swift refers to many of the public figures and the politics of his day. Cervantes' work is in part a reaction to the limiting chivalric conventions that governed story-telling in the Spain of his time.

Remember to begin writing promptly, even if you are just jotting down notes. Don't let too much thinking and planning prevent you from *writing*.

11 *The sculpture, the photograph*

Remember your approach towards writing about a painting? Choose a sculpture to which you have access in a gallery, park or square and sit with it, walk round it, touch it, see it against its background. Write about it, but only if you feel something from it; only if it has that tingle of fascination for you. If it hasn't, seek another that does, or shelve the idea in your subconscious and do other things while you think about possibilities. Remind yourself of sculptures you know: the Clement Meadmore piece in the forecourt of the AMP's St James Building in Melbourne; Rodin's *The burghers of Calais* and the Henry Moore sculptures at the National Gallery in Canberra; the Debra Halpern ceramic figure and Inga King's black waves outside the National Gallery in Melbourne; the Webb Gilbert statue of Henry Lawson in the Sydney Domain; the Tom Bass sculptures in Canberra.

Do the same with a photograph that fascinates you, one to which you return time and again, or another that you haven't seen before, but which intrigues you at first sight in a collection, an exhibition, newspaper, magazine, or book. Look back again if necessary at the approaches of William Carlos Williams and W. H. Auden to painting. Get your impressions of the photograph down on paper as quickly as you can, and then work, hone, fictionalize, compress from there, until you begin to feel the rhythm and tone of voice that is natural to the piece and that comes from the meeting of your experience and what the photograph conveys. Don't neglect the importance, the integrating effect of a title, in the piece. Your title could be a starting point.

12 *The kingdom of touch*

Take an object you can hold in your hands, something that has been made by hand rather than machine, or perhaps something from an earlier technology or an older way of doing things. Again, choose something that fascinates you—hand tool, figurine, fine China cup, metal forged in a country smithy, tobacco-tin, old lead soldier? Close your eyes and feel it slowly with your hands, then your feet, then your cheek, then your belly, then your chest and soon. Write about what it tells you through touch. Use the name of the object as the title of the poem or the piece of short prose, and begin each section with a statement about another part of the body that appraises it, thus:

It tells my fingers . . .
To my thigh it says . . . etc.

You might write about materials and objects that are familiar, but relay only what they say through touch, their associations through touch (their uses, history, value to you and others). Write about a jute wheat bag (if you can find one!), a piece of lace or velvet, a leather jacket, an oilskin, sea-washed sandstone, quality paper, tent or tarpaulin canvas, a farm water-tank of corrugated iron, the bark of an ironbark. These things may spark many associations, in which case you might number a first, touch-based section 'I' and the descriptions of the object's associations 'II'.

13 Serendipity or Did you miss something?

I suppose all of us have been so preoccupied with something that we have not realized until it was too late that we have missed something else, that the world has taken several turns that it will never take again in the same way. William Stafford describes this in a beautiful poem of his, called 'The Woman at Banff'. In an essay significantly entitled 'Writing the Australian Crawl' he describes the process, the serendipity of the poem's origins:

Doodling round one morning, I found myself with the aimless clause 'While she was talking'. This set of words led me to add to it, by a natural dog-paddling impulse, a closure for the construction; I wanted to have something be happening—just anything. I put down 'a bear happened along'. I remembered the bears we had seen at Banff—swaggering bears, dangerous and advertised as such, but valued. They were violent, or potentially so; they were protected by British laws. I began to put together phrases from that trip to Banff, from that set of impressions; the result was a poem, which appeared in *The Saturday Review*. Here it is—the simple, even poverty-stricken phrasing of it. Where I could not think of anything new to say, I repeated:

> The woman at Banff
> While she was talking a bear happened along, violating
> every garbage can. Shaking its loose, Churchillian,
> V for victory suit, it ripped up and ate
> a greasy 'Bears are Dangerous' sign.
>
> While she was talking the trees above signalled—
> 'Few', and the rock back of them—'Cold'.
> And while she was talking a moose—huge, black—
> swam that river and faded off winterward,
>
> Up toward the Saskatchewan.

When I look at this, it appears to move inevitably; and I see that my failure of invention—about describing the woman—has turned into the main invention; she has become demonstrably talkative.

Choose a place and occasion as Stafford had one chosen for him. Write from 'that set of impressions' as Stafford did. Construct a first line that sets the tone thus:

While he or she was (verb: studying the form guide? sunbaking? reading? gardening? sleeping? or some other) . . .

and write something carrying the same sense of experience missed, to which you give a title.

14 From music

Music is an ideal subject or prompt for writing. It is a language of broad appeal that easily crosses frontiers. It has been dubbed 'the architecture of dreams' or the language that begins where other languages end. Tolstoy observed that music has such a mysterious influence that it can make you believe you can do things that you cannot in fact accomplish.

It is not easy, nor desirable, to be too prescriptive about suggesting ways of writing about music. No two people share the same musical taste, although they may hold dear certain types of music. Think about your own preferences, think of music that fascinates you, but which nevertheless is not too familiar, has not lost its mystery, does not seem to have explained its all to you.

There is a distinction between writing about music and writing *from* it; at this stage we are writing *from* it, so it is better to use non-choral music as a starting point, to ensure that words do not intrude to distract you. If you like classical music, choose a shorter rather than longer piece for this exercise. You may find you can write more readily about music that suggests region or clime or palpable subject-matter or philosophy or cause. Now, choose a piece of orchestral music, jazz, or rock and, while you listen to it, jot down where it takes your imagination. Then work your jottings up into a first draft. Continue to listen and write until you have a coherent set of impressions or a 'landscape' suggested to you by the music. Let your imagination run free. Your final piece may have few direct links to the music, but that music will nevertheless have inspired it in ways you cannot map.

You could also write *about* music, perhaps, or both from and about it at the same time—Paul Robeson's voice and the negro spiritual; Kathleen Ferrier or Janet Baker and the songs of the British Isles, for example. Your 'music writing' might arise from the inimitable 'style' of the composer or group; the personality underlying the music; childhood memories of that particular music. It will send you searching for metaphor. It may urge you to create pictures of a group in performance, prompt a piece about something only remotely connected with music —the yellowed keys of a piano; someone playing a Jew's harp; a piano tuner, record seller, disco organizer, conductor, choreographer.

15 *Writing about photographs*

There are many fine books about the work of individual photographers. These are rich in interest. You have already been asked to write about a single painting, a single photograph. Here, you will write about a collection, the range of photographs produced by one mind, one eye. You may find that you are writing not only about the photographs but about the sensibility that produced them, seeking the common element, theme, or point of view that runs through the photographs. Arnold Newman, the American photographer, is a good case in point, with his portraits of the famous, his way of capturing people within the context of what has made them famous. But what about these famous people? What do they betray before the searching, camera? Perhaps that's where your story lies.

There are many other possibilities. Look at photographers' collections in a library, begin by writing about or from *one* collection first, probably in poetry, but not necessarily. Remember that this is *not a review*, but something subjective, personal and perhaps even fanciful. *You* are reacting to the photographs, getting 'inside' them.

A book of Arnold Newman's portraits
He likes footnotes, faces
in corners apologising for rooms.
There are no laughs.
A few heads
think with a jaw on a fist.
And here come all these skins, some
plump with the thought, others
Pre-Cambrian with years
of cold trying, with thousands
of cigarettes.
Most of the foreheads know
it's only temporary—they'll hear
time thud again.
And the hands itch to get away.

None of them is absolutely sure, but
he converts them.
Stravinsky finds all his notes
in one black piano lid.
Marilyn
looks through her hair
across white space and dreams
at Miller's insolent foot.
They are all, I suppose, admirable

yet must have trodden
other faces.

Only a few are famous
because they have forgotten
all but one thing.
Their dress says it.
They leave themselves notes.
They are lovable.

Keeping a journal

By now, you have probably discovered several things:
• You are much more skilful at writing quickly in response to an idea, without going through that stage of vacillation, hesitancy, paralysis, and non-writing, because you realize that writing has to start somewhere and that your first halting words are not sacrosanct, but merely a way of clearing the deck for action, enabling you to make choices, defining and refining what *fascinates* you.
• Writing's subject-matter can be anything: the effectiveness of your work depends on how astute you have been in discerning what fascinates you, as Ted Hughes says, and how adroitly you have conveyed this to a reader or listener through words.
• Knowledge is valuable for writing, but not knowledge for its own sake: rather knowledge for its human fascination, for its illumination of the human condition. Hence reading, viewing, listening.
• You are capable of having more than one piece of writing on the go at the one time. Your 'computer' sometimes benefits from the electrical abrasion between two fascinations at once. That abrasion sometimes helps it choose, or it can suddenly throw up the solution to a problem in one piece after thinking about the other.
• After that initial casting about when ideas first go on to paper, you realize that you have caught something worth pursuing: then the joy and the work lies in drafts and redrafts in search of the most effective way to tell the story.

Keeping a journal can help with all this.

Journals can be defined in as many ways as there are writers keeping them, but for the sake of discussion we can say that a journal is a repository of writings and adjuncts to writing that is not a diary and not necessarily written in daily or even weekly. It will be used with reasonable regularity, and when something excites the writer: a news report; a snippet of gossip; a description of an event, a family reunion, a change in experience, a landscape, an urban ghetto, the drift of a film, a death, a conversation. A journal is a collection of disparate facts and atmospheres, all subjective; they reflect you and your fascinations and movements through life and no one else's, although of course they will include details about many other human beings.

I have kept a journal now, with waxing and waning enthusiasm, for thirty-five years. It represents me from an uncertain and eager university student to the uncertain and eager writer I am now! The notebooks I use are reasonably strong and portable, with pages large enough for my looping writing, or for typewritten or printed-out thoughts cut out and stuck in, that will bring occasions, stories or ideas to mind.

Why all this bother? Why keep a journal? First of all, it is no bother. If it were a chore, I'd give it up. Keeping a journal is a pleasure. In it I can dredge my mind and my life, think about things on paper, store them so that I come back to them weeks or years hence, as though they were someone else's experience. In part I'm 'computer-feeding' when I enter material in the journal—storing things away before I lose my sense of them, so that they can be resuscitated later. It is also part therapy, a way of working through personal crises, and adding to the self-knowledge that will strengthen my stories. Out of self-knowledge comes convincing story-telling.

Thomas Mallon, in his fascinating book, *A book of one's own: people and their diaries*, describes keeping a journal as 'savour[ing] experience in the curious pleasure of writing it down'. It is important to be aware that the journal is a tool to the main purpose and not the main purpose itself, which is writing stories at a professional level. The journal, unlike the daily diary, loses much of its point if one becomes a slave to it.

The entries in my journal are labelled with date and place. At one stage I even made a rough table of contents on the cover of each notebook. When I have been pursuing the one subject through the account of many years—what I have written about my birthplace, for example—I have cross-referenced the notebooks in a rough way. It is clear that what goes into your journal depends on you, your interests, your bent in writing, your psychology, your personality, your sense of humour. Mine contains an incredible mixture, including this news report about a confidence trick reported in the *Geelong Advertiser* of 21 February 1936. It has for me the fascination of near-fantasy, and one day I'll write about it. You might also:

ASTOUNDING STORY OF LAND SALE
TRANSACTION WITH HALF-WITTED SON
ELDERLY FATHER SIGNS CONTRACT IN BADLY-LIT MOTOR CAR

An astounding story of how a Melbourne land-salesman allegedly in-duced an elderly father and his sub-normal son to sign contracts to buy blocks of land was told to Judge Winnecke and a jury in the County Court today. Counsel said that about two years after the son had signed a contract his father was asked by the salesman to take over half the land bought by his son. The man consented and, without his spectacles, and in a badly illuminated motor-car, signed a contract which he afterwards found was for the purchase of entirely different land . . .

How strangely and interestingly journalism and possible fiction come together!

How you use the material in your journal depends again on you and the types of writing you find yourself involved in. I have built many of my poems, stories, and articles on ideas, descriptions or cuttings committed to the journal long before I could see how they would issue in writing for publication. Some snippets are written in a very telegraphic form understandable only to me. In other passages in the journal I have quickly crafted prose descriptions to capture the essence of something and have then had to leave the impressions dormant. Some of these unpremeditated pieces have a freshness that makes it possible to come back to them and turn the prose version of the event or situation into a poem. That is one of the advantages of the journal: it is not often self-conscious in the way it is written, and holds some of the writer's freshest phrases— phrases worth preserving, which might seed larger stories one day.

Perhaps you will think of beginning a journal and experimenting with the form that is most appropriate for you. Keeping a journal applies to many other forms of writing also—reviewing, journalism, copywriting, biography, autobiography and so on.

Transition: the poetry of prose

We have now reached the divide between poetry and prose. We are close to the territory of prose fiction—the short story, the novel and a number of other forms—but the divide is not clear-cut. Travellers in this border country cannot be certain on which side of the divide they stand, because imaginative prose has its poetry too.

The prose poem

One of the greatest exponents of the prose poem in English is the American poet Robert Bly. You might like to seek out his book, *The morning glory*, published in 1975, which collects his prose poems of the previous ten years or so, or his collection, *Sleepers joining hands* or his recent *Selected poems*. In 1985 Bly visited Australia, gave lectures and poetry readings, and conducted workshops. What follows is modelled in part on one of those workshops where a number of writers gathered to write prose poems. This writing works well in a group, so if you can, organize a group of your own. The idea works well for the solitary writer too, which is the usual condition of most of us.

You will need, again, an object that is inert but interesting. Choose another object with similar qualities to the one you chose in the earlier exercise but with which you are not particularly familiar. You might be able to get someone else to produce one for you that will be new to you. You will write about it in three stages, with a time limit of eight minutes for each, writing rapidly to make a first draft, but not polishing any of the three until later. You should write in prose lines—where the length of line *is* governed by the position of the right hand margin!

1 (eight minutes) As in the earlier exercise, write about the object using all your senses and all the imagery you can to conjure up its presence for someone who has no chance to see, hear, feel, smell or taste it, or to know the way it sits, what it weighs, how it catches the light. You should have one paragraph of prose when you finish. Allow yourself a pause with your eyes closed.

2 (eight minutes) Now write about the object and the way it relates to your mother or your father. This requires honesty and an imaginative leap. Again, your piece will reach for imagery (but not too often) to convey how you feel about the connection between the object and your parent. Write rapidly towards a first draft and round the piece off as the time to stop approaches. Begin this paragraph of prose with the words, 'This (name of object) reminds me of my (father or mother) . . .' When you have finished, pause again with your eyes closed.

3 (eight minutes) Now write about the object as it touches your loneliness. Again honesty; again free your reactions and write quickly and intensely in imagery. Begin your paragraph of prose with the words, 'The (name of object) touches my loneliness . . .' Again, try to round off your statement as you see the time limit approaching.

Robert Bly's Blighted Log

It is a chunk of redgum from the paddocks, large enough to fill a third of the table top, sitting there on its sawn edge, but rising like smoke or perhaps wilful grey flames. Years have cracked its hide, frost and sun have sprung fissures. In them, and in a pocket of black where fire has pried, the spiders have made white purses. The wood tastes of sunlight and dust, of unhurried drying. There is grit in the torn flesh, exposed when a tree rended. It is rough and impassive to the touch, a quarter of the way to the uncompromising stab of schrapnel.

This wood is as gaunt as my father, now in his eighty-third year—a face indifferent with age's indifference. It is itself and neither likes nor dislikes that. But it is much more massy than the man who took me swimming, his thin legs in the bulky togs, his face surprising without his glasses, his fingers careful to place his towel before he dived. This log can outstare the sun as my father has never been able to do. I can imagine it laying down the woody law, while my father, the son of ministers and Scottish doctors, is fine-balanced, thin like a reed, uncertain.

This grey wood is as heavy and lonely as the five minutes, the lights full on still, when everyone has gone to bed and I sit tired of written words—mine and others'. The tap runs with a silver whisper for a moment upstairs, then stops. The wind wraps the house in webs. I put hands on my knees to think, and know I am alone. But what are these scars of fire? How many years do they go back? The log seems to have absorbed them just as we must the fact that we are essentially solitary. To touch others; to know they are there in the clutter, is freedom. Their yearning is outward, also—stiff upper lip. To touch again and again, and yet walk with the moon, is all we'll know. Unique, unique says the log in its silent whorl of statement.

Allow yourself a longer break without touching what you have written. If you have written directly and honestly you will have captured a spirit. Let it lie for a time. Go and do the dishes or milk the cows or clean the car. Go and plant those herbs. Hold off until the evening, or the next day. Then read it afresh. Rewrite the sections of it that are awkward, but do not extensively redraft it. Appraise what you have—a piece of prose with a poetic intent and imaginative leap; an economic, finite and structured musing; a prose poem, in fact, using the imagery of poetry and the form of prose on the page.

You will realize that you can ring the changes on this idea, and practise writing further prose poems, keeping the three-part structure for the time being, but using subjects other than static objects as your centre-pieces. The requirements that you set for the second and third paragraphs must put you under pressure, must cast you into yourself. (Writing about my parent? What darknesses lurk there? Writing about my loneliness? What have I to declare about that?)

The Australian poet Andrew Taylor has also written some fine prose poems that appear in his collection of poetry called *Parabolas*. Tomas Tranströmer, the Swedish poet whom Robert Bly has translated into English, has several of them in his collection, *Truth barriers*. Others who write in the form are David Ignatow, Russell Edson, Christa Wolf, Osip Mandelstam, Michael Benedikt, Richard Shelton, and Robert Francis. Many literary journals—*The Paris review* and Melbourne's *Scripsi* are two of them—quite often carry prose poems and experimental prose writing from which you will gain a deeper impression of what is possible in the form.

There is an illuminating and intriguing piece on the writing of prose poems by the American Russell Edson. He writes about the prose poem in an essay, 'Portrait of the writer as a fat man: Some subjective ideas and notions on the care and feeding of prose poems', in *A field guide to contemporary poetry and poetics*, edited by Stuart Friebert and David Young. Edson manages to capture the element of artlessness that is

WRITER

necessary to the prose poem—'to find a prose free of the self-consciousness of poetry; a prose more compact than the storyteller's; a prose removed from the formalities of *literature* . . .' Edson describes the prose of the prose poem as a 'cast-iron aeroplane that can actually fly, mainly because its pilot doesn't seem to care if it does or not'. What makes us so fond of the form, he says, 'is its clumsiness, its lack of expectation or ambition'.

Following are the original full versions of the poems 'Night sowing' and 'Diver' which you worked on in the exercise on pages 37 and 38:

Night Sowing
O gentle, gentle land
Where the green ear shall grow,
Now you are edged with light:
The moon has crisped the fallow,
The furrows run with night.

This is the season's hour:
While couples are in bed,
I sow the paddocks late,
Scatter like sparks the seed
And see the dark ignite.

O gentle land, I sow
The heart's living grain.
Stars draw their harrows over,
Dews send their melting rain:
I meet you as a lover.

Diver
Alone on the tower
I'm not confident.
The water is black
And distant.

I think of style
And raise my arms and aim,
Holding back the plunge.
It's mostly a game

That touches terror,
Then terror goes—
I view my fingers,
My toes.

'Defiance, love and revolt
Make the diver dive
And prove, through dying,
He's alive,'
A voice preaches in my head . . .

And so I dive.

Water gulps me down,
Chilling me with its grip,
Then arms pine up and up
Like worship.

PART THREE

Prose fiction

Truth's elder sister—fiction

Rudyard Kipling

I think a lot about a story and jot down notes and work my way towards it, almost looking in the other direction. You know what you want to do and you sleepwalk towards it, as someone once said. You know subconsciously that you're getting there, but you don't want to get there too deliberately because then you might lose it . . .

Beverley Farmer

Only that which does not teach, which does not cry out, which does not persuade, which does not condescend, which does not explain, is irresistible.

William Butler Yeats

Prose style

If you are writing a fictional story in prose, or your own story as autobiography, or a 'colour piece', a feature article for a magazine or newspaper, or a commissioned chapter for a book on conservation—if you are involved in any of these things, there are a number of different ways of doing it.

Read aloud these extracts from prose fiction.

---

1 The shot was fired about 4.30 in the morning. An hour before dawn, and a little more than an hour before the time set for the rising of the family. Poultry-farming involves early rising, but not necessarily 4.30. Everybody and everything was sleeping. Not a feather had shuffled in the long rows of white-painted pens perched terrace-like on the hillside. Not a twitter had come from the starlings and sparrows crowding the cherry-plums and boobiallas behind the homestead.

For several seconds after the shot had broken the silence its echoes rumbled along the shallow valley and crackled back from the opposing slopes. Everybody was awakened, but they kept still for a moment, as people do at such a time, collecting their wits, separating dream from fact, waiting to see what would happen next. There were five of them: Arthur Brady and his wife Margaret, their thirteen-year-old son Lance, Grandfather Brady, and Hugh Griffiths, an itinerant labourer who had been doing some draining and was due to go on his way that day immediately after breakfast.

First reaction came from the Bradys' bedroom, the voice of Mrs Brady in an excited whisper:

'Arthur, did you hear that?'

'My oath I heard it!' There followed the sounds of a man hurriedly getting out of bed, and the click of a light-switch.

It had been a hot night, with all doors left wide open for free circulation of air, and the sudden flood of light in the bedroom dispelled the darkness all through the house.

In that opening to John Morrison's short story, 'Morning glory', the language is plain and unambiguous. The sentences and paragraphs contribute to tight, economical story-telling, in which a physical context and characters are established, tension is sown, and questions are raised to which the reader is eager to have the answers. It is written in a social realist style, a style of which John Morrison is one of Australia's most skilful exponents.

Now read and hearken to the rhythms and word use of another Australian writer of fiction, as he describes his character, Theodora Goodman, travelling across America by train.

2 Sometimes against the full golden theme of the corn and the white pizzicato of the telephone wires there was a counterpoint of houses. Theodora Goodman sat. The other side of the incessant train she could read the music off. There were the single notes of houses, that gathered into gravely structural phrases. There was a smooth passage of ponds and trees. There was a big bass barn. All the square faces of the wooden houses, as they came, overflowed with solemnity, that was a solemnity of living, a passage of days. Where children played with tins, or a girl waited at a window, or calves lolloped in long grass, it was a frill of flutes twisted round a higher theme, to grace, but only grace, the solemnity of living and of days. There were now the two coiled themes. There was the flowing corn song, and the deliberate accompaniment of houses, which did not impede, however structural, because it was part of the same integrity of purpose and of being . . .

The train rocked the track.

Lying on her shelf at night, listening to the dying wind of many sleepers, Theodora was afraid that this movement might end in an intolerable clash of cymbals. So she compelled her stockings. So she unfolded herself from the narrow shelf. Her hat, with its large black gauze rose, more a sop to convention than an attempt at beauty, was easy to manage. It knew her head. She soon was ready.

There were bells in the night, wheels, and a long gush of steam.

Theodora trod down, out of the high, stationary train, on to the little siding . . .

Patrick White, *The aunt's story*

The aunt's story was one of his novels that was closest to Patrick White's heart. It was first published in 1948. Having just come from the writing of poetry, you will see that this prose story, like poetry, is conducted almost entirely at the level of imagery and imaginative possibility. It is written in what we might call a prose-poet's style. Patrick White, in his novels, novellas and short stories, is perhaps the most revered writer of that type in Australian fiction. White's prose doesn't 'explain', it reveals action and thought and motivation through suggestion, leaving the reader free to interpret on the one hand, but also with work to do to follow the depth of the story; it uses prose rhythms that match the story's movement forward; it has an idiosyncratic sentence structure, not unlike poetry; it suggests the inner life of the mind, the place of memory and instability and intuition.

What is prose style? What is style? Is it simply the way words are used or is it the level of imagery? sentence structure and variation? paragraphing? rhythm? Is it governed by whether the writer frees his or her imagination, or is that the realm of the writer's preliminary thought rather than style? Interesting questions, to which you might give different answers at different times. What is the relationship between thought and style? Is style partly a cultural thing? How much does it depend on what the writer chooses to include in the story? How much has style to do with subject matter, with a writer's preoccupations? Are the preoccupations of writers in one country rather different from those in others? How much is style a product of personality, of individual psyche? How many styles has the one writer?

Writing and its details seldom allow for any hard and fast answers to such questions, but the implications will touch you as you write—to raise the questions is to keep aware. Katharine Anne Porter, the great American writer of short stories, hazards an opinion based on her own experience (despite the generic 'man'), in an interview with *The Paris review:* 'Style is the man. Aristotle said it first, as far as I know, and everybody has said it since, because it is one of those unarguable truths. You do not create a style. You work, and develop yourself; your style is an emanation from your own being.'

Australia: from social realism to pluralism

The extracts from John Morrison and Patrick White illustrate how writing has changed in Australia. A strong social-realist tone prevailed until the Second World War and beyond into the 1950s and the early 1960s. The reasons for this are quite complex. The history of the country since European settlement is short, and its culture is still young. White Australians were preoccupied with establishing frontiers, founding primary and pastoral industries, and waging a pragmatic and sometimes bitter battle (which we are now regretting) against a 'harsh' natural world. Henry Lawson's blunt, ironic, laconic prose style, which was also the dominant style of the *Bulletin's* other writers, was popular and influential. Australia's literary style was almost certainly affected by our physical distance from the centres of European and American culture where writers of prose fiction were exploring other ways of setting down human experience. While Australian writers like Katharine Susannah Prichard, Vance Palmer, Frank Dalby Davison, Leonard Mann, Gavin Casey, John Morrison, Ruth Park, Judah Waten, D'arcy Niland, Kylie Tennant, Alan Marshall, Dymphna Cusack and others were telling Australian stories in basically social-realist terms during the 1920s, 1930s and 1940s, writers in Europe and America were opening to ideas that were influencing the arts in general—particularly painting—and therefore writing's way of re-presenting the world.

None of this is to say that social-realist writing is necessarily less valuable or less moving than other styles. In its purest form it is a style of plain statement, different from the work of those we have already called the 'prose poets' and different from more recent writers who are

56

sometimes called 'fabulist' or 'speculative' or 'metafictional' or 'reflexive' writers. It is difficult to generalize, since any one writer may employ several different styles and narrating positions in his or her oeuvre, or be at different times social realist, prose poet, or something altogether different.

Patrick White, the first Australian to receive the Nobel Prize for Literature, played a vital part in changing the Australian approach to story-telling. When he returned to Australia from Britain and Europe in 1948, with two novels and some plays published, White found himself reassessing his country and its portrayal in fiction. In the four or so years he worked to perfect his novel, *The tree of man*, his instinctive view of the continent urged him to produce a story unlike any other in Australian writing, in reaction to the dominant social-realist strain he found in Australian novels and short stories. In an essay, 'The prodigal son', published some years later, White discusses prose style and ways of story-telling as products of the writer's sensibility; he also hints at the influences of English and European writing, painting and music:

It was the exaltation of the 'average' that made me panic most . . . I wanted to try to suggest in this book [*The tree of man*] every aspect of life through the lives of an ordinary man and woman. But at the same time I wanted to discover the extraordinary behind the ordinary, the mystery and the poetry which alone could make bearable the lives of such people, and incidentally, my own life since my return . . . I wanted to give my book the textures of music, the sensuousness of paint . . . Above all, I was determined to prove that the Australian novel is not necessarily the dreary, dun-coloured offspring of journalistic realism . . .

The novels and short stories that White produced in the ensuing years were not at first readily accepted in Australia. They were wrought like poetry; they had indeed the textures of music, the sensuousness of paint, but perhaps more importantly they penetrated the boorish, swaggering, independent and intellectually complacent Australian and discovered in him or her perhaps gentleness, or fatuous materialism or xenophobia, vengefulness, cruelty, violence, or a muddled, groping sort of religion. All this ran counter to the matey norm of much Australian realist writing, which sometimes seemed to feel obliged to document events such as the Great War, Labour and its battles with Capital, the Depression and the Second World War. The differences between what Australian critics and readers expected of an Australian fiction writer in the 1950s and what Patrick White offered them in his stories and novels underscore the point that 'style' in prose story-telling is grounded in the way the writer sees human nature and its exemplification in society. That is what determines what the writer will concentrate upon in her story, the way he will choose to allow the words to fall in telling it.

The greater acceptance in the 1960s of the quality and difference of White's vision was one factor helping to create in Australia a readiness for a much more pluralistic range of story-telling. It provided the receptive climate for, and coupled with the work of, writers who flowered later—Jessica Anderson, Murray Bail, Marion Campbell, Peter Carey, Anna Couani, Peter Cowan, Blanche d'Alpuget, Beverley Farmer, Helen Garner, Kate Grenville, Rodney Hall, Barbara Hanrahan, Shirley Hazzard, Janette Turner Hospital, David Ireland, Elizabeth Jolley, Angelo Loukakis, David Malouf, Peter Mathers, Frank Moorhouse, Sally Morgan, Gerald Murnane, Mudrooroo Narogin (Colin Johnson), Ania Walwicz, Tim Winton, Amy Witting—the list goes on. There is a richness and greater balance of the sexes now in Australian fiction that did not exist in earlier decades. You could do worse than take the list of names, and follow their work in your reading. They will help you sample the flavour of current Australian writing. With this list you can appraise prose and story-telling 'style': it gives you a landscape to explore. You will find that Australian prose fiction is written in a very different context in the 1990s. Fictional and imaginative prose includes elements of poetry—in fact, as Jorge Luis Borges says, quoting Mallarmé: 'There is no such thing as prose; the moment you care about rhythm, it becomes verse.' It is worth pondering this implicit argument for crafting each sentence in prose.

The range of prose fiction

Prose fiction ranges from the short story to the novel. *Novels* are commonly 100 000 words long, but may be as short as 50 000 words. Xavier Herbert's novel, *Poor fellow my country*, was an astounding 850 000 words long, one of the longest novels ever published in the English language.

If you are going to write a novel, you might find four books, among a number of others, illuminating. The first is John Braine's *Writing a novel*, in which he stresses Hemingway's advice about getting down a first draft any way you can, probably in imperfect form, so that you have a story to work on and refine. The second is John Steinbeck's *Journal of a novel*, an account in letters of work on his novel, *East of eden*. The third and fourth are also Steinbeck's: his recently published journal of the writing of his great novel, *The grapes of wrath*, called *Working days—the journals of The grapes of wrath, 1938–1941* and *The harvest gypsies: On the road to The grapes of wrath*. Like many another solitary writer, Steinbeck despaired of the novel as he wrote it. And yet, it has since sold more than fourteen million copies and still sells one hundred thousand paperback copies each year in the United States!

The *novella*, a short novel, contains between 12 000 and 35 000 words.

The *recit*, as the French call it, falls somewhere between 18 000 words and 50 000 words. It is strongly autobiographical.

Next comes what the French call the *nouvelle* and the English call the long short story. It might commonly contain between 8000 and 12 000 words.

The *short story* most commonly contains some 2000 to 8000 words. *Short short stories* often contain 1000 words or less.

Short fiction

'Storytelling is as old as campfires,' according to *The short story: An introduction*, and yet as H. E. Bates points out, the history of the *written* short story 'is not vast, but very brief'. Like the novel, which originated two centuries earlier, the short story as a written form has developed in different languages and cultures, first among Russian, American and French writers from the 1830s to the 1870s. English writers took it up somewhat later, by which time the Frenchman, Guy de Maupassant, the Russian, Anton Chekhov, and others had strengthened and compressed the form.

The short story: An introduction, by Stone, Packer and Hoopes, follows the history of the short story's development in detail, providing many examples. You can add to it books like Sean O'Faolain's *The short story*, Frank O'Connor's *The lonely voice*, T. O. Beachcroft's *The modest art*, and Clifton Fadiman's *The world of the short story*, but go to those books *after* you have written some short stories yourself.

Every commentator on the short story suggests different precursors: one sees the form's beginnings in Sir Walter Scott's work, others in the American Nathaniel Hawthorne, or in Edgar Allan Poe, or in the Russians Nikolai Gogol and Ivan Turgenev. Some find them as far back as King Alfred's time or in Chaucer's *Canterbury tales*. Despite these disagreements, commentators and writers of the short story generally agree about the modern short story's major distinguishing features—short stories are *not*, they stress, merely short novels or bits of novels.

When the short story developed and was refined during the nineteenth century, its writers—the Americans first among them—knew the form was not akin to the novel. Because of its length, the novel can afford the development of a number of characters whose fortunes might be followed through different environments, and whose personalities might be revealed in detail. The novelist can afford to create a main plot and perhaps several sub-plots; can develop background, setting, landscape; can craft scenes sequentially, so that each arises out of the former, or even out of several earlier scenes. Novelists can often move their story forward by raising questions and then answering them, each resolution forming a climax in the story-telling.

The short story, with its 2000 to 8000 words, can afford few of these things. Edgar Allan Poe, the early American short-story writer, thought deeply about its essence. Writing as early as 1842, he stressed several things about the form. He knew that the short story could only afford 'a certain unique and single effect' and emphasized that this 'unity of effect or impression' meant that the story must be able to be read 'at one sitting', in contrast with the novel which takes much longer to read and absorb. 'In the whole composition,' wrote Poe, 'there should be no word written, of which the tendency, direct or indirect, is not to the one pre-established design'.

Many writers have endorsed Poe's view that the short story's power and intensity came from this singleness of effect, this compression. Other writers have recognized that the short story is closer in essence to the poem than to the novel. Writing about the short story, Elizabeth Bowen said that 'poetic tautness and clarity are so essential to it that it may be said to stand at the edge of prose.' It should have, she said, 'the valid central emotion and inner spontaneity of the lyric [poem] . . .'

Writers repeatedly remark that, after the poem, the short story makes the sternest demands as a form. Seemingly easy in its single-mindedness and simple lines, yet it demands greater control, economy and powers of suggestion than the novel or short novel.

The American novelist, William Faulkner, in an interview with *The Paris review* said, partly tongue-in-cheek, 'Maybe every novelist wants to write poetry first, finds he can't, and then tries the short story, which is the most demanding form after poetry. And, failing at that, only then does he take up novel writing . . .'

The Argentinian writer, Julio Cortazar, wrote a luminous essay, 'On the short story and its environs' in *Around the day in eighty worlds*. Referring to Edgar Allan Poe's descriptions of the modern short story, he adds that the modern *shorter* story is distinguished by its 'insistent race against the clock'. Its success, he says, has been through the

---

relentless elimination of all the elements proper to the novella and the novel: exordiums, circumlocutions, situation development, and other techniques . . . What is always astonishing in stories that race against the clock is the overpowering way they employ a minimum of elements to transform certain situations or narrative territories into a story with ramifications as extensive as those of the most developed novella.

Cortazar finds that writing such stories puts a tremendous strain on the writer; when he writes it is like an obsession and then an exorcism, after which he can return to the everyday world:

Anyway, that's how I wrote many of my stories, including some relatively long ones, such as 'Street weapons': through an entire day relentless anguish made me work without interruption until the story ended, and

PROSE FICTION

only then, without even reading it over, did I go down to the street and walk by myself, no longer being Pierre, no longer being Michele . . . My experience tells me that in a sense a short story like the ones I have been describing does not have a *prose structure*. Every time I have undertaken to revise the translation of one of my stories (or tried to translate a story by another, as I did once with Poe), I have been struck by the degree to which the effectiveness and the *meaning* of the story depend on those values that give poetry, like jazz, its specific character: tension, rhyme, internal rhythms, the unexpected within the parameters of the anticipated, that *fatal liberty* that cannot be altered without an irrevocable loss . . .

He goes on to say that modern stories are 'affixed like indelible scars on any reader who can appreciate them: they are living creatures, complete organisms, closed circles, and they breathe. *They* breathe, not the narrator, like poems that endure and unlike prose . . .'

Reading

We have examined the short story rather than other prose forms at this point because of its affinities with poetry and poetry's compression and singleness of purpose. It's a personal choice where you go next. You can write your own stories; you can read others' stories for the way they are told; or you can move from writing to reading as the need takes you.

If it's example you are after at this stage, you can follow up the stories of some of the writers who have been important in the development of the short story: Edgar Allan Poe, Nathaniel Hawthorne, Bret Harte, Robert Louis Stevenson, Thomas Hardy, Rudyard Kipling, Nikolai Gogol, Ivan Turgenev, Herman Melville, Gustav Flaubert, Alphonse Daudet, Giovanni Verga, Guy de Maupassant, Stephen Crane, Henry Lawson, Thomas Mann, E. M. Forster, James Joyce, Virginia Woolf, D. H. Lawrence, Isaac Babel, Katherine Mansfield, Katherine Anne Porter. You will find their stories in reputable anthologies of the short story, or in collections of each author's work.

Rather than pursuing the history of the short story, you could begin with contemporary short prose fiction—examples of the *modern* short story, the *short* short story and the experimental short story. Remember, the writing should come first.

Good examples distilled from among Australian short-story writers appear in Murray Bail (ed.), *The Faber book of contemporary Australian short stories*; Laurie Hergenhan (ed.), *The Australian short story*; Brian Kiernan (ed.), *The most beautiful lies*; Frank Moorhouse (ed.), *The state of the art*; Don Anderson (ed.), *Transgressions*; Sneja Gunew (ed.), *Displacements: Migrant story tellers*; Sandra Zurbo (ed.), *Stories of her*

61

life; Frank Moorhouse (ed.), *Fictions 88*; Anna Gibbs and Alison Tilson (eds), *Frictions.*

For overseas examples of work from the recent past or from contemporary writers you might look at Donald Allen and Robert Creeley (eds), *New American story*; Philip Stevick (ed.), *Anti-story: An anthology of experimental fiction*; Cyril M. Gulassa (ed.), *The fact of fiction*; and Don Anderson (ed.), *Enchanted apartments: Sad motels.* Select from writers such as Italo Calvino, Marguerite Duras, Donald Barthelme, Thomas Pynchon, William Gass, Susan Sontag, Walter Abish, John Barth, Colette, Alice Munro, Raymond Carver, Janet Kauffman, Marilynne Robinson, Gilbert Sorrentino, Katherine Mansfield, Jorge Luis Borges, John Cheever, Gabriel Garcia Marquez, Jane Bowles, Margaret Atwood, Carlos Fuentes, Isobel Allende, Angela Carter, Alain Robbe-Grillet, Joyce Carol Oates, Janet Frame, Saul Bellow, Bernard Malamud, Edna O'Brien, Jamaica Kincaid, John Updike, Grace Paley, Doris Lessing, V. S. Pritchett, Ernest Hemingway, Frank Sargeson, Nadine Gordimer, John O'Hara, Flannery O'Connor, J. D. Salinger, Eudora Welty, William Faulkner, Leonora Carrington, Heinrich Böll, Carson McCullers, Sean O'Faolain, Willa Cather, Jane Gardam and others.

Most of the Australian writers listed on page 58 are writing short fiction; others include: Zeny Giles, Gillian Mears, Garry Disher, Carmel Bird, Olga Masters, Gabriel Lord, Amanda Lohrey, Barry Hill, Liam Davison, Thea Astley, Fay Zwicky, Michael Wilding, Kerryn Goldsworthy, Glenda Adams, Finola Moorhead, Richard Lunn, Barbara Brooks.

The stories of others may cut across your single-minded involvement with the story you are making, and you may not want to read anything while you are writing in case your own voice is stifled.

On what do stories rest?

Vance Palmer, the Australian short story writer and novelist, wrote about the 'modern short story' in 1944:

Because of its length, the short story must move on more delicate lines of implication than the novel. It should suggest more than it states, lure the reader into co-operating by the use of his imagination. Its solidity may rest, not on an array of detail, but on the integrity of its style. And, lastly, it should move with a dancing gait, not with the dogged, pedestrian step of a traveller out to cover a long distance . . . We no longer demand that [the short story] shall have a formal beginning, a middle, and an end: that it shall contain a plot as easily extracted as the backbone of a fish; one able to be served (to juggle a little with the image) as an anecdote at the dinner-table. Nowadays a short story may be a dream, a dialogue, a study of character, a poetic reverie; anything that has a certain unity and the movement of life . . .

The short story today, he might have added, may not even have a 'climax', after which, traditionally, the story used to quickly finish.

It is difficult to be definitive about what makes short fiction work these days: there is such a variety of forms, content and interaction between tone, style and storyline. That is why it is perhaps better to speak of the pivot, or perhaps several balancing-points, on which modern short fiction rotates as it is told to us. Frank O'Connor helps to explain this notion when he says that between the beginning of the story and the end 'an iron bar must be bent and be seen to be bent'—something must break, something must be resolved, come to a head, be denied, be disclosed, released, answered, changed, deepened, tightened. This is best illustrated by looking at what makes stories irresistible, and by thinking about the pivots or balancing-points of stories that you might write. Here are two story-lines.

1 Marjorie Barnard, 'The persimmon tree'

This story can be found in both Murray Bail's and Laurie Hergenhan's collections of Australian short stories. It is classic story-telling but surprisingly modern for the 1940s. It is only three pages long. It contains no one's voice, no dialogue, and yet it 'breathes', and once you have read it, it haunts you. If we analyse its story-line, it appears deceptively slight and evanescent. A female narrator, about whom we are told little, recovering from an operation which has saved her life, takes a flat in a suburb in late winter. She observes the neighbours in the street, but becomes intrigued with only one of them, a lone woman of about her own age, reserved and self-contained. On a sill opposite the narrator's own window is a line of persimmons ripening in the spring sunshine. Soon the narrator, through observation, realizes that the sill belongs to her lone neighbour, who lives behind the fine, thin curtains that are never drawn back. She ponders on her own loneliness and that of her unknown neighbour. Days pass, spring advances, the bulbs in the neighbour's bowl sprout on the sill. The narrator as she convalesces, watches the shadows of a tree cast on the wall of her room as buds turn to leaves. One day, looking out of her window, she sees that her neighbour is standing, just inside the curtains' shadow, in a dark gown. As she watches, the woman raises her arms, the gown falls, and she stands there naked and still. The story concludes: 'I turned away. The shadow of the burgeoning bough was on the white wall. I thought my heart would break.'

I apologize for summarizing such a story in this way, but it might help you to explore what I mean by the very slender bases on which many stories balance. Look at the wording, the absolute simplicity and elemental nature of the story's final lines: it demonstrates how close to poetry a short story can come. Make sure you read the full story for yourself.

On what does the story balance? Rather than a single pivot it rests on a number of things: loneliness; the idea of the sadness of unfulfilment; the idea of common humanity and suffering set against beauty; the way life mixes autumn and spring, decline and stasis against burgeoning and sensuous possibility and renewal? There is a lot we don't know but merely glimpse—that is part of the story's power.

Write

Try writing an account of an incident between two people which depends on deliberately withheld contact and absence of dialogue, but where contact is eventually made.

2 Bernard Malamud, 'Angel Levine'

You will find this story in Malamud's collection, *The magic barrel*. He is a New York Jewish writer. The story-line of 'Angel Levine' concerns a Jewish tailor, Manischevitz, in New York. His business has declined; he has back pain that limits his work; his adult son has died as a soldier; his adult daughter has deserted him; his wife has gradually become weaker and is now terminally ill. The tailor, a devout Jew, prays to God with all his heart for her recovery. Soon after, he comes home to find a 'Negro' relaxing in his kitchen. The 'Negro' declares himself to be Jewish also and something of a freelance angel on probation. He offers the tailor assistance in his suffering, but the tailor, without rancour, tells him he thinks he is a fake, believing also that he is being mocked. The 'Negro' leaves, suggesting where Manischevitz can find him in Harlem if he should change his mind. After a brief respite from Manischevitz's back pain and a slight improvement in his wife's condition, things become worse for both of them. The tailor decides to go in search of Angel Levine, has great difficulty tracking him down in Harlem, and then has to confront a drunk Levine before a honky-tonk joint full of jibing 'Negro' friends. He eventually summons enough courage to declare that he thinks Levine is an angel from God. Levine, purporting to be embarrassed before his friends, accompanies the tailor home, sweeps through his house and seemingly disappears in a whirr of wings from the house roof. Downstairs, Manischevitz returns to find his wife up and about, cleaning the bedroom.

On what does this story rest? At what point is the 'iron bar bent and seen to be bent'? Is it not a story balanced around an act of faith that is particularly difficult for a character to make? Again, read it yourself, and you will discover that it is also modelled on a tradition of Jewish story-telling, of Jewish suffering and Jewish humour, often jokes turned against the self. You will find that Malamud exploits the differences in culture between the Blacks and Jews in New York. You will find that much of the story's delight comes, unlike 'The persimmon tree', from the dialogue which acutely records the idiosyncratic way both the Black and the Jew use the English language. It also depends on Malamud's skill in building the tailor's suffering, creating tension in the reader, to the point where he makes his declaration of faith. Then, for protagonist and reader, the tension is released.

Write

Write a story outline and then perhaps the complete story, in which the pivot is an act of faith, or in which someone is forced to act against his or her better judgement or firmly-held beliefs and in which good flows from the act.

Often the elements upon which stories balance are quite undramatic and common in human experience. In John Updike's story, 'The Happiest I've Been', available in his collection, *The same door*, these are an accumulation of simple things that make for a feeling of self-worth in the college-age man who is the story's narrator: the feeling of being young; a sense of adventure; the experience of whiling the night away at a party; the enjoyment of travelling in the dark by car across his familiar home State; satisfaction at being invited to take the wheel of a car; and importantly, in the one day in the life of this socially uncertain young man, the sense of self-worth engendered in him when two people he values trust him enough to go to sleep beside him!

The invitations to write to which you have just responded are in some ways unrealistic. Often a writer does not know at the start of a story what its balancing point, its central tone and revelation, is going to be. The writing of the story is often an exploration to discover that 'point'.

Stream of consciousness

Most novelists and short-story writers proceed by sentence, paragraph, chapter and part towards a whole. Most eavesdrop on a character's thinking from outside, as it were, in third-person narration, or make the character admit thoughts in a first-person narration.

In the period immediately preceding the First World War, however, three writers began to doubt the conventional way of representing in fiction how people think and make decisions for action. Like scientists coming to the same finding in their separate laboratories, each explored separately how better to represent human thought in words on the page, each arrived at a similar basic conclusion, and each began to employ a similar way of narrating the novel. The three were the English writers Dorothy Richardson and Virginia Woolf, and the Irish writer James Joyce, by then living in Zurich.

We cannot explore here the cultural climate in Europe that allowed new ground in writing to be broken, but developments in painting and photography, the advent of Freudian analysis and the recent availability of new writing from France and Russia combined to emphasize the person, the character, as individual and unique. These three writers questioned 'reality', how life really worked and how writing could approximate it more closely. Virginia Woolf expressed, more cogently than Richardson or Joyce perhaps, the ideas that led to the new way of looking at the world in fiction. How does time advance? How do human beings think about what has happened, is happening, will happen to them? Is it any use pretending that there is one reality and one only? How do writers represent life in action, and the process of human thought and emotions?

In an essay in her book, *The common reader*, Virginia Woolf suggested that the writer of novels hitherto had been at the mercy of a tyrannical expectation that the novel should provide plot, comedy, tragedy, love interest and, as she says,

an air of probability embalming the whole so impeccable that if all his figures were to come to life they would find themselves dressed down to the very last button of their coats in the fashion of the hour. The tyrant is obeyed; the novel is done to a turn. But sometimes, more and more often as time goes by, we suspect a momentary doubt, a spasm of rebellion, as the pages fill themselves in the customary way. Is life like this? Must novels be like this?

Woolf, Richardson and Joyce were convinced that life was far from being like that in reality. Virginia Woolf asked her readers to consider an ordinary human mind on an ordinary day, and the myriad of impressions it receives in a plotless and haphazard way:

Life is not a series of gig-lamps symmetrically arranged; life is a luminous halo, a semi-transparent envelope surrounding us from the beginning of consciousness to the end. Is it not the task of the novelist to convey this varying, this unknown and uncircumscribed spirit, whatever aberration or complexity it may display, with as little mixture of the alien and external as possible?

You should read Virginia Woolf's *To the lighthouse*, James Joyce's *Ulysses*, or part of Dorothy Richardson's novel sequence *Pilgrimage*, to see how this new vision of reality translates into practice. In these novels we are inside the characters' minds, present with them as life bombards them and as they react in a flowing and continuous present, a 'stream of consciousness' as it became known from a review of Dorothy Richardson's novels at the end of the First World War.

Write

Experiment with this form.

• Make sure you can be alone for forty-five minutes or so, and go for a walk to a place you know well where there are people—the supermarket, a shopping centre, a library, the docks, a gallery, an industrial laneway, a college or university union building. Walk through the place. You are there to absorb, listen, think on a free rein. Don't speak to anyone. Come back remembering all the *thoughts* you had, and the things you noted through your senses while you walked. Return to a place where you can write uninterrupted. Write down all the *thoughts* you can remember having as you walked and observed—even the most trivial and seemingly irrelevant. Record the story of your movement, too, as you write. Try adopting Joyce's narrating position in his novel *Ulysses*—make yourself a third person on whom you look down as 'they' take the walk.

• No punctuation. Write the sequence of someone's thoughts as they lie almost asleep and thinking about all the friends they have ever had and what drew them to such differing people. Write the passage without any punctuation, and yet include dialogue and snatches of poetry or song in the piece. Then read the celebrated final thirty or so pages of Joyce's *Ulysses*.

Writing by cut-ups

Many writers besides Woolf, Richardson and Joyce have, of course, pondered about reality and how to represent it. The American novelist, William Burroughs described how he wrote as writing by the 'cut-up'. His writing method consisted of various ways of catching the conjunction of events that comes when one is thinking at two levels:

Somebody is reading a newspaper, and his eye follows the column in the proper Aristotelian manner, one idea and sentence at a time. But subliminally he is reading the columns on either side and is aware of the person sitting next to him. That's a cut-up ... I was sitting in a lunch-room in New York having my doughnuts and coffee. I was thinking that one does feel a little boxed in New York, like living in a series of boxes. I looked out the window and there was a great big Yale truck. That's a cut-up—a juxtaposition of what's happening outside and what you're thinking of ...

This is close in essence to the conclusions of Woolf, Richardson and Joyce about the way the human mind actually works, but with Burroughs it has a greater sense of serendipity.

Burroughs went on to explain that he made notes of all these instances, not certain when or if he'd use them, and kept a diary as well. 'In a sense it's travelling in time', he said. He sometimes kept a three-column account of his travels—one column simply an account of the details of travel, arrival at the airport, what the clerks said, what he overheard on the plane; the second column containing memories and thoughts activated by his encounters; the third column containing details, quotations from the books he was reading. He also kept scrapbooks of photographs he took at the time, and postcards from his destinations. So Burroughs gathered the material for his novels.

You can see from these examples that we are at the interesting point where a writer's 'philosophy' or world-view intersects with their writing method. The Australian novelist, David Ireland, for years used a card system to capture short vignettes, dramas, conversations that made up novels like *The unknown industrial prisoner* and *The glass canoe*. Having preserved the separate but related incidents on the cards, Ireland honed them, and shuffled them to experiment with different orders of presentation. The method reminds us of Patrick White's statement that novel-writing is more like oxy-welding than writing—oxy-welding elements in different configurations to see how they work most effectively. Of course, the world-view and the methods of Burroughs and Ireland make for unusual arrangements of their work on the published page.

The New Journalism

The first generation who learned to turn naturally to television and film as well as to reading for their stories are already middle-aged, and the world has become faster, more technologically complex, harder-edged. Story-telling in the visual arts—particularly film and television—has become tighter, faster and more fragmented.

In the last twenty or thirty years all these things seem to have changed the way human beings see themselves, their lives, and what they regard as possible. In the past, such change introduced the novel in place of the fantastic 'romances' of the sixteenth and seventeenth centuries; Virginia Woolf perceived a change of the same order just after the turn of the twentieth century, and reflected it in her 'stream of consciousness' prose.

Change during the 1960s, 1970s and 1980s has resulted in 'The New Journalism' and then 'Post-modernism'.

The New Journalist writers—Tom Wolfe, Terry Southern, Hunter S. Thompson, Truman Capote, Gay Talese, Norman Mailer, Joan Didion, Barbara L. Goldsmith and others—developed what Capote called 'the non-fiction novel'. He was speaking of his novel, *In cold blood*, based on exhaustive research and interviews with two young murderers and the police, lawyers, and other death-row prisoners with whom they interacted after their conviction and up to the moment of their execution.

Other writers—mainly New York journalists—in the 1960s began writing reports and features that read like fiction in the style of the novel or short story. In New Journalist writing, all the techniques of novelistic story-telling are applied to contemporary factual material usually considered the subject of journalism.

Tom Wolfe's book, *The New Journalism: With an anthology edited by Tom Wolfe and E. W. Johnson*, contains a selection of New Journalist writing. You could read Truman Capote's *In cold blood*, which we will return to later, and also his collection *Music for chameleons*; Tom Wolfe's *The mid-Atlantic man*, *The electric Kool-Aid acid test*, and *Radical chic and mau-mauing the flak catchers*; Hunter S. Thompson's *The Hell's Angels: A strange and terrible saga*, *Fear and loathing in Las Vegas: A savage journey to the heart of the American Dream* and *Generation of swine: Tales of degradation and shame in the 80s*; Norman Mailer's *Armies of the night*; and Joan Didion's *Slouching towards Bethlehem*. Among Australian writers Thomas Keneally comes closest to this technique—in his novels *Gossip from the forest* and *Schindler's ark* among others. As Keneally says, in writing *Schindler's ark* he used 'the texture and devices of the novel to tell a true story'.

Write

A manageable exercise is to try writing a novelistic account of a local council meeting, an industrial negotiation, a confrontation of interests. You will soon find yourself thinking in part as a journalist and also as a conscious novelistic story-teller who is looking for the personality of· the participants and the atmosphere of the events.

If you have more time, brainstorm on paper about situations that might provide the material for a New Journalist novel. Adopt one idea and plan how the tale could be told. If the subject-matter of the novel is in its early stages, you might, if you were to write it as a novel, be committed to follow its course for some time, note-taking, interviewing, thinking, planning.

Post-modernism, metafiction, reflexive fiction

These are more or less interchangeable terms for recent writing in which the writer or narrator steps back from the story in order to write about or comment on the creative process of the story-telling; this commentary then becomes part of the story itself in some way. But metafiction or reflexive fiction (taking its name from the anatomical term 'reflexion': the folding or bending of a thing upon itself) can be much more than that. The one character in the story may, at different times, be the story's writer, narrator, main character, even the Muse that presides over all writing—the possibilities are endless.

69

Julio Cortazar's story, 'The continuity of parks', in his collection, *The southern thruway*, is a short, immediate and highly condensed piece of reflexive fiction. Kerryn Goldsworthy's story, 'North of the Moonlight Sonata', in her collection of the same name, is another. There are reflexive elements in Peter Carey's *Oscar and Lucinda*, Marguerite Duras's *The lover*, Mark Henshaw's novel, *Out of the line of fire*, and in John Fowles's *The French lieutenant's woman*, both as a novel and a film. In the film script made from Fowles's story, the reflexive elements are very strong, with actors playing the role of actors playing the role of nineteenth century lovers. There are many parallels between the different 'levels', and the viewer is offered two possible endings for both the twentieth-century couple and for the nineteenth-century characters they play.

You will find further examples of post-modernist or metafictional writing in Don Anderson's rich collection of recent American short fiction, *Enchanted apartments: Sad motels*. Seek out the stories by Walter Abish, Susan Sontag, William H. Gass, Gilbert Sorrentino, John Barth, Donald Barthelme and his 'minimalist' writer brother, Frederick Barthelme. As one American writer says, such stories are concerned with 'the very act of writing fiction and the difficulties of using language to reflect a reality that in itself may be unknowable'.

Write

1 Write a piece of fiction in which you as narrator write about a writer who is engaged in telling a story in which he becomes a character despite himself.

2 Write a story in which a writer is telling a tale from which she steps back to write about herself and her difficulties in dealing with truth and fiction.

People and situations

As Australian novelist Elizabeth Jolley puts it: 'Writing is always an exploration of human behaviour.' All of us are fascinated by what happens to other people, how other people behave and react; we consume stories about people each day from newspapers, books, magazines, radio, television, the stage, the screen—or around the kitchen table over a cup of coffee. All the arts take as their most common subject a person or people in context. Readers and viewers are interested in beauty, joy, sin, sadness, injustice, love, fear, envy, jealousy, conflict, grief, embarrassment, fun, lies, generosity, fantasy, redemption, forgiveness, compassion.

Writers do not, of course, sit down to write about one of these human qualities, but often conjure up people and their trials—a person, a situation, that fascinates them—and ultimately the story develops a life or presence of its own.

It's hard to generalize about how stories begin; each one is different, as any writer will tell you. So let's enter stories from three of the most likely starting points.

1 Social worlds

Start by thinking of particular social worlds that you know, rather than those you will have to research—it's often better and easier. Many writers do research social worlds: Patrick White researched the Jewish community in Australia before writing *Riders in the chariot*; Thomas Keneally steeped himself in the military and political caste in Europe in order to write his story of the Armistice negotiations, *Gossip from the forest*; Kylie Tennant travelled and camped with people searching for work during the Depression before she wrote her novel, *The battlers*.

Write

First, make a list of the social worlds you know. One section of it might deal with worlds you know well, the other with those you have brushed against briefly. It might include the world of racing or parenting or motoring, medicine, music, religion, conservation, the visual arts, motels, offices, surfing, fashion, motor repairs and towing, merchant shipping, forestry, the airlines, bookselling, and so on. Include the worlds of different Australian cities and towns in which you have lived or stayed.

Make distinctions. Think of the influence of place or environment on the 'worlds' you know. Make notes or begin writing a short piece on the touchstones, the atmosphere, of one of your particular worlds. Think of Rumpole's London as portrayed in John Mortimer's series, 'Rumpole of the Bailey'. Think of Dickens's London in *Oliver Twist* or *A Christmas carol*, of Chaim Potok's Jewish Brooklyn in *The chosen*, of the Nigerian village in Chinua Achebe's *Things fall apart*, or of the remote Western Australian cattle station in Katharine Susannah Prichard's memorable short story, 'The Cooboo'. Consider the coastal towns of Southern New South Wales as Frank Moorhouse captures them in his short stories and his book, *The electrical experience*. Think of Helen Garner's portrayal of inner-city Carlton and Fitzroy in her novel, *Monkey grip*.

Now, from one of those worlds you know well, choose a person whose story arises out of that particular world and fascinates you. How would you tell that person's story in prose fiction? Begin to make a plan. You are not going to write the person's whole life story, but just one main incident or moment of time. How would you make the story endemic to that world, that situation? What vital point might that story centre about? Write yourself detailed notes on how the story might unfold. Remember, the human interest, not the documentary details of the world must take centre stage, and the two must work together. Your person can be based on someone you know and yet be almost purely fictional.

You don't have to know the ending of the story, but write until you know how the story might tend and the tone in which it will be told. Then write an opening few paragraphs of the story, developing the nexus between character and world.

That is one way into a story, but not the only way. 'I find that most of my stories come from anecdotes,' says Jorge Luis Borges, 'although I distort them or change them.' When asked how he knows when an anecdote may be useful to him, Borges replies:

When I hear an anecdote that I think is interesting, I tell it to my friends. Then, somehow, I feel I should write it down. This happens years and years afterwards. If you tell me an anecdote today, it wouldn't find its way into print until some four or five years from now, because the process is a slow one. I suppose other writers may hear an anecdote and the story is given them at once, but in my case I have to sit back and wait, and then, when the moment comes, I have to be very receptive and try not to tamper or tinker with it.

2 The person

Katherine Mansfield, that great New Zealand-born writer of the short story, was so fascinated by people, by personality, that she wrote in her journal in May 1919: 'It takes the place of religion. It *is* my religion of people.' We can follow how she planned the story, 'The weak heart', which was never completed. In her journal notes she sketches first Roddie, and the flash of an idea for a possible story. Then she notes the way she must handle time in telling it. Finally, Mansfield prays that she as author can simply become a self-effacing medium to bring the story into existence:

A weak heart. Roddie on his bike in the evening, with his hands in his pockets *doing marvels* by that dark tree at the end of May Street . . . Today I began to write seriously The Weak Heart—a story which fascinates me deeply. What I feel it needs so peculiarly is a very subtle variation of tense from the present to the past and back again—and softness and lightness, and the feeling that all is in bud, with a play of humour over the character of Roddie. And the feeling of the Thorndon Baths, the wet moist oozy—no, I know how it must be done. May I be found worthy to do it! Lord make me crystal clear for Thy light to shine through . . .

Write

Model your approach on Katherine Mansfield's. Dredge your mind for the people you know or have known, making notes on the ones that most intrigue you. Write a plan or notes about the two or three that remain strongly in your consciousness, beginning to detail how you would tell, in prose, a story based on them.

File your notes, don't throw them out; they may grow to be fully-fledged stories!

3 The eternal dramas

Think of examples *you* have known of human envy and its results; of injustice; jealousy; greed; embarrassment; cruelty; achievement of great happiness against difficult odds; love; a struggle for power; suffering through deprivation; and so on. These experiences are as old as humanity, and yet are always new, and powerful in well-told stories, because in them readers recognize parts of their own experience.

Write

Make notes on three or four human experiences or emotions that might develop into stories. Work out the people involved in each, how they interact, suffer, triumph, fail, separate, come together. In short fiction you need *at most* three principal characters. Make notes on their background, and on the changes you must make to reality before using them as people in a fiction. Think through your possible story-line. Where will you enter it (in short fiction you can't tell it all)? Where do you think it will conclude? What do you want to discover in writing the story? What impression do you want it to leave on the reader? How will you change the events in transmuting real life (experienced, recounted, read about) into fiction? You can think about all these things, sleep on them, revise them—knowing that when you begin to write, you may make quite drastic changes. Fiction develops through plans that build on broken (but still valuable) earlier plans.

The resources of fiction

Resources work cumulatively; they are interconnected; they seed each other. The suggestions for writing that arise out of them will involve you in writing exercises that bring into play some of the story-telling techniques used by short-story writers, some that apply to the novel and the novella, and others that apply to both. They stem from the opportunities and experience life has made available to you—your 'resources' in other words. They must interpret the notion of the writer's resources pretty widely, because it is difficult to generalize about the range of very different stories that writers, including you, might produce.

Character

Characters—the human beings you are going to focus on in your story—are basic to story-telling. Thoughts of women, men, children, in perhaps several situations (the novel or novella) or a single situation (short story, short fiction) will often be your starting point, the influence on your first notes, the background to the first exploratory paragraph you write.

You should know your characters well. What does she look like? You should have a picture of her, even though you might never make a full physical description of her in your story. Does she smoke, eat out a lot, wish she were living in the country, dislike reading books? Is she obsessed with cars? How does she speak—quickly, indistinctly? What about him? Is he shy? Is he racist? What is his room like? How does he interact with his parents? What is their household like—a place of communication by grunt and monosyllable only? What body-language quirks has he—the scratching behind his head with an absent-minded hand when he's thinking, embarrassed? What does he think about personal commitment, marriage as against career? How has he been hurt in the past—in a relationship, by a relative? What, to him, are the sheer joys of life? What is his unattainable ideal? What is his sense of humour? What does he find funny?

You need to know all these things and more in order to create a believable person, whose actions are not strangely or unnaturally motivated and who is not a stereotype—the typical man, the typical woman, the stereotypical hippy; the dry, bespectacled teacher; the mug cop; the slimy politician; the barber, who's small and flash, as barbers mostly are. Out of her or him must come something deep, complex, individual—not something predictable. Character development and motivation for action and decision go hand in hand. Your he or she will be flawed, as we all are, and yet will have redeeming qualities, and perhaps one strong trait that will decide their fate in the story.

Your characters' behaviour must be believable given what you, the manipulator of the story, have allowed us to know about them, and yet they must have enough individuality and freedom of choice to be interesting.

Write

Describe two characters: one male, one female. He is lying on the beach, his head under a wide hat. She is sitting quietly in the front room of a beach-house some 100 metres behind him, listening to music. They have never met, but they are destined to before the day ends. You are describing each in the fullest detail, one at a time initially, then perhaps moving from one to the other, only returning to their physical presence beside the sea every now and then, as you reveal their lives, their past, their aspirations. Start with a physical description in each case, then work from that.

Character and situation

Situation is not physical setting. Situation is the human dilemma, stage of life, area of indecision in which the main character in your story (short fiction) or main characters (novel, novella) find themselves—and it is this that will interest the reader and you as you write. What will happen to this character in this situation?

Write

Write three character profiles for short fiction that put your one or two or three—no more—characters in a specific situation, and explore how you would tell your story about them, making notes as you go, from the set of experiences or memories that put them in your mind in the first place. For instance: the maiden sisters; whole life in the valley; the family graves on the hillside behind the house; nursing elderly relatives in lieu of marriage; unfulfilment; finally partly mad; dutiful; reliance on each other, yet hatred; visit from nephew; active; from the world outside; disturbing; how do they act while he is there? afternoon tea; photographs; and after he has gone?

Write

Now, in order to explore the broader scope of the novel or novella, write a plan of character and situation that does not deal simply with one 'spot of time', but treats several important characters and one main one, and covers a considerable time—twenty years? fifty years?—in their interactions with each other, and throws up several crisis points, times of change, tension and resolution. For instance: passage of time; aspirations of group of university students; 1960s; dreams; ambition; follow them through until 1990s; what do they become? how do they decline from their youthful ideals about work, marriage, sex, social responsibility? how do roles reverse? Apparent central figure ADRIAN—aspires to be academic; strongest personality among group of five; JOAN, daughter of Hunter's Hill businessman; KEITH, Adrian's 'mate' of schooldays, and at university, scholarship student from Kensington, impressionable, naive, easily put upon; VALMAI, daughter of painter, no father, allowed greater freedom than other four, already more mature socially, politically, sexually than the others, 'girlfriend' of Adrian when story opens; PETER, from grazing family in Hunter Valley, ambivalent sexually, uncertain relationship with Keith, who is later to marry his sister Connie; Adrian intelligent, self-centred, dominating, charming, becomes increasingly ruthless. High points imposed on each life by Vietnam ballot, marriage, relationships, separation, divorce. In their stars—Peter's suicide, Adrian's conviction as drug distributor, Valmai's move to Melbourne, affair with Keith, who emerges as strongest figure, lawyer, involved in Adrian's trial, etc. How balance the account, with advancing time, of each of the five's fortunes? Third person omniscient narration? Or each character speaking for themselves? Rotation?

This is one way into a novel, but there are others.

Character, situation, and plot

Plot is the order behind your story, the way in which it unfolds. The way you choose to manipulate incident depends on how you wish the reader to view your characters, their situation, and their decisions and actions. The revelation of events need not be sequential. In an increasing number of fictions, influenced by film and television, time sequence is not progressive. To have the past or future intrude upon the present can intrigue the reader, colour the experience of characters' actions, and raise and maintain tension.

Character, situation, plot, and tension

'Without contraries is no progression,' said William Blake. Conflict, or the tension of decision-making or the agony that follows the wrong action are all of interest to readers and writers, to any curious human being. No human quality is dramatically interesting unless it bounces off something approaching an opposite, either implicitly (where comparison is left to the reader's knowledge of the world and how it goes) or more explosively and explicitly. 'I am going to borrow your car,' contains no story. But the response, 'Over my dead body!' opens up a tale.

Georges Simenon, the prolific French writer of serious novels, and his less serious Maigret detective novels, describes for the Paris review how he comes to his novels. He commonly has two or three ideas or themes for novels in his mind. 'I never even think that they might serve for a novel; more exactly they are the things about which I worry,' he says. Then he settles on one, finds some atmosphere, conjures time of year, place, until a small world comes into his mind, with a few characters about whom his original theme hovers. 'They will have the same problem I have in my mind myself. And the problem—with those people—will give me the novel,' he adds. Then he fills an envelope with detail about his characters and places; looks for names for his characters in a telephone book; consults maps to plan where the events of his story will happen. Then, with his writer's experience, he explains:

And the beginning will always be the same; it is almost a geometrical problem: I have such a man, such a woman, in such surroundings. What can happen to them to oblige them to go to their limit?' That's the question. It will be sometimes a very simple incident, anything that will change their lives. Then I write my novel chapter by chapter.

'What can happen to them to oblige them to go their limit?' With the answer to that question enters the tension necessary to make the story intriguing.

Write

Try Simenon's method. It applies equally to the novel and short fiction. Adopt one of the things about which you 'worry', create characters that exemplify it somehow, make yourself familiar with them and with the places where things are going to happen to them—and then put them under pressure! Make notes for a story or a novel that arises from this pressure.

The narrator

You are the person in control of your story, but yours may not be the voice telling the story. The voice, the narrator, the viewpoint from which the story is told, is most likely to be someone you have invented. That narrator may in part be you, but could also be someone whose view of the action is directly opposed to yours.

To see how this might work in practice, let's consider Thomas Keneally's novel, *Schindler's ark*. Based on research, but told as fiction, it won the prestigious Booker Prize in 1982. In it he decided to 'use the texture and devices of a novel to tell a true story'. Set in wartime Poland, the central character is Oscar Schindler, a German businessman and speculator living in the Polish city of Cracow, a man who, at risk of his life, organizes the rescue of Jewish forced-labour workers for whom the Nazis plan deportation and either forced labour, summary execution, or more systematic execution in the gas chambers. Keneally's fascination for Schindler came from meeting a *Schindler Jude* (a Schindler Jew), in a leather-goods shop in Beverley Hills, California, thirty-five years after the war's end, learning of the debt of so many survivors to the enigmatic and contradictory Schindler, and then following up other survivors and Schindler's post-war friends for their stories in Australia, Europe, the USA, Israel, Argentina and Brazil.

After his research, when he knew he had the ingredients of a fascinating story, Keneally, like any story-teller, had to decide on several things, amongst them the position and 'person' of the narrator.

How would Keneally narrate the story? The 'I' could be someone who knew Schindler: 'I didn't see Oskar Schindler after that for several weeks ...' or the 'I' could be Schindler himself: 'My first meeting with the SS Commandant ...' If Schindler were to tell the story we would be limited to his view of events, to his view of himself. How much, Keneally had to ask himself, should the narrator know? In a story told from what point of view will the reader be most intensely involved in Schindler's activities and their success or failure?

If the narrator were to be an 'I' (a first-person narrator), then their knowledge would consist only of what they had experienced or been told, even though that could be quite sufficient to tell the story. Keneally presumably decided that a first-person narrator would have been unnecessarily limiting; he chose a third-person, omniscient (all-knowing) narration. At times, the narrator withdraws temporarily from the action, takes the reader aside, as it were, and reports updates or recapitulates:

In observing this small winter scene, we are on safe ground. The young man would to the end of his days wear double-breasted suits, would, being something of an engineer, always be gratified by large, dazzling vehicles . . . [or] So the story of Oskar Schindler is begun perilously, with Gothic Nazis, with SS hedonism, with the thin and brutalized girl, and with a figure of imagination somehow as popular as the golden-hearted whore: the good German.

These fine distinctions within the choice of third-person narration give the story a definite tone—of matter-of-factness, objectivity, even cold-ness—which makes the terrible events described even more terrible.

The choices available to Keneally illustrate the choices available to all storytellers:

First-person narration

If Keneally's first-person narrator had been Schindler, or one of the survivors, Keneally's own feelings and sympathies would run parallel to those of his narrator. There is, however, another possibility: Keneally, in an effort to plumb the thinking of such a person, could write a first-person narrative through the hideous, racially selective view of Amon Goeth, the SS Commandant. 'I, Amon Goeth, have the sacred—the sub-lime and satisfying—power and responsibility of following through the orders of the Führer and Heinrich Himmler in ensuring labour for the Third Reich and in the systematic extermination of the Jews . . .' In that case Keneally's sympathies would not be reflected in the narrator; he might reflect the very reverse. Readers might be left to come to their own moral conclusions. In this case the very choice of narrator and narrator's position might be the prime expression of Keneally's sym-pathies; all would have to be done by implication, all would depend on the reader's attention and awareness.

Think about first-person narration. Think of moral values as they might be presented·through characters or narrators in the novel or short story. Listen to Beverley Farmer as she talks about her own stories: 'My characters might make moral statements, my first-person narrators especially might, but that's not me. First-person narrators are characters like any others.' In short you, the manipulator, the story-teller can create anyone as a narrator.

Some stories lend themselves automatically to first-person narration. You might like to look at the personal intensity of Beverley Farmer's *recit*, written early in her career, entitled *Alone*, or Swift's *Gulliver's travels*. How else could Swift have written that, considering the immediacy and personal revelation he needed for his tale? Other examples include the early novel, *Robinson Crusoe*, by Daniel Defoe; Elizabeth Jolley's partly autobiographical novel, *My father's moon*; Jean Bedford's *Sister Kate*; or many of the stories of the American writer, Raymond Carver.

Write

Write the opening of a story in which your narrator is someone you hate or whose opinions you violently oppose. Make notes about how you might continue the story and conclude it, possibly sketching in several acceptable endings. Don't forget that your narrator must be convincing as a rounded person and not a stereotype.

Write

Write the opening of a story in which your narrator observes the injustices meted out to someone with whom they are completely in sympathy but incapable of helping, although they try. Again, sketch the ways you might bring the story to resolution.

There are other rich possibilities in first-person narration. Because the first-person narrator is a character, as Beverley Farmer says, and because first-person narration tends to bring the reader very close to that character, there is often great tension created in the reader if the narrating 'I' is unreliable, is a liar or a misinterpreter of the events described—if the reader, in other words, is allowed to know more than the narrator.

Such is life, the classic novel of the nineteenth-century Australian writer, Joseph Furphy, is a case in point. Its narrator, Tom Collins, who puts his name to the book as author, is a government official travelling the New South Wales Riverina. We readers come to realize that poignant human drama follows from his misinterpretation of events, or from his ignorance of the results of his actions. He does not know, for instance, although we know if we are attentive, that a man he meets on more than one occasion as a boundary rider is in fact a woman in disguise whose story he has heard earlier in a droving camp. We know, but Furphy's narrator does not, that by setting a haystack on fire he has caused another man to be wrongfully convicted of the crime and sent to gaol. We know, but Tom Collins does not, that a man he decides not to disturb because he is apparently settling down to sleep under a shade tree not far from a station homestead is in fact lost, has been without food and water for days, and dies soon after for want of the knowledge that he is close to help. So the tension for the reader is compounded, so the irony of life deepens in Furphy's manipulated account, told through a fallible first-person narrator. Such is life!

There are other possibilities in first-person narration.

The objective view

In this case the narrator simply describes what people say and do, offering only clues about states of mind or attitudes, leaving readers to infer these things from body language, voice inflexion, choice of words. This is camera-like first-person narration.

The observer

Here the narrator as character serves to observe others' relationships, although she or he may of course be a pivotal character in the outcome.

Narrating with hindsight

This narrator is casting back in time, and applying present experience and wisdom to events that occurred during a time when he or she was not so wise and understanding.

The diary

A novel or short story can act out its drama, make its point, through a string of entries in a diary revealing actions, decisions, and attitudes. Furphy uses this device in part to tell his story in *Such is life*, but employs diary entries selected at random to begin his musings on life's ironies. *The diary of Anne Frank* reads as a novel, but is in fact an actual and tragic diary kept when the author was hiding from the Nazis in Holland.

Narrator 1 and Narrator 2

In this way of telling a story, Narrator 1 might begin the tale, and then be told a story by Narrator 2, either speaking or writing in the first person also. One narrator may comment on the other as the story proceeds, and the tension created by the differences in their standpoints may become important.

Multiple narrators

Given a central event or a set of key events, it is possible for each of several characters to describe the action in first-person accounts. Like evidence to a court about the same crime they will vary from participant to participant. It is possible for these separate accounts to bounce off each other, creating tension and interest, and to mount towards a climax or denouement. William Faulkner's *As I lay dying* is a case in point.

Speaking quietly to one's self

In this form of narration, often called an interior monologue, the narrator alone speaks, revealing intimate thoughts, recollections, assessments. Others are seen only through this one pair of eyes, their actions and speech reported. Virginia Woolf's *The waves* is a good example of this mode.

The dramatic monologue

This mode may occur in short prose fiction but is unusual if used at any length in the novel. In it the narrator speaks aloud, without the response of others being recorded. What the narrator says on the phone or to the silence beyond the door or the grave, how he chooses his words, the level of his voice, and other things, may help the reader to guess what the person on the other end, or beyond the door, is saying or might feel. You could look at Frank Moorhouse's pieces, 'Tortures, jealousy tests and getting tough', 'Mechanical aptitude' and other pieces in the section 'The oral history of childhood' in his collection, *Room service*. In these pieces it is not only what is said, but the childish tone of voice, word choice and order in the one and the carping, derogatory tone in the other that fill out the picture. The dramatic monologue comes into its own on the stage, of course, as we shall see when we come to the writing of drama. Barry Humphries often used it in his early stage sketches and in his recent revival of the character Sandy Stone: 'I went to the RSL the other night and had a very nice night's entertainment . . .' Jack Hibberd's play, *A stretch of the imagination,* is in the form of a dramatic monologue.

The letter writers

A letter can tell a story in itself, so can a sequence, so can an exchange of letters. They can deal with the passage of time, changes in attitude, decisions, etc. Other novels or short fictions incorporate letters as part of their way of telling the story; examples include Helene Hanff's novel *84 Charing Cross Road,* Samuel Richardson's early English novel, *Pamela,* Frank Moorhouse's 'Letters to Twiggy' in his collection, *The Americans, baby,* and A. S. Byatt's *Possession,* in which letters, poems and other devices are used.

Warts-and-all subjectivity

This position is much more common than that of the objective view mentioned first. The narrator is more than likely to be a character in the story, bound up in its action, changing with it, declaring himself, unaware of her failings here, completely in control there—a rounded person.

Obviously, despite its rich possibilities, first-person narration has certain disadvantages. The most obvious are the limitations on what the narrator can know, can reveal, or is likely to reveal. She cannot possibly know details of something that she has not experienced or heard about, whereas a third-person narration can include anything, because it can make itself all-seeing if it chooses. Think about other limitations. How is the first-person narrator to describe himself if he is to be convincing and natural? How else can that information be given? Will the repetition of 'I' become wearisome? How directly should the narrator address the reader, if she is to remain convincing?

Second-person narration

The use of a 'you' by the narrator is often a veiled way of telling a first-person story:

You sat on the sand with the towels and watched them splashing in the rock pool. Peter's angular arms and legs chopping the water, Nicky's laughter bubbling, Joan standing arms akimbo, waist-deep, sun-hatted. Watching her broad mother's arms and shoulders you felt alone, a voyeur, uncertain of your right to be there . . .

The use of the second person can invite the reader to come close, to share and empathize: 'As you skindive, you keep a weather-eye out for sharks. In the ocean, on Victoria's coast, it's always possible that one is cruising through the shallower water near shore. You hope it's not a Great White . . .' There need to be compelling arguments for using 'you' in place of 'I'. It can confer distance, if that is what is needed, but the 'you' and 'your' to which it commits the writer and reader can become very irritating if used at length. Second-person narration is rare outside short fiction and is not often chosen as a mode there.

Third-person narration

This is the choice that Thomas Keneally opts for in telling Oskar Schindler's story, the voice used most by Patrick White, Christina Stead, Elizabeth Jolley and Helen Garner. Peter Carey's prize-winning novels are told in this way. It is the mode that vies with first-person narration in short fiction, where the circle of the story has to be relatively close and intimate. But the larger scope of the novel means that more are written as a third-person narration than any other way. The narrator has the advantage of knowing literally everything, if they wish, and the reader can come very close to the characters, especially the one or two key characters. After meeting them as 'he' and 'she', readers very soon forget the distancing of third-person narration and, if the writer is skilful enough, inhabit these people and rejoice and suffer with them.

There are several forms which third-person narration can take. One is third-person narration disguising first-person narration. As with second person, the third person can mask what is basically a first-person, close and limited view of the action:

As the young man he had never seen before rattled on to him, as he put the lens cap back on, he caught a glimpse of the heavy black face of the policeman standing squat at the building line that gave on to the Fifth Avenue pavement. He was watching, his face closed, mouth flat and unrevealing, eyes undisclosing black currants, and yet . . . Now the young man was speaking to him again, quietly, standing close, both of them kneeing the seat that ran along the raised flower-beds of Rockefeller Center.
'This your first visit to New York?' he was asking. Trevor struggled with the camera bag, an obvious tourist.
'Yes, this is my first time in the Big Apple,' he said, smiling, but sneaking a look at the young man's face. There was nothing he could put his finger on, but he felt a tinge of disquiet about the youth's approach, about the policeman's bland attention. Was it resignation or waiting that was flattening that mouth?

A second form of third-person narration is all-seeing and expansive. In this way of telling it is possible to take in the whole cosmos if the writer wishes:

Manhattan lay like a dark spine rearing out of the copper sheen of the Hudson river. The sun flashed intermittent jewels from its bridges, over which, in a stream of automobiles and stolid trucks, the city's committed commerce inched out along grey arteries to the east, to Queens, to Brooklyn, to JFK.
Deeper in the noisy fastness of its canyon-avenues, just where the old skyscrapers of Rockefeller Center cast shadows down to Fifth Avenue, an Australian, only twenty hours in the city, heard a voice at his elbow as he replaced the lens-cap on his Minolta . . .
'Hello, sir. I hope you're having a good day.' . . .
Since hitting New York he had only been spoken to by a taxi driver, a postal clerk, a bellhop.
As he turned to respond the Australian caught a glimpse of the heavy Black face of a New York cop, who stood flexing his legs just at the building line giving on to the Fifth Avenue pavement. New York cops seemed to form a grey-brown statuary in the city: statues that occasionally flashed keys absent-mindedly, but otherwise melted against the buildings, or into wired and littered corners. The Black cop was watching this new transaction, his face closed . . .

In the latter version, as distinct from the closeness of the first, we seem to be looking down on the Australian from a great height. We seem to be waiting for his fate to be played out below us, and his fate will become part of the fabric of New York. The frame within which the Australian's story is set here is larger than in the first version. It feels like the view through a telephoto lens, and yet it can zoom in to a close-up if necessary. It is much better suited to a novel than to the compression required in a short story. For other examples of this technique, you could read Thornton Wilder's *The bridge of San Luis Rey*, Patrick White's *Riders in the chariot*, Ruth Park's *The harp in the south*, Murray Bail's *Holden's performance* and *Homesickness*, Gabriel Garcia Marquez's *One hundred years of solitude*, Christina Stead's *The man who loved children* or Helen Garner's stories in *Honour and other people's children* among many others.

Between the two versions above, and beyond them, there are many other possible third-person narrative voices that can be used.

Write

It is interesting (and educational too!) to try your hand at some of the range of voices, some of the almost infinite range of ways of presenting human experience. The fiction shelves of any library will provide your raw material. Sample some novels and short stories, pick those with distinctive narrating positions, and copy them—write something in the same way, perhaps working from their openings only. Do they begin close and intimately, or are they expansive, drawing in the sweep of time and history? Listen to the rhythms of sentence structure, short and long sentences, balance of close detail with hints of the wider world. Try something similar of your own, without using a novel to set you off.

All this might seem more oppressive and bewildering than it really is. You will find that the choice of narrative voice and point of view is soon made after a bit of casting around, governed by the nature of the story you want to tell. You will find that you fall on the right 'sound', perhaps immediately, perhaps after some experimentation. The requirements of the story may dictate: do you need a learned narrator, an adult view, a naive and innocent child's view of events? Many writers simply write themselves part-way into an opening and then, as that process reveals things about characters and the way they seem compelled to tell the story, they put down telegraphic notes so that they don't lose ideas; the notes are not binding, they are only starters.

You will see that when you have developed for yourself an opening profile for a novel, there is bound to be a lot of rethinking ahead. The novelist, as Vance Palmer would say, is the long-distance runner and needs staying power and the ability to maintain interest in the story, while avoiding the highs and lows of self-esteem as the work progresses.

Novelists, like Ernest Hemingway for example, learn strategies to maintain their sharp edge, since writing is an exhausting task. Hemingway used to begin writing as soon after first light as possible, reading over what he had written the day before, then going on from there:

You write until you come to a place where you still have your juice and know what will happen next and you stop and try to live through until the next day when you hit it again . . . When you stop you are as empty, and at the same time never empty but filling, as when you have made love to someone you love. Nothing can hurt you, nothing can happen, nothing means anything until the next day when you do it again. It is the wait until the next day that is hard to get through.

Many novelists keep track of the number of words or pages they write in a day's work. Working five hours or so a day Norman Mailer found that he wrote seven typewritten pages. This produced an average of twenty-eight pages a week. Even at that steady rate, the first draft of his war novel, *The naked and the dead*, took seven months to write. Steadiness and discipline are the ideals for the novelist, but these are not necessarily easy to achieve. Pamela Frankau, the American novelist, explains:

An awful lot of people have said to me, 'I imagine you can only write when you feel like it'. The answer to that is 'bosh'. If you left it till you felt like it, you'd never do it at all. Writing is a demanding, exacting, lifetime labour. It can never come easy.

Narrative devices

Narrative can be broken down into its elements:
- *Time:* When do things occur and in what order?
- *Space:* Where do events take place? Why there? How important is place? Does place suggest change, travel in a spatial and experiential sense? Does it suggest a journey?
- *Person:* Whose voice is heard telling the story? Is it an 'I'? Is it an all-seeing third-person narrator?
- *Tension:* Where is the human problem? When is something going to snap? Who is under stress? What is going to happen to them?
- *Point of view:* What happened and according to whom? How are we allowed to view what happened? Who is telling us and are they reliable?
- *Words' power:* This is the only vehicle: words on pages. There is no vision or image otherwise.

Consider these ingredients. You will soon realize that there are many other ways to write an account of human behaviour beside those we've mentioned: the writer can play with time, space, speech, thought, point of view, truth, the conventions of publishing and page lay-out!—even play with the reader.

Time and person

Writers can do virtually anything they want with time, so long as their manipulation of it is effective in the telling of their story. Unfortunately, many new writers see the handling of time as a difficulty. They forget that the reader finds little trouble accepting the passage of time denoted by a paragraph break, a multiple line break that demarcates a section of work, a row of asterisks, or the simple jump forward in time indicated by the phrases, 'Three weeks later . . .' or 'In the evening . . .'. Look at a wide range of novels to see how writers handle time.

In her novel, *The lover*, the French writer, Marguerite Duras plays with both time and person, telling her story in both the first and third persons and in past tense and present tense. The chief character, who begins as a girl of fifteen in Saigon, sometimes narrates, and sometimes is described in a third-person narration as 'she'. Sometimes she is describing her present; at other times she is an older woman looking back at herself as a girl at the French boarding school. Sometimes the girl falls into the future tense: 'It's a year and a half after that meeting that my mother takes us back to France. She'll sell all her furniture. Then go one last time to the dyke. She'll sit on the verandah facing the setting sun, look towards Siam one last time . . .' Sometimes the narrating voice of the girl anticipates events—her brother's death, for instance—that we will hear more about later in the story. We accept all this naturally. The book is written in discrete paragraphs rather than chapters or sections: each paragraph is a picture and may be from a different time from the ones before and after it.

George Johnston manipulates time in his novel, *Clean straw for nothing*, the second in his Meredith trilogy that began with the more conventionally-constructed novel, *My brother Jack*, but Johnston's narrating position does not change.

Write

Take a story from your own family's larger narrative and experiment with the effects you can achieve by playing with time and voice. You probably know in general terms what members of your family were doing at the outbreak of the Second World War for instance. Write a selective fictionalized account that reveals its impact on one adult family member in the first person. Then, allowing several line spaces to indicate passage of time and shift of person in narration, write about another 'spot in time' showing how the war has affected her two years later. This time you will be examining a changed person, writing about her in the third person. You could then write a third piece picking up your character's reactions, feelings, and actions at the war's end in short, intercut passages of five lines or so, alternating first and third-person narrations that merge with each other and yet allow the third-person pieces to show up some subterfuge and masking of emotion in the first person accounts.

Beginnings and endings

Study the beginnings and endings of short stories and novels. Both beginnings and endings are important and may take longer to ponder and polish than other parts of the story you have to tell.

In the short story the opening should promise interest, tension, conflict that is to come, and must be economical—the story must get underway quickly. This is not so vital in a novel, where there is more space to develop character, situation and sense of place.

With the short story, it is often important to enter the story in the middle of action, or conjecture, or tension. The Welsh short story writer of the Second World War years, Rhys Davies, speaks of that necessary instinct 'to dive, swift and agile, into the opening of a story' as being half the technical art of the short story. 'One must not on any account loiter or brood in the first paragraph,' Davies says. The story writer, he added, should 'be deep in the story's elements in a few seconds'. Anton Chekhov would have agreed. 'Beginners', he said, 'often have to . . . fold in and tear up the first half [of their stories] . . . The first half is superfluous.' This is where the 'flashback' serves its purpose: employed later in the story, it reveals, generally in a condensed form, important information that would have held up its opening or its more dramatic moments.

In a sense it is not important exactly where the story begins, but it is important that it leads promptly into the 'meat' of the story. Thornton Wilder's famous novel, *The bridge of San Luis Rey*, follows the same advice. It begins: 'On Friday, July the twentieth, 1714, the finest bridge in all Peru broke and precipitated five travellers into the gulf below . . . ' We as readers see those figures falling and want to know more about the accident, and who the bridge's victims were. One of Hal Porter's short stories, 'Revenge', on the other hand, begins in an intriguing way which, with the story's title and the unusual imagery, have us in thrall:

The woman (expanded, velvety, a dahlia) and the boy (unexpanded, formal, a cold bud) each with a reserved seat, were the only two in that compartment of the country train. He knew who she was. She had not the faintest idea, my love, who the little brat could *possibly* be . . .

It is more difficult to be definitive about a story's ending. It is often predetermined to some extent by the direction of the story and its point of balance. If the story is well structured and the characters have been convincingly portrayed then the writing contains the germ of the ending. The ending may be a revelation, a denial, a realization, a *rapprochement*, a failure, a question that won't be answered, a relaxation, a promise of fulfilment, a prediction of dire consequences, the suggestion of a new direction. It should not be an essay-like recapitulation. Its wording may be as refined and precise as a poem, requiring much redrafting to bring it to its full power.

Write

Try writing two story beginnings that could introduce situations that you have experienced and which might become short stories or pieces of experimental fiction. Look at Hal Porter's opening again, considering the way it involves the reader so quickly. Emulate it. Make each opening no more than two paragraphs long. You may well return to them later and complete them as stories.

Dialogue

Writing convincing, natural and informative dialogue is an art in itself. Most stories contain some dialogue, since it is the most obvious way for characters to communicate, but dialogue in fiction, as in drama, should earn its keep.

Dialogue can reveal elements important to the story:
- character and personality
- characters' ages and attitudes
- level of sophistication in a character—education, social class, breadth of experience, wealth or poverty
- where a character was born and brought up (perhaps France, perhaps Italy, perhaps Australia)
- a character's honesty or dishonesty.

Dialogue also brings immediacy, the sense of a person's physical presence or emotion to a scene. It can dramatically *show* rather than flatly *tell* or *explain*, as in the following examples. We will return to showing and telling in more detail later.

Telling

When Joyce came home from the meeting, her father wanted to know what had happened. She sat at the kitchen table and tentatively suggested to Jim, whose response she feared, that she thought the conservationist move against the idea of the pine plantation might have something to be said for it. She told Jim that they should perhaps reconsider the idea of selling the farm, and that it would be the end of farming in the valley. Jim's angry response was immediate. He accused Joyce of becoming a greenie and of wanting to ruin him at the end of a long farming life . . .

Showing

When Joyce came home from the meeting, she sat at the kitchen table.

'Well?' said her father. 'What'd you learn?'

'Quite a bit,' she said, watching his hands fingering the pages. 'Dr Benton from the Foundation was there. He spoke for half an hour or so. People asked a few question afterwards.'

'And I suppose he told you all to go out and plant eucalypts along the coastal side, did he?' asked Jim. His hands were still now.

'No!' she said. 'What he *did* say was that the timber people's offer to buy us up for pines will end farming right up the valley.' Joyce breathed deep, waited. Now it was out.

'God! I never thought I'd be harbouring a greenie on this place!' Jim exploded. 'You talk as though I had a choice! This is all I've got to trade with. It's too late to start again. What sort of offer do you want for it, for God's sake? We won't do better than the money the timber blokes are putting up.' He ran his hand through his hair. 'You want to ruin me, eh?'

Dialogue is not the only difference between these two examples of course. The second version, as you'll see, is better in movement, has an ebb and flow of emotion, is rhythmic, and carries with it the physical presence of the two protagonists. The first is flatly reported, cannot be felt, has few highs and lows in intensity and the observations of characters' feelings lack subtlety.

The dialogue serves other purposes, suggests other things. You will notice that it can effectively draw in the characters' tell-tale body language: 'his hands fingering the pages' and 'his hands were still now'.

Some writers have no difficulty in making their dialogue ring true; others may write strong descriptions or passages of action but find natural-sounding dialogue difficult. One novelist used to quit work at five every afternoon and head for the pub—not to drink, but to sit with a beer and listen to his mates argue, kid each other, recount experiences, talk about their families. Then he went home and spent an hour rendering their dialogue on the page, until he had the rhythms right, the colloquialisms true, the changes in tone from pleasant to argumentative captured convincingly. Even professional writers of fiction, even experienced dramatists, have to practise rendering dialogue to keep their hands—or their ears—in.

Dialogue *can* be used to provide the reader with necessary information, but here lies danger. The dialogue that reveals the information must also sound convincing, support character and personality, and perhaps forward the action, otherwise it will sound artificial and false. If it does, then it is an indication that the information should have been provided in another way, or a little at a time rather than all in one parcel.

Write

'Are you so mad at Harry today because he used your ghetto blaster at Deidre's party last night without permission, even though he knew you would disapprove?' asked Jerry.

'Yes,' said Jennifer, frowning. 'But more importantly I'm going to ask him why he spread the word that I'm going out with Jack, when all I said to his mother was that Jack is a whizz at Maths and on the tennis court.'

Try rewriting this overblown piece of dialogue, so that it unfolds naturally and reveals its information more gradually and dramatically. Think about the motives, positions and feelings of the characters and establish the relationship that exists between them. People in conversation generally work towards what they want to know by a series of short questions, rather than one heavily-loaded one, and they may go to great lengths to conceal the reason for their curiosity.

In fiction, dialogue can vary the rhythm of the story-telling, or lighten or freshen the writing after a passage of exposition or description. Look at Henry Lawson's stories to see how he handles dialogue apparently effortlessly—stories like 'Send round the hat', the Steelman stories, 'Telling Mrs Baker', 'The Union buries its dead'. You will notice in 'Send round the hat' another function of dialogue: a figure of speech, or a mode of address, when repeated, can become the 'signature' of a character. For example, the character known as the Giraffe always prefaces his entreaties for money on behalf of the poor with something self-effacing and insistent like: 'Is it any harm to wake yer?'

Dialogue need not be spoken; it can be internal: a character can *think* in dialogue, with the distinctive flavour and word choice of real speech:

Thaddeus wasn't going to get involved. He was rapt in the music, yeah, but if they thought he was going to the Billy Joel concert to deal drugs they had another think coming. Thaddeus the pimp, eh? Didn't he know where all that took you? The ruthless, cold look in Clem's eyes, and the way he grabbed Benjamin's wrists to show the others the needle marks. Shit! Clem was way over the top. He was bloody dangerous. You'd never catch Thaddeus as Clem's bloody servant, Clem's little yes-man. Ben was down the tube, and that was that. But not him. Not Thad Thomas!'

Allied to dialogue, is the jolt, the directness of the human voice coming suddenly out of a section of story that relies on movement and action only:

Just as we were marking time, before marching up those indestructible brick steps and into school, a small figure rushed round the corner and then slowed and sidled up the bricks towards the taps, smiling all the while. It was Jerry McColl.

The two teachers, judging that this was a ruse to hide his lateness, began to advance on him. But Jerry had gone to the corner to look back again to the far yard under the pine tree. There was a strange excitement in his movements that we couldn't understand. Then he turned to see Mr Johns and Mr Stephens bearing down on him. Despair, frustration, disappointment swept his frame.

'No, Sir. No! It's Ralphie,' he rattled out.

The teachers stopped in their tracks. A shadow projected round the edge of the building. Shoulders working, and school bag, and then, slowly, the symmetry of crutches—and there stood Ralphie.

'See, sir, it's Ralphie. He's come back, sir.'

Write

Write a passage of fiction which describes a physical setting and a group of inactive people. Build tension through their refusal to act and the impatience of two of their number. Allow two pieces of short dialogue to spur them to action.

Practice in making spoken words carry the burden of the tale is important here and vital in writing for the stage, for film, or for television.

There are a few do's and don'ts that might be useful. *Don't* explain mechanical detail in dialogue. *Don't* fill dialogue up with pleasantries, or with social clichés and requests unless these give evidence of character or feeling. *Don't* use dialogue to provide information in an obvious way. *Don't* let characters speak in great mouthfuls.

Don't feel obliged to substitute fancy words for 'said'—averred, queried, questioned, uttered, muttered, stuttered, announced, explained, etc. Each of these has its place every now and then, but 'said' is usually sufficient.

Do read your dialogue aloud to test its verisimilitude and rhythm. Be ruthless with parts that you doubt. *Do* study a selection of novels and short-story collections to see the different methods of setting out dialogue. Some publishers use quotation marks to encompass direct speech, some simply use a dash at the start of each new speech in dialogue. The golden rule, whatever method you choose, is to start a new line for each alternate speaker in the conversation. *Do* study the stories of Ernest Hemingway for his minimalist dialogue, which has a distinct and convincing ring to it. *Do* listen to radio or television comedy sketches—Barry Humphries, Fred Dagg, Kylie Mole, Peter Cook and Dudley Moore, Con the Fruiterer, John Cleese, Warren Mitchell, etc.—to hear how words are used to suggest the person's background, prejudices, limitations, foibles, obsessions. *Do* look at the plays of David Williamson—'Don's party', 'The department', 'The club'—to see how he makes every word count in dialogue. But not all stage, film or radio dialogue is naturalistic and vernacular. Look at the plays of Samuel Beckett or Eugene Ionesco. Here you will find dialogue that is self-absorbed, obsessive, aberrant.

Write

- Develop a dramatic situation that is surreal and strange, in which the characters are obsessed by the motor vehicle and all its concomitants. Develop dialogue for two of them in which they speak obsessively about these things in long tirades.
- Write dialogue for three characters who are unnaturally preoccupied with transporting huge volumes of files from the filing cabinets in one high-rise city office block to the filing cabinets in another.
- Write a passage of dialogue in which the two speakers cannot see each other, but the reader, via a third-person narration, can. Make the words each speaks belie their actions.
- Write a passage of 'persuasion' dialogue in which character A eventually persuades unwilling character B to do something.
- Write a passage of 'faceless' dialogue between two people, where no names are mentioned, where there are no 'he saids' or 'she saids', but in which the words exchanged tell us a great deal about the people. The two should begin apart in some sense, but come together by the close.
- Listen to two or three conversations in a public place and then write them up as dialogue, fictionalizing where a story suggests itself to you.

Curiosity and satisfaction

If you are telling a joke you watch your listeners to see how they are taking it. You want to tell it well enough to make them laugh. You are disappointed if they don't. There is great satisfaction in a well-told joke or story, but how can you best hold your listener, your reader, your audience?

The Australian novelist, Ruth Park, spoke to me some time ago about her prize-winning and popular novel, *The harp in the south*. She admitted with great candour that when she wrote it (her first novel), she did not know the art of structuring a long story:

> As any reader could see I wrote a simple chronology, which is the very simplest form of novel-writing . . . I hadn't written a novel before and I realized then what a truly arduous labour it is . . . The very simple chronological form does not permit the writer to take advantage of every dramatic and literary ploy. If you know more about it you can make things far more forceful and of far greater interest. You learn that absolutely essential trick of all novelists of first stimulating reader-interest and then gratifying it and then stimulating again. I think until you do that you can hardly call yourself a novelist: you write books, you write long stories or chronologies or histories, but you are not exactly writing a novel.

This question and answer (stimulation and gratification) structure is not the only valid one for a novel by any means, but it has the advantage of fitting the psychology of the reader who wants to know the answer, wants to learn and understand. A good example of this structure is Truman Capote's 'New Journalist' novel, *In cold blood*, in which the reader's attention is caught and held from the outset. Will the police find the killers? Yes. Now that they are in custody, what will be the nature of the trial and the evidence? Will they be convicted? Yes. What, then, will be the sentence? It is to be death by execution. How will they react to it? How will the killers come to terms with their crime, with those around them, with their death? The book is a model of the method of telling a story that Ruth Park disarmingly outlined.

Write

Take a piece of drama that has been acted out in your own family's story—present generation or past—and mock up a plan of how you would tell it in novel form by using the sweet lure of question and then answer, stimulating reader interest and then gratifying it. Your initial notes might be simply a list of basic questions. Block out the opening sections of the story, each governed by a different question building on previous questions.

Prefiguring

Prefiguring an event is an effective device in story-telling. It stimulates reader interest in the same way as a question, but it has to do with the chronological order of events and with openings. It casts forward intriguingly.

When Peter Carey opens his novel, *Bliss*, with the words: 'Harry Joy was to die three times, but it was his first death which was to have the greatest effect on him, and it is this first death which we shall now witness . . .', he is prefiguring a crucial event in the story, whetting our appetite. When Patrick White opens *The aunt's story* with: 'But old Mrs

Goodman did die at last . . .', he is doing the same thing, but for the purposes of the first section of his novel only. When a television drama or a film opens with a court-room scene that mentions a crime and then fades into a long flashback leading to the criminal act at the story's centre, it is prefiguring. It is also putting the final act of the drama first, then leaving it, in order to build towards it: it is playing with chronological sequence.

Write

Construct in your mind a story that centres about a key event—a birth, a crime, a reprieve, a declaration of war, a terrorist attack, a reconciliation, a natural disaster, the first encounter of a strong love—and write an opening that hints at this event and whets the appetite of the reader. Then make the jump in time to where you begin to tell the story of that event and write a few paragraphs of that.

Show, don't tell

There is no more important skill in story-telling than suggestion or implication, once you have established the basic strength, structure, and interest of your story.

Write for an intelligent and imaginative reader, then allow that reader's imagination room to work as the story progresses. In most fiction, the reader should be touched as directly as possible, which means that the writer or narrator should only intervene where it is absolutely necessary. Usually the writer aims to 'put the reader there', in the midst of the story. That generally requires more words, more effort in the writing, more attention to detail, than a method that merely states or explains. 'Showing' is just as desirable and useful in journalism, film scripting, drama, and advertising as it is in prose fiction. As William Carlos Williams said: 'No ideas but in things.' Don't forget the telling detail!

Look at the following example. It could remain a basic piece of exposition, or it could become human drama.

---

1 In Geelong the Great War came to an end when an announcement was made late on Monday 11 November 1918, soon to be followed by the ringing of bells and shrieking of factory whistles. The word spread. People gradually became aware of a great sense of relief and release and a crowd grew in the streets outside the City Hall from about 6.30 pm. The men, women and children were intensely happy as the City Band played and marched to the Town Hall. The Mayor declared a holiday for the city for the next day but found it difficult to hold the attention of the rejoicing people who seemed to have forgotten everything beyond the fact that the War was over at last.

2 The first hint came on Monday 11 November. The bell of the City Fire Brigade began to peel across the town as darkness fell, then the bells of the borough fire brigades took up the message. People began to come out on to the street. The big post office bell sounded, then the post office clock began to chime: it went for half an hour. More and more people were gathering in the streets, even though it was eight o'clock. The City Band, which had been practising when the news broke, turned and marched to the City Hall playing patriotic airs, which were almost drowned by the shriek of factory whistles. The crowd in the streets near the City Hall swelled to eighteen thousand people and more, milling, singing and dancing to the sounds of Messrs Hawkes Bros. Gala Day Band in Moorabool Street. At a little after nine, the Mayor, Councillor Hitchcock, addressed the mass of faces and flags before the City Hall. Tomorrow would be a public holiday! Even the hotels would close. The flag-waving mass of people cheered and heckled the Mayor good-naturedly. Some businesses must be kept going, said the Mayor. No, no, said the crowd, not tomorrow—the War was over!

Look at the two versions. The second is longer, and contains much more detail, which brings the momentous evening alive. It is more concrete. It does not contain vague words and phrases like 'intensely happy', 'relief', 'release', 'rejoicing'. It leaves the reader to infer that these were the feelings of the crowd. Instead of telling us that the implications of the War's end gradually dawned on people, it lets us experience it with the crowd.

There is a mounting sense of excitement in the second version that is absent from the first.

Write

Using your own experience, completely recast and expand the following flat piece so that you eliminate the italicized words and imply actions or feelings instead. Don't forget that dialogue and body language add immediacy and subtlety. Consider ways of indicating human interaction, how verbs can be made more active, how actions can be made more immediate so that they seem to happen before us.

Callum's first day of school was a *severe emotional trial* for him. He was *frightened*, felt *lonely* and was *confused* when confronted by *so many other strange children*, even more *intimidating teachers*, and a *succession of demands* to do *things he was not used to*. His mother was there for the first half-hour, but she was *visibly upset* too, *her disquiet transmitting itself to Callum*. The upshot was that when *she departed* and Callum's *teacher approached him to suggest* he might like to draw and paint with the other newcomers he *withdrew into himself* and tried to *escape from the room and go home* when her back was turned. When *she discovered this* and *brought him back,* his *unhappiness* was so great that he *would not communicate with her* at all. He *wept* and *called for his mother.*

Note, as you recast this piece, that it makes the mistake of shooting off its biggest gun—'severe emotional trial'—in the first sentence. Once you have been 'told' that, rather than being allowed to see it for yourself, anything that follows is an anti-climax (if not irrelevant).

The experiential journey

> I am a part of all that I have met,
> Yet all experience is an arch wherethro'
> Gleams the untravelled world whose margin fades
> For ever and for ever when I move . . .

Thus wrote Alfred Lord Tennyson in the poem 'Ulysses'. Something of that sense of journeying or maturing should be invested in your characters as they move towards the make-or-break point of their story. Not only should they have doubts, but their perceptions and ways of handling situations should change. All these must be credible. You as writer–manipulator must 'feel' for your characters and plan to mention these changes and advances as you pursue the main story-line.

How this happens depends sometimes on the length of the story. Hemingway's characters in his clipped and brutal short story, 'The killers', do not advance experientially as characters in a novel might: the moment is too short and concentrated for that. The three men tied up by the killers have nevertheless made an unforgettable experiential journey. At the story's ominous end they see the world differently from the way they viewed it before the killers walked in. If you haven't read the story, look for it in Hemingway's collection, *Men without women*.

Write

Make a plan or notes for a story in which a key character sets out in search of something or someone, so that the search is paralleled by an interior journey, a 'growing in knowing' for the character. In some ways this is an artificial way to begin a story, so you may not wish to pursue your plan, but note that this allegorical element logically develops from character and situation, as does John Bunyan's *The pilgrim's progress* or Swift's *Gulliver's travels* or the story of Ulysses or James Joyce's gloss on that Greek story.

What if . . .?

Some new writers find they are tethered to events in their own experience, and cannot disengage from them. As Carlos Fuentes says, one wants to create a 'slice of the imagination' and not simply a 'slice of life'. Listen to Kate Grenville: 'The fiction I like is that which makes the world look slightly different afterwards. It's like living through it to find experience . . .' or Hemingway:

From things that have happened and from things as they exist and from things that you know and all those you cannot know, you make something through your invention that is not a representation but a whole new thing truer than anything true and alive, and you make it alive, and if you make it well enough you give it immortality. That is why you write and for no other reason that you know of.

Hemingway stresses 'invention' and not simple representation, making a new thing rather than transcribing life.

So this is a reminder to keep asking the question 'What if . . .?' to modify real-life's offerings. What if the person on whom you are modelling your principal character were not to experience this, as in real life, but that? What if the intriguing incident on which you are loosely basing your story were to happen not on the coast, but in an inland town.

Yes, write *from*, but not necessarily *about*, what you know. Allow yourself to include in what you know your own imaginative life, your ability to see possibilities, your dreams and your passions.

Editing

A second or third draft—even an eleventh or twelfth draft—of a story is not ready for submission unless you are satisfied that it is as good as you can make it. To be sure of this, you must put on your objective editorial cap—different from your story-writing cap—and go through it with a fine-tooth comb, as though it were the work of someone else. You will discover and correct the mistakes, infelicities, unintended puns, mixed metaphors, poor punctuation and ludicrous dialogue of which we are all capable. No professional writer, no Nobel or Booker prize winner, can afford to omit this stage, which should be slow and thorough. It may help to read the sentences out loud. Try to miss nothing. You should give your sentences the same attention as Thea Astley:

Sometimes I've been so filled with envy of a particularly long sentence of, say, someone like Updike, I've analyzed it and I've broken it down into its structures: conditional clause, noun clause, you know, object and adverbial clause of time. I've put all these things down and, because I love the rhythm of it, I've tried to construct another sentence using exactly the same structure.

From my experience, you will find that the mechanical things most commonly needing correction are those listed below.

Punctuation

Look out for:
- sentences that are not sentences, that unintentionally lack a verb, or trail off without a conclusion
- use of the comma where a full stop is necessary because a sentence is complete and a new thought has started
- obsessive use of a particular punctuation mark (comma, exclamation mark, dash, semicolon, colon)
- use of 'and' to join thoughts that are not closely or causally connected, each of which should be accorded a separate sentence
- if you know that your sense of punctuation is weak, make a special study of it to learn its distinctions, or ask someone whose punctuation is good to read your manuscript before you finalize it.

Echoes

Look out for:
- the unintentional use of the same word or phrase within a few lines, so that it clangs unattractively on the reader's ear—this can very easily go undetected unless you concentrate and read aloud
- the use of the same sentence structure in quick succession and unintentionally (subject, verb, object: subject, verb, object: subject, verb . . .)
- excessive use of the present participle to begin sentences ('Crossing her toes as she walked up the steps, she fell over . . .').

Dialogue

Look out for:
- words in the mouth of a character (possibly a narrator) that they would be most unlikely to use, given social position, education or other factors.

Inappropriate word selection

Watch for:
- words that leap out of a piece because they don't match its tone, perhaps because they are too colloquial or slangy, or too formal
- use of clichés and jargon, unless it is something a character or narrator says which is consistent with their make-up (listen to news or current affairs reports in which the text consists almost entirely of news-speak clichés strung together: 'raging inferno', 'at this point in time', 'pinpoint accuracy', 'a big plus', 'the bottom line', 'walking away from their White Paper', 'the impending clash', 'strained relations', 'egg on their faces', 'ball-park figures', 'an all-time high', 'buffeted by the winds of change', 'the wash-up of all this', 'thinly-veiled threats' and so on, and so on)
- Americanisms in Australian mouths. Language is constantly changing, and many Americanisms have become or are becoming part of Australian speech. As a writer you need constantly to monitor this change, and

judge whether your characters or narrators would use phrases such as: bus depot; regular toothbrushes (normal toothbrushes); flashlight (torch) train station; sleeping over, etc. It will depend on such factors as your character's age, social background, job, and home. Avoid putting Americanisms (or other foreign phrases) in the mouths of unlikely people, or using them in unlikely situations.

Paragraphing

Watch for unreasonably long paragraphs, or unreasonably short paragraphs (possibly under the influence of journalism, where paragraphs are seldom more than one or two sentences). Fiction is not journalism.

Accuracy

This is part of knowing the 'world' of your story, or spending time researching it. The weather should be appropriate for the place in which the story is set (biting wind and sleet at Port Douglas?); mealtimes and food should be appropriate to the class or the country of the characters (a judge's dinner at 5.30 pm sharp? a breakfast cafe in Nice without croissants?); people should use local names (a New South Welsh family who insist on calling bathing suits togs, bathers or trunks instead of swimmers?).

Spelling

Last, but by no means least, your manuscript will benefit from a careful reading for this alone. As with punctaution, if your speling is weak, make a list of worsd you find trickey, work with a dictionery so that you can check, and persuade someone with a good spelling sence to check you draft for you. (Remember, even if your spelling is strong, you are reading as a proff-reader for unwitting mistakes in word processing or typwriting which will occur in spite of you; they should not be allowed to go through to an editor.) Now, for proof-reading practice, correct the complete paragraph of which this is the last santence!

Summary

We have now discussed most of the resources in writing fiction. The list is not complete or comprehensive: other writers would add and subtract items and place emphasis here rather than there, but it is a list that all writers would understand. It involves experiences all writers have been through. Let's summarize the main points.

1 Observe, be curious, take notes, and know your fascinations. Ezra Pound said:

I don't know that you can put the needed qualities in hierarchic order, but [the writer] must have a *continuous curiosity*, which of course does not make him a writer, but if he has not got that he will wither. And the question of doing anything about it depends on a *persistent energy.*

As John Morrison puts it: 'If you're a writer, you're always thinking of how you can convert what you see, what happens to you, in words. It's the old story of seeing something fascinating and wanting to tell someone.'

2 Cast around, let the subconscious work, make a mess in order to clear your thinking, to see the path come clear. Don't be dismayed by false trails and ineptness. Jessica Anderson says,

I try to get a tone of voice and sometimes, if the tone of voice is right, the whole thing is all right, and at other times I get off the rails, and I'll write on and on and have to throw away all that part and start again.

3 Know your characters well, and be fascinated by them. Here's Jessica Anderson again:

I get a big piece of cardboard, and when all my characters are there, which is usually after twenty pages or so, I write their names on this card, or sometimes in an exercise book, but I prefer a big card, and I attach a few biographical details to each. Then I write on until I feel the need of a plan . . .

4 Know the 'world' of your story in detail. Don't be satisfied with generalizations, don't be satisfied with not knowing how sheep are shorn, how a bank teller opens up, how wine is made, how a private detective earns her keep, which galleries specialize in which art forms, etc. You need to know and understand a great deal more than you can ever afford to include in your story. Look at Ernest Hemingway's knowing tale, *The old man and the sea.* His knowledge of the life of such fishermen, of the Gulf of Mexico, of its tides and seasons, of human motivation and satisfaction is not presented in the novel as knowledge, but nevertheless underlies every word he writes. He explains:

If it's any use to know it, I always try to write on the principle of the iceberg. There is seven-eighths of it underwater for every part that shows. Anything you know you can eliminate and it only strengthens your iceberg. It is the part that doesn't show. If a writer omits something because he doesn't know it then there is a hole in the story.

5 Show, don't tell. Reveal, don't explain. Let the story unfold with the reader as witness. As W. B. Yeats put it: 'Only that which does not teach, which does not cry out, which does not persuade, which does not condescend, which does not explain, is irresistible.'

6 Maintain a sense of a journey being undertaken, a feeling of movement, of personal progression and growing enlightenment in your story.
7 Be specific, use telling detail, and describe for your reader, but not to the point of clogging up the story's momentum. Generalizations are opaque.
8 Ensure that the pivotal or make-or-break point of your story, when you reach it, is believable, moving, disturbing, intriguing. You may not know what it is going to be until you are well advanced, but character and situation will eventually suggest it.
9 Become your own editor. This can determine whether your work is taken up by a publisher's editor or not. Everyone receives rejection slips, of course, but some writers receive them more often than others. It may be that they have not bothered to complete the final stage of the writing process—that they have not edited their own work before submission.

Stories for children

Children are very particular and critical readers. If you want to write fiction for children—a subject that deserves a separate book of its own and cannot be treated in detail here—then the best advice is to spend time with children of all ages, from very small toddlers to teenagers. Talk with them, play with them, listen to them, observe them. Read stories to children and see how they react, study what fascinates them, what leaves them cold, what imaginative world they live in. Begin to discriminate between age groups—the six to eight-year-olds who enjoy animal characters and fantastic worlds; the nine to twelve-year-olds who have begun to look ahead to the teenager as model, but who are still spellbound by mystery, danger, adventures, even though they are beginning to be moved by the more complex elements and joys and sadnesses of life—ostracism, loneliness, injustice, hard-won success, marriage breakup, and so on—but not presented in these terms, of course.

You should also read, read, read, especially if you haven't written for children before, or if you haven't a good working knowledge of the latest books written for these distinct age levels. Read books written for children by writers of proven ability; read children's magazines and consider the age-groups at which they are pitched. Study the structure, the pivot of the kind of story they use. How conservative are the stories? How much do they engage with social issues? Are they the type of story that *you* would like to write?

Children's likes and dislikes

Children read to find out, whether they read fact or fiction. Therefore, they are interested in stories that move forward, where the action is persistent, where the rules of the story or game are constantly changing, and new vistas, conflicts, tensions are offered.

By and large children are not attracted to reflective or atmospheric stories. These are for adults, who make moral judgements, think intellectually about issues and reflect about experience more deeply.

Children appreciate complete and rounded and fallible characters rather than stereotypes.

Stories that move about in time are less appealing to children; they want a straight chronology. They do not analyse stories: a story either strikes them and holds them, or it does not.

All children, but particularly those at kindergarten and primary school, enjoy the sound of words, onomatopoeia, rhythm and repetition, but not for their own sake: these things must enrich the story-line and the characters.

Children are fascinated by the way people speak. They have a good ear for false dialogue or the wrong key struck in the current vernacular or the argot of a particular pastime or special world—skateboarding, space fiction, rock music, school-ground conversations.

Today's children, in contrast to those growing up, say, at the time of the Second World War or in the 1950s, mature much earlier physically. The average age for the onset of menstruation in Australian girls in 1992 is between eleven and twelve years. Romance and an interest in boys begins earlier than it used to, and girls in their early teens seek these things in the stories they read. Boys generally seek them a little later.

In general, children are possessed of a more sophisticated knowledge of the world and of sexual practices than their counterparts of three decades ago, but this apparent sophistication does not mean all is understood. Children still read to find out. Among the most popular books for teenagers are personal problem novels that tackle youthful relationships, family discord, single-parent families, moving house and school, parental separation and so on. You would do well to read the latest books for older children and teenagers by writers such as Gillian Rubinstein, Robin Klein, John Marsden, Victor Kelleher, Tim Winton, Nadia Wheatley and Paul Jennings.

Humour is always popular with children, but not sarcasm, ridicule, or irony. Kids like slapstick, eccentricity, absurdity, stories where people operate by their own idiosyncratic sets of rules, stories of mistakes and mistaken identity.

If you are thinking of writing for kindergarten children (books and stories that will be read *to* them, and not *by* them) or for early primary school children, then get down on your knees, or at least on your haunches. See the world from their level. It consists of Shetland ponies, puddles, bikes, tricycles and their shadows, ants, water, cracks in the pavement, mysteries, sand-pits, small cars and trucks, dolls and their houses, sand-castles, mud pies, television screens level with their shoulders, animals, bed, high shop counters, towering adults, balls, a bath for sailing, food handed down from on high. The stories you write for small children will come from these things, and particularly from animals—both the domestic familiars and those exotics at the zoo—as well as from toys that move or develop personalities.

Most of the elements we have already discussed in talking about adult story-telling can be applied successfully in writing for children, but some situations are particularly apt for young people:

- accidents, danger, adventure
- revenge, triumph of good over evil, paying out the villains
- overcoming hardships
- the picaresque, following the trials of characters moving physically (and metaphorically?) from A to B
- folk tales, fairy stories, myths, the fantastic, supernatural powers
- seeing the high and mighty tumble, the perfect fall
- emotions: stories for teenagers often trade heavily on the emotions and may be relatively limited in their social geography and action compared with those for younger children.

You will find that overt propaganda, proselytizing, moralizing, the clinical portrayal of contemporary violence, an overall tone of depression, desperation and bitterness are unwelcome. Young readers will also identify these elements in *covert* form, and leave you.

Despite all this, the challenge of writing for children comes back to *you*. If you *want* to write stories that you think children will treasure, then make sure you *know* children, and that you are still in touch with the child in yourself, then write for them without looking over your shoulder. Some of the most cherished 'children's stories'—Alan Garner's *Red shift*, William Mayne's *Earthfasts*, Kenneth Grahame's *The wind in the willows*, Randolph Stow's *Midnite*, A. A. Milne's *Winnie-the-Pooh*, Mark Twain's *The adventures of Tom Sawyer* and *Adventures of Huckleberry Finn*, and stories by Rosemary Sutcliff, Russell Hoban, James Thurber, J. R. R. Tolkien, C. S. Lewis, and others—are riveting for children and for adults. They were written from deep knowledge of story-telling and the nature of children, but they were not written to a prescription.

Writing for the young is not a mere addendum to writing for adults: it is an art of its own. You must be honest and sincere in writing for children. As Gillian Rubinstein, the Australian children's writer, says: 'It is in "Children's Books" that I feel free to ask the basic questions that adults no longer dare to ask themselves aloud: Who am I? What is the world? Why are some things (selfishness, greed, hatred) life-destroying and others life-giving?'

Write

1 Try developing a world round an animal or bird and write a story for five to eight-year-olds. It should be book-length, but not wordy—say,

one thousand words spread over twenty-four illustrated pages. How would you illustrate it? What would you leave up to the illustrator? Make a page-by-page mock-up.

2 Study children's magazines produced by the various ministries of education or education departments and write some short stories for different levels—for eight-year-olds (Year Three), for eleven to twelve-year-olds (Year Six), for thirteen to fifteen-year-olds (Years Seven and Eight).

3 Research and write a story—on computers, on conservation, on writers and writing, on palaeobotany, on spiritual beliefs in different cultures, on stamp-collecting—for children in Years Seven and Eight. Suggest illustrations and sources for them.

4 Develop the story-line or synopsis for a teenage (fourteen to sixteen years) novel centring on a personal problem of that age-group. Write the opening and first chapter.

Study the market

Some hard-headed advice about how to market your work might well be useful at this stage. Many of the general principles here will also apply to marketing the types of writing you will attempt later—scripts, stage plays, feature articles, public relations pieces, and so on—although each type of writing has its own distinctive requirements and methods of marketing.

By now you might well have a number of pieces of writing that you are planning to offer for publication. How do you go about it?

First, study the market. Just as you should read widely to get an idea of fiction for children, who publishes it, at what levels and with what illustrations, so you should adopt the same habits for adult material.

If you intend to submit your work to a particular magazine, study its issues over a couple of years to see what sorts of stories it uses and in what context. You can then submit knowledgeably, and not risk having your manuscript rejected unread simply because it falls outside the magazine's publishing guidelines. Seek statements of these guidelines if they are available and build up a file of possible outlets for your work. If a particular magazine publishes your fiction, study the journalistic articles they publish and perhaps submit some journalistic stories as well.

Submitting a manuscript

Editors of magazines and newspapers receive many more unsolicited manuscripts than they can publish. Some of their page space is taken up by commissioned articles or poems and short stories from established writers. Of the pile of unsolicited manuscripts that arrive on the editor's desk each week, less than one tenth might be accepted. Among the rejected manuscripts there are almost certainly some whose storytelling and content are of similar quality to those that have been accepted. They have been rejected, nevertheless, because they are poorly presented and the editor would have to put in too much work to prepare them for typesetting.

It is in your interest as a writer, therefore, to edit your work carefully before you prepare a final manuscript for submission, and then to make sure that your submission is set out and conveyed to the editor in the best way.

Presentation and layout

- Use white A4 paper of medium or heavy weight.
- Use one side of the paper only.
- Type lines double-spaced.
- Type the manuscript or print it out on a word processor, making sure you use a good black typewriter ribbon, or a relatively new printer cassette on your word processor. Make a carbon copy as you go, or save the document in memory or back it up on a floppy disc. Do not submit handwritten manuscripts to editors.
- Leave the editor liberal space around each page to make editing changes and to write in instructions for typesetters, designers and illustrators—4 cm on the left margin and at bottom and 3 cm at top and on the right margin.
- Wherever possible make yourself familiar with the 'house style' of the publisher to whom you are submitting. Contrary to what you were taught at school, there is no single and 'correct' way to spell all words (realise? realize?), to signify figures in a text (10,000? 10 000? ten thousand?), to capitalize words (Parliament? parliament?), to express dates (16 November? November 16?), to abbreviate (Mr.? Mr?), to hyphenate (wood-cutter? wood cutter?) and so on. Each publishing house, magazine, newspaper and television channel has a house style, set down in a sheet or booklet to maintain consistency in its publications. If you want general guidance, consult *The Oxford dictionary for writers and editors, Hart's rules for compositors and readers*, or, best of all for Australian publishing, the Australian Government Publishing Service *Style manual* or *The Australian writers' and editors' guide*, edited by Shirley Purchase.
- Type lines of roughly equal length, avoiding awkward word breaks at line endings. Leave the line short and type the word complete at the opening of the next line.
- Type up a title page. It should contain no text but carry all the information to identify work and author—title of story, author's name, address, telephone and fax number, pen-name if used, number of words, and the © as a copyright sign beside the author's name repeated at the left foot of the page with the date of writing beside it (© 1992 Bertrand Balranald). Calculate the number of words in your manuscript by

sampling several lines on a typical full page to find the number of words they contain, average them, and multiply by the number of lines on the page. Repeat this for several other sample pages to calculate an average number of words per page. Then multiply this by the number of pages in your manuscript. If you are using a word processor, its software package will probably do an accurate word count for you.

• Your first page should carry the title centred in its top half and only half a page of text below it.

• Indent each paragraph of text some six letter spaces from the left margin; begin each book chapter or part on a new page; indent quotations that are longer than fifty words rather than allowing them to 'run on' in the text; number each page in the top right corner.

• In most instances you should centre titles and main headings on the page. Place sub-heads hard against the left margin.

• Don't submit messy pages. If you have more than a few corrections, retype the page; otherwise type corrections or write them clearly above the line.

• Type the word 'End', centred a few lines below the last line of your final page. You might like to repeat your name and contact details again in the lower left of the final page.

• If your manuscript is a book, type up separate pages after the title page to carry a table of contents, acknowledgements, and sources of illustrations.

• If your article or story is to be illustrated, post the illustrations in an envelope bolstered with stiff card to protect them in the mail, and indicate by a numbering system on each illustration, matching numbers in the text, where each is to go. Add a list of numbered captions.

• Ensure you have kept a copy of the manuscript for yourself. Manuscripts *do* get lost in the mail and in editorial offices. Editors are happy to work with good photocopies, enabling you to keep the original in your file.

• Fasten your manuscript securely with a fastener strong enough to preserve it intact through some rough treatment by several hands.

• An increasing number of magazines, newspapers and publishing houses will accept and even prefer stories submitted on floppy discs using a software system compatible with their editing and typesetting equipment. You should enquire whether this is necessary or appropriate before submitting a disc.

• Try to post your manuscript flat, or if you have to fold it, make the fold lengthways.

• Send with your manuscript a self-addressed and stamped envelope for its return if necessary. Few editors will return manuscripts without this. Enclose a covering note—not a long letter—stating the titles of the pieces you are submitting for publication, that you are offering first use

Australian rights only, that you have enclosed an addressed and stamped envelope for return of the manuscript, and that you would appreciate any comments the editor can find time to make on your work. This covering note, often separated from the manuscript by the editor and kept as evidence of receipt, may be the means of finding a lost manuscript in an editor's office awash with paper!

• Keep a running list of the titles of poems, short stories, and articles submitted to editors, when sent, when returned, and with what result. Do not have the same piece under submission to two publishing houses at the same time, unless you make it clear that you are submitting it elsewhere. Be prepared for publishers to refuse to consider it if it is submitted elsewhere.

• Best of luck in your submission. Do not be deterred by rejection slips. They are a means of learning, and editors are not infallible. There are several cases on record in which books that ultimately became best-sellers were rejected time and time again before being taken up by insightful publishers.

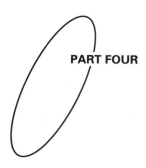

PART FOUR

Autobiography, memoirs and life histories, biography

This inescapable duty to observe oneself: if someone else is observing me, naturally I have to observe myself too; if none observes me, I have to observe myself all the closer . . .

Franz Kafka

. . . the further I go back, the better I remember things— whether they happened or not . . .

Mark Twain

[These personal essays] record what seems to me important about my own life, and try to treat this life, this massive datum which happens to be mine, as a specimen life, representative in its odd uniqueness of all the oddly unique lives in the world . . .

John Updike

Writing from life

Autobiography is personal writing; it is self-centred, and yet universally interesting if it's well done. It may not be for public exposure at all: it may be a pursuit of style and artistic satisfaction. 'Not to enchant anybody,' writes the Polish poet Czeslaw Milosz; 'Not to earn a lasting name in posterity. An unnamed need for order, for rhythm, for form, which three words are opposed to chaos and nothingness.' The English diarist, Gail Godwin, writes:

The prospect of people reading my diaries after I am dead does not disturb me in the least. I like to think of pooling myself with other introspective hearts: madmen (and women), prudes, profligates, celebrities, outcasts, heroes, artists, saints, the lovelorn and the lucky, the foolish and the proud. I have found so many sides of myself in the diaries of others . . .

All of this is true, at one time or another, of the writing of diaries, journals, memoirs, life-histories and autobiography. So, let us first make some distinctions, and then go on to discuss life histories and autobiographies in more detail.

A diary is not a journal. If often contains notes of events, and need not aspire to style, depth, complexity or drama, although in some hands it may: *The diary of Anne Frank* is an example. A diarist writes daily or at least relatively regularly.

A journal is not a diary, but when is a notebook a journal? A journal is generally used to record what is fascinating, dramatic, moving, stranger-than-fiction. It may spend many words on a brief episode in life, engaging style, sentence structure, and paragraphing—elements that the diary may largely ignore. At other points the journal or notebook may devote only a few spare words or notes to something that will be developed later. It is episodic in its compilation. See Thomas Mallon's book, already mentioned, *A book of one's own*; the excellent *Antaeus —journals, notebooks and diaries*, edited by Daniel Halpern; James Boswell's *Journal of a tour of the Hebrides*; V.S. Naipaul's *Congo River diary*; Beverley Farmer's *A body of water—a year's notebook*; or *Necessary secrets: The journals of Elizabeth Smart*.

A life history is something less high-flown than an autobiography or memoir, and is a form of writing that has become very popular in Australia in the last few years. More people are being encouraged to write about their own experience, and oral history has become a genre of its own, as we become more aware of what we lose if the details of people's lives go unrecorded. A life history is a natural piece of story-telling, something that might be written by a grandmother in response to questions from her young grandchildren. It almost always has a strong element of family in it.

Memoirs may be born out of diaries or journals, but they are selective, carefully structured and composed. Generally intended for publication, they are often worthy of it mainly because they are the literary reminiscences of someone famous or at least well-known, or because fate has made that person's experience unusual and interesting. Writers are especially well-placed to write memoirs, but they may resist it because they prefer to invent. Examples of literary memoirs include John Updike's *Self-consciousness—memoirs* and the recalling of Melbourne's artistic circle by the expatriate Australian writer, Alistair Kershaw in his book *Hey days: Memories and glimpses of Melbourne's Bohemia 1937–1947.*

Autobiography is akin to a set of memoirs, and yet is less formal and consecutive in many cases. In both autobiography and biography there is much more scope for variety in the story-telling than is commonly realized. See, among classic international examples, Cardinal Newman's *Apologia pro vita sua*, Gorky's *My childhood*, Alfred Kazin's *A walker in the city*, *Starting out in the thirties*, and *New York Jew*, Ernest Hemingway's *A moveable feast*, William Gosse's *Father and son*, Walt Whitman's *Specimen days* and *Song of myself*, and among many Australian examples, Patrick White's *Flaws in the glass*, Dame Mary Gilmore's *Old days: Old ways*, Henry Lawson's 'A fragment of auto-biography', Albert Facey's *A fortunate life*, Kylie Tennant's *The missing heir*, Bruce Beaver's *As it was*, David Malouf's *12 Edmondstone Street*, Barbara Hanrahan's *The scent of eucalyptus*, Mary Rose Liverani's *The winter sparrows*, Dorothy Hewett's *Wild card* and many others.

Then there is that vast and shifting array of writing sometimes described as 'autobiographical novels and short fiction'. George Johnston, for instance, describes the first part of his trilogy, *My brother Jack*, as an 'autobiographical novel', even though he makes a number of drastic changes to 'real life'. Elsewhere he deals with experience very directly, and models the two succeeding parts of the trilogy quite closely on his own experience. Alan Marshall, in *I can jump puddles*, was clearly writing from his own childhood experience but said he went beyond the facts to get at the truth. Often readers are unaware of how deeply writers have drawn on their own experience, or of how it is imperative that they do.

Your life history

The American Jewish writer Alfred Kazin said: 'So one writes to make a home for one's self on paper . . . But to write is to live again, and in this personal myth and resurrection of our experience, to give honour to our lives.'

Telling a life history is not just for the elderly, as the diary of Anne Frank shows. Older people can record and secure the details of an earlier and very different world, take stock, and make sense of their lives; the young, writing about their lives, embark on the sort of self-discovery that is endemic to every field of writing. All autobiography salutes and celebrates humanity.

In telling your story you will find that you inevitably become involved in telling the stories of your relatives, friends and others biographically.

Write

1 Have one large notebook in which you can write quick notes, and another in which you can work in 'life sections', so that a structure emerges when you begin to draft your story. Have a small tape recorder, if possible, to catch other people's impressions and information.

2 Learn to plan diagrammatically. As a start, draw up on a large sheet a family tree that goes back as far as possible. Give it plenty of room so that it can be amended and expanded. Work in pencil first, then ink it in if necessary later.

3 In this writing, you will find it best to move from the centre outwards, from the particular of yourself, to the general of the context, the time, the other people involved.

4 With the family tree near at hand for reference, turn to your notebook. Start with your beginnings. Leave plenty of space around your writing for later additions, and write in note form, then perhaps in sentences and paragraphs, all you know about your birth. Was it difficult, a hard pregnancy for your mother? Who was the doctor or midwife? Where and when were you born? Describe the hospital if you can and its environment. What was your parents' position economically and socially at the time? Describe your father and mother as they were in the year you were born. Don't forget details: age? jobs? relatives? interests? hopes? fears? habits? rituals? Describe your father's character and family background in detail and then your mother's. What were her family origins, what differences in upbringing, class and attitudes did she exhibit in comparison with your father? What bound them together? What set them apart? Describe your sisters and brothers, if any, and your grandparents. What sort of a home, street, suburb, town, farm, did you come home to? What sort of a reception? Leave ample space for additions after these initial jottings.

5 Expand from the centre of your birth. What country were you born into? What sort of wider world? Who was Prime Minister or leader of the country? What party was in power? Was the country at peace or war? Economic conditions and their effects on people? Employment? Relationships between city and country? How widespread was your extended family? Their strengths, weaknesses, callings, living places, peculiarities?

6 First plan, diagrammatically, a widely spaced step-by-step chronology of how you moved from your situation at birth to your present situation. What were the changes—geographical, emotional, aspirational, economic, employment, family, religious and spiritual, sexual and physical—you went through? Centre it on a sheet so that additions can be made easily. This plan will probably give you many of your chapter headings. Your first draft of this plan will not be your final one—there will be steps that you have forgotten.

7 Second, plan a diagram of all the near family and others who closely affected your life in your first twelve years—siblings, male and female cousins, uncles, aunts, grandparents, godparents, neighbours, family friends, employers (did you do a paper-round? help in a shop? a stall? a garden? a farm?), teachers, ministers or priests, doctors, etc. Write a one-line note describing *your* feelings about each. Like? Dislike? Interest and why? Jealousy and why? Fear and why?

8 Tap into your memory and begin research. List those people mentioned above who closely affected your young life and describe their physical contexts, homes, households, jobs, and so on. Then seek out the people themselves, if possible, as well as others who knew them, and talk about what you remember. Don't neglect humour; don't neglect the unpleasant. You should be honest in what you write later, even if you decide against including some stories of family bickering and bitterness. If memory is obdurate, think again of where you lived, where you played as children, with what toys, what rituals you shared—Christmas, Hanukkah, Ramadan, New Year, picnics, fishing trips, your mother's or father's work place, Grandma's house, outside the pub, the park, the creek.

9 Now, in your life-sectioned notebook, under a new heading, 'Childhood', write a distinct anecdote or story about each of these people, or at least those who at this moment seem to loom largest. Leave plenty of space after each sketch. You will most likely write about parents and grandparents, running to several stories on each. You will finish with a series of small sketches, each of which centres about your experience, but does not parade it. This story repository can be enlarged almost indefinitely.

10 You are now on your way to an extended piece of autobiographical writing. As this stage you will need to plot your life by topics and by order of events. You will have to think hard about what categories might contain the various events of your life, and be honest in the questions you are prepared to ask about yourself: What are you proud of? Ashamed of? What do you fear? What have you failed to do? What would you like to do? What were the turning points in your life? What has shaped your life? And so on. You can make your own schema, asking further questions under each of these headings. When we approach the development

of characters in play-writing and script-writing in Part Five of this book, similar searching questions about yourself and your relationships with others will become important. Here are some suggestions, to which you will add questions, themes, life stages of your own:

Life-stages: Childhood
                Kindergarten, primary school
                Secondary school
                Tertiary education
                Relationships with the same sex/the opposite sex
                Teenage years/sexuality
                First job
                Living together/marriage
                Children
                Ambition/adjustment/trials
                Change of viewpoint—your 20s, 30s, 40s
                Mid-life—'so this is all there is; so this is what it is about'
                Ageing—job, retirement, adjustment, wisdom, looking back
                Old age—benefits, disadvantages, feelings, new allegiances and paths

Some of the life-questions you should ask and answer honestly and the life-areas you should consider and even research further are listed below. Read through these more than once. Use both these and the life-stages as a check list when writing and seeking information from other people and other sources. Then try writing autobiographically out of them following the structure for the telling of the story that is suggested below. But first the broad questions:

—Those places other than home; holiday places; walking places; swimming places; retreats, and their value to you?

—What has love meant to you? Different sorts of love?

—Have you met the famous, and what resulted? Have you met the obscure who proved to be luminous?

—How close have you been to politics of your time? Write about it.

—Artistic expression—has it been merely vicarious in influencing you, or has it been an undeniable appetite—books, radio, records and CDs, film, music, television, crafts, painting, sculpture, ballet, dance?

—What do you do to unwind? What have you always done? What pattern is there to it?

—Where has death entered your experience? What have been your attitudes to it? Grief, understanding, regret?

—Physical discomfort, illness, operations, recovery—what have these been for you?

—Are you a spiritual person? In what senses?

—When has life been hard for you and those around you? How does the experience appear to you in retrospect?

—What makes your family distinctive? Rituals? Traditions? Tension? Religion? Closeness? Fulfilment? Unfulfilment?

—Technology—at what points has it impressed itself on your life? Memories of first using new technology?

—Balance-sheet. Of what are you most proud? What would you do differently, given a second chance? In what respects have you failed your own standards?

—Has war influenced your life? How? When? Your attitudes to it?

—Sport or physical pastimes—how do these loom in your experience?

—What sort of national or ethnic sense of belonging do you seem to have hearkened to in your life? Has it been challenged? Is it easy and rewarding to adhere to or does it provide tensions?

—Sex. When did you first become aware of it? How would you describe its place in your life? What is your sexual history?

—Which two or three of all the people you have met have/had the greatest influence on you? Why?

—Think of the touchstones of spirituality—the centre, the gift, the initiation, the turning-point, trance, dream, God, uniqueness, time, movement, stasis, the inexplicable, supernatural happenings, prescience, foreknowledge, non-violence, asceticism, aloneness. Write short statements that reflect these touchstones or others as they have affected you.

—How has your gender influenced the course and detail of your life? How aware are you of gender issues, injustices, divisions, cleavages?

—Your life set against history. What sort of person were you when war broke out, when it ended, when man first walked the moon, when the stock market crashed, when Whitlam was dismissed?

—What have the necessities of life—shelter, food, clothing—meant in your experience?

—What role have children played in your life? How do you regard children and the process of growing up?

—What are your views about education, formal or informal? Write about yourself as you were when you first went to kindergarten; primary school; what the beginnings of secondary school were like for you; the novelty of that fresh start in a tertiary institution, if you experienced it. Dig deep into memory held in the senses and emotions in making these stories.

—How has your life led you to view work? How has it led you to regard property?

—What have you *not* yet done or experienced in your life which you would dearly love to do?

Autobiography

You might do further talking, interviewing and research about your life. Look up the section on research to be found in Part Eight on Journalism. It may be helpful.

You can write about yourself autobiographically in several ways. You can simply write a sequence of small sketches arising out of the life stages, life questions and life areas above, without concerning yourself too much with chronology, leaving the tone and detail of each sketch to place it in your life. Alternatively, you can write a series of chronologically arranged sketches, casting forward and back in some of them to other points of reference in your life. A combination of these two approaches might suit you best, allowing your life story to be carried forward chronologically, with space for atmospheric sketches and incidents that give the telling universal dimension. One model for this is John Steinbeck's novel—it is *not* an autobiography—*The grapes of wrath*. In that story Steinbeck traces the trek of the 'Okies' (Oklahomans dispossessed of land and work in the Depression of the 1930s) as they travel to California in search of work, pausing as he pursues the narrative to include what have been called 'intercalary chapters' that draw together the common and simple pleasures, sufferings, rituals and emotions of the travellers. In a similar way, you could intercut your story with carefully selected pieces of atmosphere and incident.

Write

Choose an approach among the ones above, or another that appeals to your personality, style and subject-matter. First, try writing a short (1000 words) opening to the account of your life. Where and in what style should you begin the story?

Next, move forward in time and write 2000 words or so telling the story of an incident or incidents connected with your coming to terms with the adult world, not forgetting that this and other segments of your autobiography depend for their interest on being revealed through action and not merely through explanation.

Finally, again moving in time, choose the significant year when you experienced the greatest change in outlook. Write 3000 words or so about it.

Biography

Now, from your own life to those of others. We yearn to know about people and how they use their lives. If they are famous, so much the better. Churchill? Simone de Beauvoir? Bob Dylan? How were they made what they became? Joseph Furphy? Barbara Baynton? Louisa Lawson? What drove them?

For those who want to tell the story of a life it is now possible to do it in sound, on video, on film, on stage, in print. We will speak mostly about print, although the methods and strategies used in producing a book-length biography are closely akin to those necessary to tell the life in other media.

Biography may be short or long or somewhere in between. Womens' magazines, newspapers and specialist magazines often thrive on the short forms of biography, but these articles are a far cry from the book length academic or journalistic biography, the full political, historical, literary, scientific, business or sporting biography. A person need not be famous to be the subject of a biography if their experience is interesting enough. Such biographies challenge the biographer's story-telling skills more, perhaps, than those whose subjects are well known.

The biographer and 'truth'

Biography and history often intersect and interact, and the biographer is willy-nilly an historian. 'Truth', whatever that means, is the biographer's aim, but accuracy is the best she can hope to achieve. Experienced biographers will tell you that an event never comes through to the researcher pure or unmediated: the time of day, the date, the place may be well documented, but the *nature* of the event appears different to each person involved with it, even if they share some common impressions of it. In writing a biography from a mass of gathered detail, the biographer selects, decides that this is more important than that, and is swayed by his own prejudices, past experience, fears and loves in making these decisions about another person's life. Exit 'truth'.

Nevertheless, biography is a fascinating and very important form of research and writing, which is open to a greater range of writing styles and techniques than most of us realize.

Principles and a method

Will your fascination last?

In deciding whether to write a biographical study of a person or persons you should be guided by the principle of story-telling in general—does the person's life, their character and times, truly fascinate you sufficiently to carry you through months, perhaps years, of study, research, travel, correspondence, interviewing, photography, checking details, and then a long bout of writing in which the need for accuracy puts a steadying hand on your wish to write openly, stylishly, fluently? If so, proceed. If not, think about other possible subjects.

Possible publication and market

Your thoughts at this stage might also be tempered by practical, personal and commercial considerations. Whether you are writing a biographical profile article of, say, 10 000 words for a magazine or journal, or are contemplating a book-length biography, you are well advised to discuss the idea with editors and publishers. Some biographies are more publishable than others, because they are more interesting to a wider range of readers. If a magazine editor or book publisher says yes, it will do wonders for your commitment.

Angle

Is there an 'angle', a basic point about your subject, that will underlie much of what you write? Does one basic fact of their life go to explain much of its course and preoccupations? Did your subject fall from grace? Was her life one of a rise from obscurity and lack of education to one of intellectual prominence? Was his life governed by an early belief about the spiritual in human life? Your 'angle' should not obscure other possibilities and directions in your subject's life, but it should help you make sense of the life and help the writing and arrangement of material.

The work involved

When you have satisfied yourself on these three points, your work starts in earnest. It involves research on a number of fronts. If your subject is alive, and agrees to co-operate with your project, it probably means interviews with her or him. You will also want to interview as many as possible of the people who know or knew your subject well. As you become more deeply involved in the work, it will be as if you have developed antennae that discover sources of information about your subject. Each source will seed others. It is vital that you gather information efficiently and organize it well—it could consist of notes, clippings, tapes, videos, photographs, letters, diaries, bank accounts, articles, official documents, and much more. Look at the sections on research and on interviewing in Part Eight of this book and use the suggestions there to help organize your work.

Research methods

Keep a list of possible sources of information, and draw up an expandable time line of your subject's life. Write in the main events, knowing that you will add notes to the outline as you discover more detail. You can use this to check and double check the order of events and what might have influenced what in your subject's life. Keep exhaustive details of where you found material in case you need to reproduce it or to go back to it in the light of later evidence.

Diagrams of a life

Draw diagrams of your subject's life and the patterns of it, the influences on it. Map out the contexts in which the subject has operated, friends and colleagues, social worlds in which they moved, work situations, enemies, supporters, major events and turning points, the elements of the person as a private individual and as a public person.

'The facts'

Be sceptical but receptive when gathering detail about your subject. Realize that people have poor memories; that they repeat inaccuracies in which they come to believe; that newspapers, because of the speed with which they have to be put together, are not reliable sources in many cases; that errors can be perpetuated in print; that memory can be selective, blotting out elements that are unpalatable; that people sometimes have axes to grind; that names and place-names are often misspelt; that motivations for human action may be very complex.

Try to see sites in the subject's life yourself—houses they lived in; districts they lived and worked in; work places; places of relaxation; haunts for meeting friends, lovers, children, etc. Wherever possible go to official documents—resignation letters, birth certificates, house titles, financial statements, Army discharge papers—to check detail.

Fictional techniques applied to facts

The details surrounding your subject—background, geography, family, social and intellectual interaction—are in many ways as important as events in your subject's life. In writing about these you will find that you want to employ the skills of the novelist or writer of short fiction. Your biography should be alive and not dry, inert and fact-filled. Attend to pace, balance, style, word choice, paragraphing, and sentence length.

Asking the central question

Put your subject at the centre of your thoughts, asking all the while, 'What was it or is it like to be this person?' With this as a guiding question, it is often difficult to know when you have completed your research. You will find that you develop a sixth sense that urges you on to more enquiry, telling you that you have not quite plumbed the secret, have not yet asked some crucial questions. You must aim, in any case, to amass much more material than you can use in the written account; it will fertilize in subtle ways what you do put on paper. Then, as Philip Zeigler, the author of the biography of Earl Mountbatten, puts it, you will cast about and make an imaginative leap that imposes a structure on the material and guides you in the writing.

Ways of telling lives

There are often several biographies written of the one figure—a proof that interpretations of the same 'facts' can differ, that to an extent the unrealized selves of biographers come out in their accounts of their subjects' lives. Again, some biographies are much more imaginative than others and employ a variety of writing techniques and styles.

Louisa, Brian Matthews's biography of Louisa Lawson, is a case in point. It uses conjecture and dramatization to present the results of meticulous re-search and to hazard possibilities about a life that is incompletely known and documented.

Look about you at the ways of story-telling used by other biographers—see Michael Holroyd's celebrated three-volume biography of George Bernard Shaw, for example, or David Marr's biography of Patrick White—and then give some thought to how you might vary the form of what you will write to suit your subject.

PART FIVE

Writing for stage, film, television and radio

A play is what takes place.

A novel is what one person tells us took place.

Thornton Wilder

Get your character up a tree. Throw stones at him. Get him down.

French proverb

The playwright's statement

I once saw a shy, middle class couple endeavouring to separate, to wind up their affairs, of the twin hearts, so to speak, in a fairly crass Chinese restaurant in Sydney. I was touched by their politeness. I was amazed at their secret sorrow. This play is my first attempt at a Middle Class theme: Barry Williamson, I now am!

Perfect English explores the dyed-in-the-wool Anglophobia (Anglophilia?) of old-fashioned, well-intentioned, middle-class Australians. They are good people who don't swear, who don't laugh much, for whom interest rates and the blind terror of loneliness mean everything.

We commence in said Chinese restaurant. It is perhaps six o'clock in the evening, probably a Friday night. It is winter in Sydney: 1990. The couple in question are frightfully polite and eager to please. It is their very Englishness which destroys and creates everything in their nervous and terribly sedate existences. They are too nice.

Geoff and Monique Grubb are about 50. Geoff looks more. Monique has commenced 'forced tennis' and has chucked smokes and drink. Geoff is still very keen; a lush, no less. They are not quite shabby-genteel; but the Keating economy is beginning to show on them somewhat. The only other character is the ubiquitous waiter, who plays several parts, and determines time and place and even mood. The waiter is about 50. He is going through mid-life crisis as well.

Barry Dickins wrote that statement before he began work on his play, *Perfect English*. His words come with intensity. They leave no doubt about his fascination or where he gained the strength of involvement to complete the play. They reflect the play's strength and variety of emotion—from great sadness and a sense of loss to high comedy.

Story-telling for the stage

We are now in the world of illusion that is created through sound, or visible action and sound. We are in the world of drama. Although there are crucial differences between the writing techniques for stage, film, television and radio drama, we shall proceed from what those different crafts have in common—action and sound.

Your writing for this Part will explore those common elements first and then the special requirements of each medium. There will still, of course, be refinements that we cannot cover in depth.

You will, however, begin to develop dramatic skills, to uncover your strengths and work on your weaknesses in writing drama. For further guidance in these forms, a number of excellent books are listed in the Bibliography.

Write

Reread Barry Dickins's statement, then try writing a statement for a story that you can see as a stage play. Your statement—some writers call it a scenario—can be as long or short as you need. You are exploring the elements of a play, perhaps for the first time.

In this stage play script, of which this is the first step, you are allowed no more than four characters, no intervals, an indefinite number of scenes, and a running time within one and a half hours. You may wish to write a more detailed statement and divide it into parts to cover the following elements.

1 A personal statement about the experience that sparked the idea and still feeds it.

2 A statement about the play's broad subject (marriage, pursuit of power, male violence, the artistic outsider, etc.) *and* a two-line description of the play's action from beginning to end.

3 A statement about characters and setting: 'The action takes place in the adjoining backyards of two houses in the Melbourne mortgage belt . . .' Add details of time of day, month or season, year or decade, special occasion (election eve, Christmas Day, someone's wedding day), etc.

4 Biographies of the three or four characters—who they are, where they were born, their family, schools, jobs, friends, beliefs and opinions (even if they are unaware of some aspects of these), what they see as the future for themselves and each other, their relationship over the years (if any), their living place(s), their state of health, ages, experience, their personal and speech foibles, etc. This will take some time: out of your characters comes your story, and you need to know them well.

5 A paragraph about the question that will be held in tension throughout the play, and may or may not be answered within the action.

6 A couple of paragraphs about the tension and conflict between characters at the center of the play, with ideas about how it will be resolved or left unresolved at the play's end.

7 A list of scenes that you can envision already (brief descriptions of the point of the action and some of the lines in each). You might not be able to imagine all the scenes yet, but some important ones will be developing in your mind.

8 A statement about the 'tone' of the action—heavy irony, comedy, tragicomedy, naturalism, surrealism, representative slapstick, etc.

When you have completed your statement, write an expanded second statement (two or three pages at least) following up what you wrote in 2 above, and telling the story in more detail. Outline the steps in the story—'this happens and then that happens, and that changes the way that A sees B, so that what happens next is . . .'

All of this is preliminary, but very important, and will take quite a deal of time and thought. It will be changed in many respects, you can be sure, as you develop the piece. You may even decide that your idea is not suitable for drama; if so, think again, and write another statement about a different idea.

There are other ways of approaching drama, but working from a statement is one commonly used by dramatists and script-writers. It raises the inescapable issues; it can be changed and built upon; it gives you confidence in arranging the 'world' in which your story can be enacted.

Act 1, Scene i

What is necessary for an opening scene? You have an empty space or stage before you. You have actors, an audience, and a story you want to tell. The outline of that story and its points of tension are in your head and your statement or scenario.

In what setting will your characters (or single character) first appear to the audience, who know nothing about them? Where will you enter your story, keeping in mind that your setting will probably serve for other scenes, and that frequent scene changes can be expensive and awkward? How can you suggest several places while still using the same space? Can you use lighting, different parts of the set, props, or other conventions? Remember, you are dealing in space, illusion, and sounds of voices.

Choose the setting and the character(s) that the audience will see first. Write out the scene in detail for your own purposes, then condense the detail into stage directions. The play opening below is merely a worked example. The form in which it is set out is a good one to adopt initially in setting out your own. However, if you are presenting a professional script you may set out the play differently to allow quick communication with actors, directors, designers and stage crew. You might make a distinction between actors' directions and stage directions by placing actors' directions on the left of the page and stage directions on the right of the page. Louis Catron's *Writing, producing and selling your play* gives suggestions for setting out play scripts in this way.

WALKING TO THE FALLS
A Play by X
Cast

Vanessa Carlyon—thirty-five years
Ellie Carlyon—thirty-two years   maiden sisters
Mime Jennings—twenty years; the sisters' boarder; a primary teacher
Harold Blaine—Mime's beau, soon to be fiancé
Alex Warrell—thirty years; a new neighbour to the sisters, and owner of 'Caithness' farm; had befriended Ellie briefly before he enlisted;

unexpectedly returned from the Great War after being reported Missing Presumed Dead

Reg Grey—share-farms 'Pitnacree', the Carlyons' farm, and looks after stock for the sisters

Jock Eastaugh—farm manager for Alex Warrell at 'Caithness'

Time: summer, early 1919

ACT ONE

Drawing-room and verandah, (seen through french windows, stage right), of the sisters' house, set above a river valley on the south coast of New South Wales.

It is genteel, used and efficient, as befits the hillside holiday cottage of Vanessa and Ellies's father, recently deceased, and formerly a Professor of Languages at the University of Sydney.

A skirt and a pair of bloomers are stretched to dry on the fire screen before the fireplace on the left. The mantelpiece above it is something of a shrine, with photographs of officers in uniform, a polished brass cartridge case standing beside candlesticks and a portrait of the Professor. Light flows from stage right beyond the french windows in a wall cut away to allow a full view of the wide verandah and its railing.

There are two entrances apart from the french windows. One, centre back, gives into the kitchen, of which there is a dim view of table and sink. The other, left front, gives into hallway and bedrooms. Slightly left of centre, and forward, is a colonial round table and on it a lace cloth, some piano music, and three books. Beneath a silver vase of flowers at table's centre is a set of silver cruets. It is mid-morning: a warm Saturday in summer. There is the sound of water and washing, clothes being wrung out into a tub. As the curtain rises, ELLIE sits at the table writing on notepaper with a gold fountain pen. She wears a wine-coloured longish skirt, black leather boots and a white blouse. Her hair is swept up and held with a comb. She sprawls girlishly at the table, one foot trailing behind the chair as she writes, considers, writes again. She seems younger than her 32 years.

(*Voice over*: ELLIE's *voice reading what she is writing*) Madge, as I was hinting we might in my last letter, Nessie and I have been down to Kiama to see the Highland Games. Now that the War is over, there seems to be more hustle and bustle: a charabanc of visitors even came up here to the Falls a week ago, but it broke down at the foot of our hill. I took some hot water down to make tea for them. There were four soldiers. Light casualties they call themselves. Light! It's terrible. One was blind. He came from Albion. Another one had lost his foot. How can we have any idea what they've been through! Can you possibly get down at Easter? Tell me in the next post if you can. We'd love to see you. We can ride—it should be good weather.

You'll never guess. Leila Petrie is getting married—to that manager from Dubbo. She'll be the lady of the manor, the lucky girl. What about you and Tom? Ness and I have missed the boat here, it seems. Nessie is better than she was; it's three years now, although it doesn't seem anywhere near so long. Seeing Keith's brothers in the village all the time must keep raking it up again for her, poor thing. And you've heard about Alex Warrell who bought 'Caithness'? He came as our neighbour just before the War started. He was such a good influence on all of us—funny, gentle—and he handled horses so well. I only knew him for five weeks, off and on, before he enlisted. I can't think of it. He was posted missing in the last days of the War. The Germans gave up just two weeks later. His mother is a widow and lives in Sydney. Jock Eastaugh manages 'Caithness' now. I've heard that Alex's mother has retreated from everyone . . .

(Enter VANESSA *from the kitchen, unseen by* ELLIE, *who keeps writing.* VANESSA *is taller, thinner, more severe than* ELLIE, *but attractive in a dark, dignified way. She is the responsible elder sister. She feels cheated by the world and the War and is repressed and resentful. It is she who has been washing. She wears an apron over a dark, worsted gown.)*

ELLIE *(still writing)*: I've often thought since the news about Keith and Alex, and now that Father's gone, we'd be better in Berry or Nowra. We're cut off here, in our valley. But I suppose if it came to the point I couldn't leave it. It's been my magic place since Father bought the cottage when I was five. Imagine! I'm thinking of starting a dressmaking business, with perhaps a little shop. Having Uncle Jim down the coast is a great comfort . . .'

VANESSA *(She stands just inside the door for a moment, her eyes taking in the table at which* ELLIE *writes, the fire screen with its drying clothes. She fights down disapproval.)*: El, have you seen my book? The Housman? *(*ELLIE *continues writing to the sentence's end, but is already turning towards her sister.)* Ellie! *(*VANESSA *waits with a just discernible toss of the head, turns over the books on the table, continues when she sees* ELLIE *has surfaced. She delays, now that she has* ELLIE's *attention. She studies her hands.)* My hands are chapped. *(She pauses.)* I had it yesterday. I thought I left it here. That book of Housman poems?

ELLIE: Oh, Ness, I'm sorry. I was looking at them when you went to bed. The book's in the hall. I'll get it. *(She caps her pen, starts to rise.)*

VANESSA: *I'll* get it, for Heavens sake. (*With studied control*) Who are you writing to?

ELLIE (*Sinking back in chair; expansive, enthused*): Madge Curtis. I'm suggesting the idea of Easter, if she can get on the train. We could ride. We have beautiful crisp days around then.

VANESSA: Minnie won't be ready for that!

ELLIE: Oh, yes she will. Mr Grey seems to think she should be able to walk by the middle of next week . . . (*sounds off, of car approaching*) and we should be able to take her for a canter the week after, he says. (*Sounds off, of car arriving, stopping, door shutting, car moving off again. Footsteps.*)

MIME (*voice from kitchen*): Signed, sealed, delivered—I'm back!

VANESSA (*picking dead petals from the vase of flowers at the table's centre*): Anyway, I thought we might invite Uncle Jim up at Easter. (*Enter* MIME *from the kitchen: She carries letters and a parcel. She is shorter than the two sisters. She speaks quickly and vivaciously, and is clearly something of a lively commentary on the larger world for* VANESSA *and* ELLIE. *She wears jodphurs and a crew-neck woollen jumper.*)

MIME: Signed. Sealed. Delivered! In Harold's Ford T. I love his motor car. He's coming down again after lunch. We might drive to the Mill and then walk up to the Falls. (*The sisters are silent,* ELLIE *having taken on* VANESSA's *negativity, but are watching* MIME's *eyes and movements.*) Well, ladies . . . Letters! (*She slaps them down on the table.*) And parcel! (*She slaps that down. She sets herself to reporting mode.*) In the grocer's I saw Mrs Bauer, and her Stewart is going to Bowral for a few weeks farm labouring. In the store I heard that the Gibsons have bought the Maher property on the Cambewarra Road. They are going to run shorthorns. And in the post office—I don't know how to tell you this. Everyone in the village is talking about it. (*She swallows with emotion, gathers herself together again.*) The sisters Carlyon are to have a visitor! A visitor they will never have expected. The sisters Carlyon . . .

ELLIE (*playing up to* MIME's *hyperbole*): And who, pray, is to visit us?

MIME: I couldn't believe it. Under his hat I didn't recognize him. He was collecting the mail, and I hear this voice behind me at the counter . . .

ELLIE (*impatient, tantalized*): Who? Who?

MIME (*not to be stampeded*): I hear this voice saying 'Remember me?' You won't believe it either. It was Alex Warrell . . .
(*The name clearly strikes* ELLIE *like a bolt. She turns in her chair to look at* MIME, *her arm sweeping pen and sheets of paper off the table.*)

ELLIE: Alex? . . . Alex? (*Her voice chokes.*) But he's . . . There was a telegram months ago. He's supposed to be . . .

MIME (*beaming down on* ELLIE): Well, he's here, large as life. Only just come home.

ELLIE: Are you sure?

MIME: I'm sure. Of course I'm sure! I don't know the full details, but there was a German withdrawal and he was taken with it, apparently. A wounded prisoner. A prisoner till the Armistice. Fancy being treated by Fritz nurses!

ELLIE: Are you sure? Are you sure?!

MIME (*ignoring* ELLIE's *question; silencing her with an assured, conspiratorial smile*): He wouldn't talk about it. He looks well. He's brown—he's been seeing the sun. He seems to walk with a bit of a limp. He has a sort of black stall over some of his left hand. (*Pauses for breath*) And he asked me to tell you that he might drive over this afternoon if you are going to be at home . . .

(VANESSA *has been arrested with petals in her hand. They drop to the floor. She is silent, looking at her sister with a mixture of interest at her reaction, noncommittal resignation and then a certain desperate determination.*)

VANESSA: What will the War offer up next? Think of his mother! How must she . . . He's back from the dead!

(ELLIE *has buried her head in her arms at the table. She is completely silent.*) . . .

At this stage, read through what you have written, listen to it, see it in your mind's eye. Generalizations about the openings of plays or scripts are dangerous: there is no sacrosanct set of rules. There is no need to reveal all in this opening scene, but it should allow the audience to know who and what they are seeing, to feel the 'tone' of the story, and to see some of its conflicts emerging. Has your opening provided this? Could it be better? Is it believable, or is it strained? How does the dialogue sound? Is it consistent with your vision of the characters and their backgrounds?

If you reached a point where you could not 'feel' what your character might say next, it probably means that you have not fully envisioned the play, or you don't fully know your characters. If that is so, think about the character and write more detail into their biography.

Annotate the scene in the margin, rather than completely rewriting it, and reread it aloud to yourself.

Write

Keeping all this in mind, return to your statement and write an opening scene, or part thereof, for your piece. Don't worry if you are still unsure about details, and remember, you are writing a play script for the stage.

Now, keep your scenario and opening scene by you and turn your skills to another way of telling the same story, with the same characters and with the action balanced on the same pivot.

Writing for film

Now, in the name of experience, you are going to assume the role of script-writer to tell the story of your play script for film or television.

There are refinements in script-writing that we will have to skate over or simplify. Writing for the camera is considerably less wordy than writing for the stage, since the camera can range near and far, recording gestures, expressions and acts that speak instead of words. On stage, much more has to be conveyed through dialogue.

A film script differs from a television script in several ways, and there are different types of television drama scripts. Unlike the playwright, the script-writer has to take her story through several different stages before it becomes a shooting script and is produced as film or television.

For the moment, however, let's concentrate on the story-telling device that film and television have in common—the camera. This machine allows you almost as much choice of narrating positions as prose fiction. You can know everything from your narrating position if you wish, and if you can afford it! The camera can be made to see all, hear all, and to treat all characters objectively; or it might tell the story from the perspective of a particular character, so that we see mainly what affects her and follow her reactions; or, more subjective still, the camera could allow us to see only what she sees, know only what she knows.

As you write your script, you will call on the camera to create illusions, just as you called on the stage and set to do. Cinematography, with its effortless fades and dissolves, its often quite drastic changes of scene, atmosphere and sound level, can manipulate and compress time and can suggest a wider world. Ingmar Bergman, the Swedish film maker remarked:

When I was ten years old I received my first, rattling film projector, with its chimney and lamp. I found it both mystifying and fascinating. The first film I had was nine feet long and brown in colour. It showed a girl lying asleep in a meadow, who woke up and stretched out her arms, then disappeared to the right. That was all there was to it. The film was a great success and was projected every night until it broke and could not be mended any more. This rickety little machine was my first conjuring set. And even today I remind myself with childish excitement that I am really a conjuror, since cinematography is based on deception of the human eye . . .

An outline or synopsis

A *story outline* or *synopsis* is what a script-writer first writes for a producer and director, before being commissioned to go on to a film treatment and later a full script. Having assured himself that the basic story-line is strong structurally, the script-writer can then expand it and write more detail into it.

A story-line generally consists of three parts:

1 The basic *conflict* or problem to be resolved, which will become evident quite early.

2 The *development*, with increasing tension and complicated twists of plot that keep the audience wondering what will happen next and how the conflict will be resolved. This section generally takes the bulk of the film's running time. Each of these dramatic twists is called a 'beat' or 'highlight' in the story.

3 In the last eighth or so of the film comes the *climax*, at which time there is a *resolution* of the conflict in an emotionally charged scene. The story then quickly draws to a close.

Write

You are about to write a film story-line. Here is a sample modelled on the idea used in the play statement and opening scene above. Use it as a model and write your own synopsis.

In early 1919 the maiden sisters Ellie and Vanessa Carlyon are living in the family cottage in a small town inland from the New South Wales south coast. They are the daughters of a former Professor of Languages in Sydney. Vanessa's fiancé has been killed in France early in the Great War, the women's father has died within the last year, and Ellie's friend of a few weeks before his enlistment, Sergeant Alex Warrell, has been reported Missing Presumed Dead on the Western Front in the final days of the War. Ellie, more generous, caring, and expansive than her sister, is attempting to remake her life by starting a dressmaking business. Vanessa is bitter, feeling cheated by the world in general and by the War. She unconsciously visits her resentment and negativity on Ellie and others.

When Alex is astoundingly brought back from the dead, having been held as a wounded prisoner behind the German lines until the Armistice and only rediscovered and invalided home after the War's end, their friendship rekindles and deepens to love. Vanessa, bitter and jealous, connives to prevent their engagement, dredging up and exaggerating Alex's alleged affair before the War with a Kiama barmaid, playing on Alex's evident physical and mental instability resulting from the War, and trading on the prospect of her own loneliness if Ellie were to marry and leave her. Ellie, doubts sown in her mind, seeks out the barmaid, finding evidence of Vanessa's dishonesty in doing so. She confronts Vanessa with her lies. She consults Alex's doctor about his erratic behaviour. He advises against marriage because of Alex's shell-shock. Ellie tells Alex that she cannot marry him. Alex is bereft, desperate. He goes on a destructive rampage against the factory of a war profiteer in a nearby town. Ellie accompanies him to court and hears character references for him from his Regimental Sergeant-Major and others who survived with him in France and Belgium. Hearing their evidence about the War, Ellie realizes the sacrifices made by these men and recognizes again the depth of her love for Alex. Alex is fined. His doctor shortly after discovers a piece of shrapnel lodged in Alex's head. He suspects that it is a major factor in Alex's fits of frustrated anger. A surgeon examines Alex and assures him that the head wound is operable. Ellie and Alex plan to become engaged after the operation and convalescence and later to marry and move to Alex's family farm. The operation is successful. The two become engaged. It is clear that Vanessa will be left, a chastened and pathetic figure, to live on in the cottage with her boarder.

Don't approach your synopsis as an adaptation of the play for film: think freely of the same basic story, but allow yourself to introduce other elements if a film treatment seems to require them. Much of your state-ment or scenario is still relevant, so go through it again, remembering that now a *camera* and *sound* will tell the story. Amend the story's structure where improvements can be made that will more fully exploit camera and sound.

Write an account in two paragraphs of the basic story idea for film, the first establishing the setting, characters and current situation; the second detailing the beginning, middle and end of the story, showing the 'conflict' that will arise, how it will develop, and eventually be resolved. This 'conflict', the central issue in the script, might be simply a choice that has to be made, a problem that has to be solved, an objective that must be achieved or not achieved.

An expanded outline

Methods of expanding an outline differ from writer to writer, production company to production company, but a professional script-writer might first write a story outline of the entire piece. The purpose of this ex-panded outline is to allow the producer and possible director to discover whether the story has potential as a visual story. If it has, the script-writer expands this account to a scene-by-scene breakdown. For a ninety-minute film this 'scene breakdown' might consist of up to ten thousand words. Producer and director can use it to make preliminary estimates of costs, set expenses, and so on. The scene breakdown might go through several revisions. It has to consider the overall structure of the story and how major, minor, and briefer scenes work together rhythmically. A script carrying specific dialogue and camera directions comes much later, and a shooting script later still.

Here is a sample opening for an expanded outline of the story in the synopsis above.

Alex Warrell, whom his neighbours think is dead (his mother received an Army telegram in Sydney three months ago—'Missing in Action: Presumed Killed on the Western Front, October 1918') is miraculously back at his farm, 'Caithness', above the river valley inland from the south coast of New South Wales. It is early 1919. The farm is still run by his wartime manager, Jock, fifty-two. Alex has spent only a few days with his mother in Sydney since disembarking after a long sea voyage from Britain with other wounded. He has been at 'Caithness' for only two days, and has not ventured out into the small community he left when he enlisted four years ago. He is wounded in the leg and the left hand and shows signs of shell-shock. Now, in the dimness of the house, he is painfully dressing his ulcerated leg wound. We identify with his pain and moroseness, even though we are yet to learn who he is, his import in the story and how he has 'come back from the dead'. Jock hovers in the background, uncertain of his role now that his boss has returned a different man. Jock is still amazed by Alex's presence: 'You could have knocked me over with a feather when I heard. You shouldn't be here, but you are!' Alex is in pain, taciturn.

Meanwhile, across the valley, Vanessa and Ellie Carlyon are stirring. They are maiden sisters, the daughters of David Carlyon, former Professor of Languages at the University of Sydney. Professor Carlyon has died of heart trouble only three months back, at about the time of the War's end. Ellie, thirty-two, is feeding hens on the hillside and walking back to the house, 'Pitnacree', via the stables. She stops in the stables to inspect the injured hack, Minnie, talking softly to her, stroking her. Ellie is warm, sensitive, caring. Minnie responds. Vanessa, thirty-six, is washing in the laundry, face set hard, complaining to herself. Neither is aware of Alex's return, both thinking him lost in action in the last days of the War. He and Ellie had been friends for only a few weeks at the time he enlisted. He had only recently bought 'Caithness' and moved into the valley.

Mime Jennings, twenty, the sisters' boarder and a teacher at the primary school in the valley, excitable and lively, is preparing to drive into the town with her beau, Harold, twenty-four, in his T Model Ford to get shopping and letters. Harold arrives, seeking the sisters' 'star boarder'. They depart in a whirl of gaiety and banter that contrasts with the sisters' reserve, although Ellie plays up to some of Harold's good-natured teasing.

On the other side of the valley, Alex Warrell climbs painfully into his car and also sets off down the country road towards the town, his first visit there since his return. He looks diffident, shaky.

Half an hour later, Ellie sits writing to her friend Madge in the drawing room of 'Pitnacree'. Voice over as she writes indicates that she is inviting Madge, an old school friend, to stay at 'Pitnacree' over Easter. As she writes we see pictures of two soldiers on the mantelpiece, including one of Alex Warrell, with the annotation: 'My Ellie—from Alex. Home soon, I hope.' Ellie's letter reveals that the deaths of her father, of Vanessa's fiancé Keith, also killed early in the War, and the news some five months ago of Alex's death in action weigh heavily on both sisters, but that Ellie is beginning to make moves towards a new life. Vanessa appears and pours cold water on Ellie's idea of inviting Madge to 'Pitnacree' for Easter. She is the negative to her sister's positive.

Amid the Saturday chance meetings and bustle in the little town, Harold leaves Mime to her shopping and goes towards the blacksmith's. As Mime shops at the grocer, and passes the time of day with friends and parents of her school charges, Alex parks further down the street. Mime goes into the post office. Alex, with walking stick and hat, comes in unseen behind her, speaks over her shoulder, introduces himself. She acts as though she has seen a ghost. Alex gives a brief explanation of how he was wounded behind enemy lines and hospitalized by the Germans until after the Armistice. He asks about Ellie, and is clearly emotionally affected by the thought of her, although he has written to her only infrequently from the Front. He tells Mime that he wants to come to 'Pitnacree' that afternoon, if he feels up to it. There is a diffidence in him that Mime can't place . . .

Write

Once you have a strong basic story-line, your next task is to write an expanded outline of how you would tell it in film, accenting the story's 'beats' or dramatic high points, remembering that the chance to use a camera on locations may change the way you make dramatic points from the way you made them in the stage version of your story.

Don't be concerned at this stage if you cannot envisage all the twists of the tale; write clear statements of where the conflicts will lie and about characterization. Once that is done, you can think about how you might begin the film with visual images and sound.

As you can see from the above example, the expanded outline you are attempting should read like a pragmatic short story, concentrating on how the story will be told visually. You can visualize the effects, the tensions and the tone you would like to create. Write in the present tense, as if the action were happening in front of you: for the moment you are the camera. Your first step is to imagine the effects, tensions and tone you want your film sequences to create. Then you can write an account of the story that would allow a director and production team to understand the story's main elements, the order in which events occur and the essence of each character.

Beginning a 'treatment' or scene breakdown

Our next step is a 'treatment'; the complex shooting script complete with fine camera instructions and lens details for each shot is still a long way off. A treatment or scene breakdown outlines what happens before the camera from the first scene of the film to the last. It is the writer's description of how the story will appear visually. In writing it you will imagine yourself as the camera and sound boom, visualizing the shots that might tell the story and the sound and dialogue that will accompany them. At this stage you do not write in camera directions, sound effects or dialogue, although some key lines of dialogue might express best the main point of a scene here and there. By and large, these things come later when a shooting script is being worked on by director, writer, and camera operator.

Your treatment should be concise, written in short sentences where possible. In each scene you should 'show' the advancing action and how characters are feeling, rather than 'tell' these things through dialogue. Make sure each scene advances the story for the viewer, that scenes vary in length, and that none is too long, obvious or repetitious. Scenes should follow each other logically. Script-writers work on the basis that each double-spaced A4 page of a scene breakdown represents roughly a minute of film time; only rarely should a scene run for more than three minutes—most run for considerably less.

Before trying the first few pages of a 'treatment', you might like to read up on cinematic technique, or look at published film scripts to remind yourself of some of the techniques and technology available.

Now here is a sample treatment, again based on the story-line used in the sample play, film outline and expanded outline. You should begin your treatment with a title, a list of characters, and a list of locations. Then each scene should carry a chronological number, and a statement as to whether it is to be filmed outside, a description of location, whether day or night, and the names of the characters in the scene.

WALKING TO THE FALLS
a film treatment by X
Characters

Alex Warrell—thirty-year-old farmer recently invalided home (head, hand and leg wounds) from the Great War; friend of Ellie for only a few weeks before enlistment, having recently bought a farm in the valley.

Ellie Carlyon—thirty-two-year-old, unmarried, warm, compassionate, impulsive.

Vanessa Carlyon—thirty-five, unmarried, Ellie's sister, who has in the past four years lost her fiancé in the Great War and her father of heart disease at home; perfectionist; worrier; responsible, suffering, and negative foil for Ellie's optimism and quick-to-act nature.

Mime Jennings—twenty-year-old, local school teacher who boards with the Carlyon sisters; lively, relatively unaffected by the War; of another generation to the sisters and to Alex. Ambitious.

Harold Blaine—twenty-one-year-old friend of Mime, soon to be fiancé; farmer's son from next valley, generous and accepting.

Reg Grey—forty-year-old local farmer who farms 'Pitnacree' and looks after stock, horses, etc., for sisters, for share of produce.

Jock Eastaugh—farm manager for Alex at 'Caithness'; a good farmer, but naïve, insular, complacent about human nature and the wider world; vehemently anti-German.

Locations

'Pitnacree' interiors—kitchen
                    drawing room
                    laundry
                    dining room
                    verandah
'Caithness' interiors—Alex's bedroom
                    bathroom/laundry
                    kitchen/pantry
Post Office interior
Mime's schoolroom
Grounds of 'Caithness'—machinery sheds, car shed
Grounds of 'Pitnacree'—hillside and sheds, stables
                    verandah
                    driveway and road entrance
Main street of shops in 'village'
Track to Mill and the Falls
Cleft of rainforest in paddocks, containing red coral trees
The Falls—subtropical cleft and waterfall

1. EXT. RIDGE-TOP FARM, 'CAITHNESS'; DAY; (ALEX, JOCK)
It is early morning on the ridge above the valley. The sheds of 'Caithness' lie quiet in the sun. Sound of agonized panting and cursing. We are drawn closer to the house and its back door. The painful panting increases in volume. We move into the darkness inside, coming along the dim hall to Alex's bedroom. He is sitting in pyjamas on the bed, gingerly unwrapping the dressings from his leg wound, panting, cursing. He dis-

closes an ugly ulcerated flesh-wound in his calf. He reaches to an enamel basin, wrings out a cloth in water, and cleans the wound slowly, gritting his teeth. Sounds of hens fossicking begin to take over from Alex's panting and grunting.

2. EXT. YARD OF 'CAITHNESS'; DAY; (ELLIE)
Sounds of hens continue. Hens are feeding near the back door of 'Caithness'. We look beyond them and across the valley and see Ellie Carlyon on the opposite hill as a distant figure in a white apron walking uphill in the grass. She is followed by white fowls. She heads towards the outbuildings of 'Pitnacree'.

3. EXT. SHEDS AND MACHINERY IN 'PITNACREE' YARD; DAY; (ELLIE)
Ellie is walking up the hill towards the house, stables and sheds, calling to the fowls. She is relaxed, walking slowly, enjoying the morning. She stoops under the farm wagon to collect an egg, puts it in her straw hat.

4. EXT. STABLE DOOR, 'PITNACREE'; DAY; (ELLIE)
Ellie comes up to the stable door, puts down the hat full of eggs in the grass, lifts the latch, swings the gate open and enters, bringing the latch down again with a thump.

5. INT. INTERIOR OF STABLE; DAY; (ELLIE)
Sounds of horse whinnying, straw underfoot. Ellie goes to the riding hack, Minnie, standing in the corner with a bandaged fetlock. She stoops and inspects the injury, admonishing Minnie in a mothering way. Minnie nuzzles her, is clearly fond of her. Ellie steps to the other wall of the stable and invites Minnie to walk. Minnie walks over. Ellie still talks to her encouragingly and feels the fetlock gently.

6. INT. ALEX WARRELL'S BEDROOM; DAY; (ALEX)
Sound of panting and painful exertion. Alex is now almost dressed, but is awkwardly tying his shoelace, his bad leg elevated on a chair. He wears a large black stall over the space where the three last fingers on his left hand should be. He is working with just the first finger and thumb on that hand.

In later versions of the script—often called a 'working script'—dialogue may be set to the left side of the page, while all camera directions appear on the right, including suggestions for technique, details of close-ups, lenses, zooms, tilts, dissolves, slow motion, etc.

Write

Take your expanded outline and work it up into a treatment. Don't worry about jargon or terminology too much at this stage.

Look back over what you have written. You will realize that in film treatment of the basic story, you can afford—in fact you need—more characters. Characters who can only be mentioned in dialogue in the stage version now appear in person—Alex's mother, Reg Grey, Harold Blaine and Jock Eastaugh, for instance. You can sense the possibilities for a sub-plot, for conflict between Alex and Jock, given Jock's attitude to Germans and Alex's direct experience of them during his convalescence. In general, therefore, character development must be deeper.

In film, the camera can suggest the physical context of the story much more fully. You will realize, as you write these scenes in, that they may be expensive to shoot and will almost certainly require research for accurate details of dress, motor cars, speech habits, terminology, music of the time, and so on.

All the above examples are generally naturalistic, but they need not be written in this mode. The treatment might become quite surreal, internalized and dream-like in later sequences, as long as this change of style is prepared for and doesn't jar or look awkward. It will be determined by the narrating position the film adopts.

Finally, although this treatment is not yet a shooting script, all your work as writer tends in that direction so that a director and production team can, in your absence, plan each camera movement, choreograph each scene's action and sound in minute detail. In some important senses it then becomes 'their film', their piece of creative story-telling.

We do not have space to proceed to a working script or shooting script, but if you are interested in this area of writing, turn to the Bibliography for books that are devoted entirely to film and television scripting.

Radio plays

The rules change again! Now you are writing for radio—you must live by sound alone. In Australia, as far as radio *drama* is concerned, that means probably Radio National or ABC FM, but your dramatic skills can also be used in radio for advertising, public relations material, humorous fillers, or documentary assignments.

Back to drama, and since this is radio, where sound is all, we will be closer to the stage in some respects than to film. A range of characters and their voices cannot be sustained in radio as they can be in film and television, for instance, and dialogue in radio is doubly important in revealing character. In film, you can hold back information without losing your viewer, but in radio listeners need to know what is happening—there are no visuals to occupy and inform them. Most radio plays are an hour in length, generally shorter than the film feature, although not necessarily shorter than a television drama. A radio play must be economical.

Nevertheless, radio is one of the most liberating of media for the dramatist. It can be naturalistic, abstract, poetic, surreal, or an interior study of an individual consciousness. Radio has been called the 'theatre of the mind'. Playwrights like John Osborne, Robert Bolt, Samuel Beckett, the Australian poet Douglas Stewart, Alun Owen and others have written movingly for radio. Dylan Thomas's unforgettable play, *Under milk wood*, was a radio play extracted scene by scene from the poet by an English producer.

Radio drama gains very little publicity. Nevertheless, before TV came to Australia, radio was the nearest approach to a 'national' theatre, transcending state boundaries and drawing a greater audience than a stage play could draw over many weeks. Dramatists learn by seeing their work exposed in performance, so radio—cheaper and therefore more readily accessible—presents an invaluable opportunity for new writers: it is still one of the few direct and available means of entry to the professional world of drama.

An outline

Below is a sample outline, based on the general story-line used for the play and the film above. Note that different techniques are necessary in the radio version to keep the story moving forward and to give the listener information convincingly and economically. Few characters can be used, because they can easily become confused in the listener's mind. In this radio outline, for example, Jock Eastaugh becomes more important than he was in the stage or film versions, as part of a sub-plot and as intermediary and conveyor of information. He now eclipses Mime Jennings in importance. You will find that you too have to make similar changes in the elements of your story and the way you tell it for radio.

The play opens with Ellie Carlyon writing a letter to her friend Madge, the details of the letter coming to us as voice over—'Dearest Madge, It has been so long, or it seems so . . .'. Ellie now and then calls to her sister Vanessa who is within earshot, to check this and that. Their conversation, together with the information in the letter, tell us that the time is early 1919; that these are maiden sisters; that their father, the former Professor of Languages at University of Sydney, has recently died of a heart attack; that the sisters have holidayed in this hillside cottage in this rural community for most of their lives and now live there permanently; that Vanessa, thirty-five, lost her fiancé early in the Great War; that Ellie's friend of only a few weeks before the War, Sergeant Alex Warrell, has been posted 'Missing, Presumed Killed' on the Western Front in the final days of the War; that Ellie, thirty-two, is a positive and outgoing person and is trying to take up her life again after these misfortunes by starting a dressmaking business: that Vanessa is negative and bitter to her sister's positive and hopeful and manages to hold Ellie in thrall by veto and disapproval much of the time. The letter complete and sealed, Ellie addresses Madge in her imagination, saying that sometimes she feels everything is lost and hoping that Madge can come for Easter as planned, as a comforting and familiar figure.

Ellie's voice over is lost to a gradual thunder that becomes the sound of distant guns. Out of the thunder of the guns come voices, as in a dream, calling 'Sergeant Alex Warrell . . . Sergeant . . . Sergeant Warrell'. The voice surfaces as a heavily German-accented voice addressing the Sergeant and saying that he is lucky to be alive; that he has been in a coma for three days; that he is a prisoner; that the War is nearing an end; that he will be repatriated when he is well. Other voices and sounds take over, each suggesting a further stage in Sergeant Warrell's recovery, the War's end, his repatriation to Britain and then by troop ship with other wounded to Australia. In it we hear Alex's voice becoming progressively more prominent and assertive, but still clearly indicating a soldier deeply wounded physically and psychologically by the War. The dream-like voices and sounds carry through disembarkation in Sydney and Alex's reunion with his mother, who lives there, a widow for many years. Alex indicates that he will spend a week in Sydney and then go down to his farm, left for the duration of the War under a manager, Jock Eastaugh. Alex hopes he can pick up the threads of his life as a farmer again. He asks his mother about the Carlyon sisters, who she has met only once and who live on the hill opposite his farm. She says she has had no contact with them. He says Ellie had written him letters at the Front.

Against sounds of a farmyard ('Caithness'), we hear Alex's panting, cursing his pain and the War as he uncovers and dresses his ulcerated leg wound. Jock Eastaugh is with him, having only returned the previous evening from down the coast to discover that Alex had arrived back at his farm. Jock is torn between talking about farm matters and his amazement at seeing his boss present in the flesh. Alex seeks Jock's help in getting basin, water and antiseptic to wash the wound and the two talk, Jock questioning Alex about his return from the dead and betraying a simplistic and jingoistic view of the War. Later, Alex asks after Ellie. He asks Jock to call in at 'Pitnacree' on his way to town to ask if he, Alex, might drop in on Ellie that afternoon.

Vanessa at the kitchen window sees Jock Eastaugh driving into the yard at 'Pitnacree'. She alerts Ellie. Jock comes in, bringing news of Alex's reappearance. Ellie is dumbfounded with an emotion that she herself cannot completely explain—she realizes that Alex means more to her than she had admitted to herself. She asks if Jock would take her back with him to 'Caithness' as he returns, rather than waiting for Alex's visit in the afternoon. Jock promises to pick her up on his way back. Vanessa, alone with Ellie, is disapproving; tries to persuade Ellie to be calm, reminding her that she scarcely knows Alex and might in any case find him very much changed. Ellie sticks to her intention, waits for Jock's return and goes with him to Alex . . .

Write

You might want to write a series of notes about how you will tell the story in sound before you tackle an outline. Remind yourself that you are not writing an adaptation of the story you have already told for stage and film, but are making a fresh start using the same basic story elements to see what they can become as sound drama. Think of possible structures for the story in this form and how it will build.

Opening scenes

With a broad radio outline at least partly developed, we move now to writing an opening scene or two. The model below is set out in typical style.

WALKING TO THE FALLS
A radio play by X

1. (MUSIC—INTRODUCTORY CUE)

2. SFX SOUND OF COCK CROWING, BIRDS TWITTERING (OFF)

3. ELLIE: (CALLING OFF) Vanessa? Vanessa! What are the dates of Easter this year? I'm in the drawing room! . . . Oh, don't worry. I'll check them later. 'D-e-a-r-e-s-t M-a-d-g-e . . . (SHE IS WRITING A LETTER) . . . Dearest Madge, It has been so long, or it seems so. It was six months ago, do you realize, when you were down for Father's funeral! In some ways it seems like yesterday, and yet so much has happened. We feel like permanent residents here now, and the cottage is plenty big enough for just the two of us. I suspect that we're known as the maiden sisters. The maiden sisters on the hill! But you know how much I love the valley.

So much *has* happened, hasn't it. The end of the War. Some of the old hustle and bustle has come back now that it's over. A party of visitors even came up from the coast to the Falls a week ago. Their charabanc broke down at the foot of our hill. I took some hot water down to make tea for them. There were four soldiers. Light casualties they called themselves. Light! One was blind. He came from Albion. His mate had lost a foot. Another one had been bayonetted in the shoulder. He had lost the use of his arm. It's awful, and yet they seem so cheerful. I feel a terrible drag on my heart every time I see the uniform. You know my friend Alex Warrell—he was the one who bought 'Caithness' and moved down just before he enlisted. He was lost only a few days before the end of the War. I liked him so much. A waste. A waste!

Oh Madge—can you possibly get down at Easter? With you here we could forget the War for a while. Tell me in the next post if you can. We'd love to see you. We can all go riding—the weather is nearly always good at Easter . . .

4. SFX DOOR OPENS (OFF MIKE)

5. VANESSA (COMING ON MIKE): Oh, you're in here. You were saying something . . . I couldn't hear . . .

6. ELLIE: Yes, I've forgotten what the dates of Easter are this year. I know it's early . . .

7. VANESSA: The thirtieth of March. Easter Tuesday is April the third. Who are you writing to?

8. ELLIE: Oh, Ness, it's been so long since we saw Madge; I'm writing to see if she can come down on the train for Easter . . . We can go riding.

9. VANESSA: Minnie won't be up to that, for Heavens sake. She's still favouring. Anyway, we were going to have Uncle Jim up for Easter, don't you remember?

10. ELLIE: Minnie will be all right, and Uncle Jim can come anyway, surely. Wouldn't it be a comfort to see Madge for a few days? She's so level. We need her laugh, Ness. She's a tonic.

What does this reveal? Probably your mind has logged a number of things as you read.

• You can afford few characters and can manage only two or three at the most in any one scene.

• There can be no silence of any great length from a character. Silence implies absence in radio. This does not mean, however, that you cannot write very dramatic one-sided conversations, where the one character's relative silence says a great deal.

• Narrators should generally be avoided in radio drama, except where the narrator has a direct role as story-teller; Dylan Thomas's *Under Milk Wood* is one of the few examples of this.

• It is important to gain the listeners' interest early, otherwise they may switch off or move down the dial to something else.

• There is no place for very long speeches in radio, and skill is required to create a rhythm (as on the stage or in film) between the longer and the shorter speeches. In most instances it is better to end a scene with a short speech rather than a long one.

- Do not reveal too much at the outset, but allow the listeners enough to go on with. Make them aware of the situation and the characters, then release information slowly, allowing action, conflict and tension to appear as soon as possible.
- Do not start the story too early. Ask yourself if your story could have been started at a later point?
- Adverbial stage directions are easy to overdo, and annoy actors. It is important to indicate, however, when the words given a character belie their meaning. Irony or lying must be indicated in a radio script: 'How pleasant it is to see you after all this time! (irony).'
- Sound effects—SFX CHISELLING (OFF)—should be specific and detailed, and often can be used to indicate a change in scene (sound of cutlery, breakfast radio). Sounds should not be gratuitous, and must have a definite role in the narration.
- Music, well chosen for its task, is vital to radio drama and also to documentary and even current affairs and news programmes. In drama it provides fades, time changes and scene divisions effortlessly. It operates at other levels too, when it is written in as an adjunct to a character's life (a Beethoven freak; a lover of Dire Straits), or suggests a place or period of history that would be difficult to indicate otherwise.
- Pauses, filled by sounds other than words, are valuable in radio drama, allowing people to react, laugh, groan, or continue working: each of these reactions reflects characters' mental states.
- A well prepared 'flashback' is effective in radio as drama, comedy and documentary. If cued skilfully the events then seem to happen in the minds of the listeners.
- Radio lends itself to 'absurd' or 'surreal' material that moves between fantasy and fact, or to stories that move in time, or that move fluidly from a broad view of events on a large scale to a much closer look at the plight or thoughts of an individual; it is ideal for horror and suspense.
- Radio can suggest distance and movement if the writer notes that a character should deliver lines ON MIKE (close to the microphone), OFF MIKE (distant from it), COMING ON or FADING ON (coming towards the microphone), FADING OFF or BEHIND OBSTRUCTION (as if the voice comes from behind a partition or window or door).

Write

Using the early part of your radio outline, write one or two opening scenes, following the style of the example above as you type out your final draft. When you have taken your radio script to a satisfactory point, reread your story in this form.

Confidence comes with practice, and knowledge comes through not merely 'hearing' next time you listen to radio, whether it be drama or documentary, but *listening* to effects that you have hitherto taken for granted and thinking about how they achieve their power. ABC Radio on its FM and its Radio National networks consumes some one hundred radio dramas each year. Although the programme titles change, the nature of their requirements do not differ markedly—Fictions, Radio Helicon, Stereo Drama, The Listening Room (which is more experimental) are some of them, in addition to comedy programmes, using pieces usually thirty minutes long, or short three-minute sketches. Stereo Drama has more specific requirements—material that exploits the stereo medium.

The elements of drama

Now that you have had a taste of telling your story for the stage, for film and for radio, you are perhaps better able to see what the three have in common and then what distinguishes them as forms of drama. The writing suggestions that follow are designed to increase your understanding of dramatic forms, and give you practice in the main elements of dramatic story-telling.

The main elements in drama are hard to rank. Some commentators say drama is character in action. That statement calls up all the tradition of theatre, from the Noh drama of Japan, the Greek stage of Aeschylus, Sophocles and Euripides, the Shakespearian plays of Tudor England, the Irish National Theatre, to the great plays of Chekhov. The statement also throws us back on something more ancient: performance. Human beings have performed for each other, told each other stories in action and sound, since they first communicated. Interest in human performance comes back to interest in our fellow humans and in what life has offered them.

In drama, we can identify the following elements:
- structure
- character
- action and sound
- dialogue and movement

There are also the special requirements of the medium in which you are to tell the story—whether it be stage, film, television or radio.

Structure

Sometimes the idea of a person or character fascinates you deep in the gut, and almost immediately you find yourself casting about for what their story will contain, in what order it will be revealed, what tone it will have, how it will end. You are immediately involved with 'structure', a structure strong enough to hold the interest of an audience. If you are unsure of your structure then perhaps you should *not* direct your energies, your thousands of hard-won words, to that person or character. Assessing a story's structure to ascertain whether it is strong enough to work is a skill that will become second nature to you if you persist with writing.

Remember, there is no formula or guarantee for the perfect dramatic structure: the test is whether it is strong enough to hold back human boredom. As Howard Lindsay once put it: 'Two things can lick a play. One is that the audience doesn't believe it, and the other is that they don't care'.

Dual structure

Consider the structure of the film, *Crocodile Dundee*, keeping in mind its primary markets: Australia and the USA. Its structure is symmetrical: the second half mirrors the first. In the first half we have an attractive New York woman completely out of context and out of her depth in Australia's wild Top End. She is confronted by larger-than-life Dundee who is disgustingly at home in this environment and looks askance at her fumbling and trepidation. A stream of incidents woven round this basic disjunction and source of humorous tension between sexually attractive male and female, completes the first half.

In the second half the gauche, parochial Dundee is plunged into the depths of wildest New York, where his bushman's skills and small-town folksy friendliness become sources of wonder and humorous disbelief among the New Yorkers he meets. He bumbles along under the protection of his attractive companion of the first half, who is now completely at home. The second half is filled out with humorous and potentially dangerous incidents woven around this basic disjunction of social systems and social mores. Doubts about whether love will burgeon between these eminently unsuitable partners maintains the audience's interest. Dundee proves to be just a bit more assured in *his* new milieu and manages to pursue his true feelings and secure his mate in the midst of the New York subway's bustle. So the bow of romance is tied and double-knotted and the audience departs with memories of a warm and funny story about two people in two places. That is one possible structure of dramatic action, but there is an infinite number of others.

Write

List twenty stories that you know in film or drama whose 'shape' and 'dramatic logic' hold you, that you admire and cannot fault.

Note how the basic structure, once cast in large blocks of content and thought, is then easily festooned with chains of incidents that arise from that basic structure. From your list, plot out the basic structure of perhaps four of the stories and some of the incident-chains that hang on them.

Three-part structure

Let's consider the traditional three-part structure of stage drama, which has been adapted countless times for film, television and radio drama.

In its pure form it is now rejected in favour of other structures as often as it is used, and yet elements of it still inhabit those other structures, because all dramatic structures are based on questions.

The three-part structure is sometimes described as a beginning–middle–end structure, a set-up–conflict–resolution structure, or a beginning–development–denouement structure.

Part 1: This is the situation: these are the characters. What else is there to know about them? What is putting them under tension? What is going to happen?

Part 2: This is what is going to happen to them. This is their problem: and look how it is consuming them inwardly! Wait—the rules of the game are changed and these new questions are posed which bear on their fortunes. What are they going to do about them? How are they going to be changed by them?

Part 3: The outcome now almost certainly will be . . . No, things have changed drastically again, because . . . This, now, is the final outcome . . . Now let's see what that does to X and how Y comes out of it—joyous, sad, resigned?

Write

Now construct two basic dramatic story structures of your own. Make sure that their 'shapes' are different. Develop a sketch from an incident-chain for at least part of one of them. Keep in mind that structure depends on tensions and questions raised in the audience's mind. If there is no tension or question still hanging by the time you reach the third act, then there is no third act. Think also about the range of your dramatic ideas thus far; if they lean towards tragedy or emotionally tense and serious material, commit yourself now to writing a structure for comedy.

Look again at familiar stories from theatre, film and perhaps radio. Consider them to see if they are arranged in a three-part structure. As a case in point, think back to the film, itself based on a play, *Driving Miss Daisy.* Its story is basically a three-part structure, although of course it is not broken into acts or parts.

Part 1: Meet widowed Miss Daisy, seventy-two years old, and her son, Boolie, members of a Jewish family in Georgia. Miss Daisy is no longer a capable driver, but is very strong-willed and dictatorial and chafes at being deprived of her car and her son's suggestion that she should have a chauffeur. Her son engages a Black driver (Hoke) of similar age to Miss Daisy and a widower, but she will have none of him, preferring to walk or take taxis rather than allowing him to drive her. He is quietly confident that he can win her over. Will he?

Part 2: Circumstances and Hoke's patience and steadiness of purpose result in Miss Daisy condescending to enter Hoke's car and from that point in the story she is driven by him. Then the rules of the game change (as a means of holding audience expectation and deepening interest) and a new question appears about the relationship between these two people from two very different strata of American society, and in the American Deep South to boot. There is a gradual thawing of Miss Daisy's social and class assumptions about Hoke until she depends on him not only for his driving, but for human security, warmth and understanding. Various sub-plots attend this central plot-line. At this point something must break to maintain audience interest.

Part 3: For the purposes of the plot Idella, the maid, dies of a heart attack. This incident, and the funeral at which Southern white Miss Daisy sits with the Black congregation and Hoke in the church, prepares the ground for the even larger break: Miss Daisy falls ill with dementia and confusion. Hoke, who discovers her distress, helps her. She declares Hoke to be her only true friend and helper. After this climactic declaration, the story, as it must, moves quickly to a denouement.

Write

Think this structure through again, then write, in much briefer terms than those above, two three-part story-lines or scenarios for a film or play, jumping on them both with heavy boots to test whether they are likely to collapse and bore your audience.

Character

The greatest of dramatists for stage and script have stressed that before you develop the knowledge to create honest and deep characters you should come to know yourself in a way that you may never have attempted before.

Write

Ask these questions of yourself and answer them fully. They are also the questions you should ask of your characters.
1 What are the six activities you enjoy most?
2 How do you feel about each of your parents?
3 How at present do you regard your own death?
4 How do you react to the death of someone close?
5 What are the six most important educative experiences you have had in your life?
6 What are your politics?
7 What are your views on formal education?
8 How do you regard formal religion?
9 Are you a spiritual person?

10   What part does sex play in your life?
11   Which of your achievements gives you most pride?
12   Who has been the greatest mentor for you? Why?
13   How do others see you as a person? Are they wrong?
14   What is your greatest worry?
15   Are you more compassionate than the average person? How does your compassion show itself?
16   What characteristics in other people disgust you most?
17   What, from your experience, are the most important things to know?
18   How idealistic are you?
19   How important is food to you?
20   How materialistic are you?
21   Why do you think the human race exists?
22   Is the world situation heading in the right direction?
23   Do you see yourself as loving?
24   In what situations have you acted with moral courage?
25   How impulsive are you?
26   What do you see as the value of travel?
27   Have you travelled widely?
28   Are you physically attractive?
29   How important is money to you?
30   Do you see your life as following an even path?
31   Are you a physically active person?
32   What phenomena in the world social order would you do away with if you had the power?
33   How would you describe the way you dress?
34   What do you consider are the most dangerous ideas abroad in the world at present?
35   Which concepts do you think give the greatest hope world-wide at present?
36   Do you work a great deal at changing yourself and your behaviour?
37   Do you feel that you can generally contribute valuably to the world or do you feel impotent?
38   What is it that you do for and with other people that gives you the greatest satisfaction?
39   How many *close* friends have you?
40   In what ways are you artistic?
41   What connections do you see between the various arts?
42   Where is your ideal place?
43   How rich in experience was your childhood?
44   How do you regard ageing?
45   What are your six major faults?
46   What actions are you morally incapable of doing, no matter what the circumstances?

47 How do you regard information, knowledge and wisdom?

48 How tolerant are you?

49 How involved are you with your immediate and extended family?

50 What major new understandings have you come to about life in the last five years?

51 Are you an optimist or pessimist or do you vacillate?

52 How would you describe your voice and the way you speak?

53 What sort of sense of humour have you? What do you find funny?

54 Which three people with whom you have constant interaction do you most actively dislike? Why?

55 Which three of those you are constantly in touch with do you most admire? Why?

The list of possible questions is virtually endless, but if you have answered those above with honesty, you will feel a somewhat different person from when you began. You should—and this is the point—be able to answer such questions truthfully about yourself and about your characters in drama. As you develop a character you should keep a growing file of notes on what you know about his fears, her likes and dislikes, and so on. Then you will know the depths of moral action the character is capable of, what his price or breaking-point is. How does this character see herself? How do other characters see him? What sort of things do you hear her saying? What speech habits, hackneyed sayings? What everyday things does the character do with relish? What people do you know who can be plundered to give characteristics to your character?

Write

Develop a character with a background that will cause ructions in one of the following situations:

- at the door of the church as the minister is farewelling his flock
- in a queue during a petrol strike
- at a military reunion
- at a fashion parade
- on the showroom floor, as a Rolls Royce is being sold
- at a school speech night
- at a sitting of parliament.

Don't write the scene, but describe what form the intervention takes, perhaps with some dialogue. Then allow the character to speak in a monologue from their background to say why they acted as they did.

Of course, at the stage beyond exercises, after you have written a first draft of a play or film script, you need to redraft, looking in fine detail at the plausibility of all your characters, especially the protagonist—the character who is the main focus of interest, conflict, tension and trial in the play. Clearly Ellie is likely to be the protagonist in *Walking to the falls.*

As you redraft, all the elements of character construction come up for review—actions, reactions, dialogue. First read the play *aloud* quite quickly to yourself, making sure you are not interrupted, to hear and feel the characters as entities, to hear when they sound unconvincing or indefinite, where they sound strong and individual. Annotate the unconvincing spots so you can rewrite them later. Then read *aloud* to yourself each character's part on its own, starting with the protagonist and then the antagonist—the character who makes life most difficult for the protagonist: Vanessa is the antagonist in the drafts of *Walking to the falls.* Later, after amending characters' actions and dialogue, read the play aloud in its entirety for the rhythm of its high points or 'beats'.

Action and sound

Just as it is better to show than tell in fiction, so it is often better in drama and film to allow characters' actions to show their states of mind, rather than have them telling an audience how they feel in dialogue. Obviously there are also many situations where words and passion are indispensable.

We shall first examine action and sound.

Write

1 Find a play in print, or a scene from a piece of drama you have written, and eliminate words in five or six of its segments of dialogue, replacing them with stage directions for actions that will convey the same message to an audience.

2 Can you devise a scene in which a 'sound off' triggers the actions of one or at most two characters on stage without any word being spoken, so that for two or three minutes you are balancing *sound* and *action* in your script? Perhaps it is fugitives caught red-handed by the police knocking on the door; their efforts to hide evidence or to escape while making no sound can constitute the entire scene.

3 Try writing the opening scene of a pantomime, with caricatured characters expressing themselves by actions only.

4 Act yourself, as a mime, and then write the directions for:

• the movements of a person coming in cold and hungry to find no warmth in the house or food in the fridge, and registering a reaction or complaint

• the movements of a person showing another how a bike works and how to mount and ride it, then watching the novice's disastrous attempts at riding, and finally having to pick up the pieces.

5 Study the directions for actions, monologue and sound at the end of Chekhov's play, *The cherry orchard.* Write an end to a scene in a play

or film that uses the same technique. Write a note of explanation about the background of the play, stressing the sound's dramatic significance and how it provides an unmistakable conclusion.

6 Try conceiving and writing a film's opening sequence that is action only without dialogue for some time, and in which the viewer is kept in suspense about the significance of the action.

These suggestions hint at the practice you can gain by visualizing carefully what your characters might do within the logic of your story and what those actions might reveal to an audience. They are simply flexing exercises. You should take every opportunity, if you want to write for stage, film or television, to sit in on acting workshops, plays, and television or film rehearsals to gain insights into what actors can do, how they train, how they use trust exercises, improvization and mime to achieve effects. It all helps you to gauge how much can be stated by action, what actions you can write into a script, and what may be asking too much of the actors.

Dialogue and movement

At this stage in dramatic writing all the elements in the creation of the story can come together. You know what your story is about. You know your characters and their backgrounds. You are presenting them page by page as living entities, although they will be slightly larger than life in some senses. You are giving them words to speak. They will not stand still as they speak, so actions and words will often unite as a forceful expression of their personalities.

Creating dialogue and surrounding it with movement is an art. This is where plays and scripts are written and rewritten many times, and where radio is a marvellous training ground, because in radio, by and large, there is only the dialogue.

Write

1 Dialogue is never independent of character and situation. Think about your characters and how they might be likely to speak. He is short, fat, breathless: he speaks in little bursts. She is languid, terribly intellectual, never utters anything unless it is perfectly thought out, incisive and immaculately expressed: she speaks in long sentences. He is trying to persuade her to act, this Saturday afternoon in a Melbourne winter. She wants to stay home and read. Determine what physical activity or activities he has in mind, then write their dialogue as a script, so that eventually their roles are reversed: he speaks in long and persuasive detail, while she becomes monosyllabic.

2 Take a theme and worry it in dialogue. A man trying to 'play the field' and finding that it is not all he had hoped? Write this for radio,

capture him with his various partners, establishing the general situation, and then add complications, or find examples of your own.

3 Write a desultory piece of dialogue between two people about the efficacy of baked beans and their place in the world order. Have one character tell the most elaborate lies. See where the exchange leads . . . Again, write for radio.

4 Write a news background report about a fictitious national or international situation using all the journalistic clichés you can muster. Allow no original English to intrude, if you can manage it.

5 Write the dialogue for an interview with a politician in which the politician is evasive and repeatedly fails to answer the question.

6 Write a scene in which character A is talking to character B. Character A, who has been involved in a particularly humiliating episode with a third and absent character, is all passion and anger against that person, while character B, who has not been emotionally involved in the episode, is counselling cool thought rather than violence.

7 Make an object (a car, a ring, a radio) become a symbol of freedom, bondage or imaginative freedom between two characters by letting us listen to their dialogue.

8 You see a lonely thirteen-year-old girl by herself in the glassed-in foyer of some high-rise flats, unaware of anyone watching her. She has organized a dance game for herself, using the space available, and is talking animatedly to herself. Convert her to drama. Add other voices. Set the scene in stage directions and write what she is saying, while reflecting the relationship between her words and thought, on the one hand, and her movements on the other. Take her on an imaginative journey with the other voices, returning her eventually to the foyer alone.

9 Write dialogue between three characters centred round the theme of the vanity that attaches to body-shape. Let envy rear its ugly head.

10 What can a single actor do when alone on stage, set, or at the microphone? He can write something, and then speak what has been written. Or talk to a mirror? Talk to an object? Soliloquize philosophically? Try writing two sketches in which characters do two of these things, so that in each case a basic theme and story development begins to appear.

11 Don't neglect nonsense. Capture the strange world of dream or first waking or intoxication when the world's rules can be changed. Build a narrative that veers from the real and actual. It's the 'What if . . .?' question again. What if, of all the people invited to a wedding, no one knows who will come out married because the vicar has a scatter-gun approach to the job? Begin a string of dialogue that is based on ambiguity from the outset: 'I feel for people with fat stomachs!'. Write dialogue for two people who are watching a third and who are weighing up her chances of success at something never clearly defined: 'I don't think she's going to make it, do you?'

12   Try writing some dialogue in loose verse form—in rhyming couplets, for example, or look again at Dylan Thomas's *Under milk wood* or Douglas Stewart's *Fire on the snow* or *The golden lover* or *Ned Kelly*. Then try creating dialogue with similar poetic or mystical qualities. Perhaps adopt a myth, as Stewart does in *The golden lover*, and tell the story as a radio play.

13   Write a very one-sided conversation between an overbearing person and someone whom he or she is always interrupting and rendering almost speechless. Then turn the tables.

14   Read this basic piece of dialogue.

A: Now that we're away, what'd you think?
B: She's too hard on . . . She's making trouble for later . . .
C: As far as I'm concerned he needs it . . . Man, if I . . .
A: I'm trying to be fair . . .
C: You saw him . . .
B: Oh, come on, what . . .?
C: (*interrupting*) You saw him throw it, just after she . . .
B: He's just like all kids his age . . . and who was talking about freedom to develop . . .
C: Yeah, but not over everyone else's dead body . . .
A: Well, on the one hand . . .
C: Listen, she needs some support . . .

Now rewrite it in three different styles. In each rewrite you can invent background and incident to some extent. First, as melodrama:

A: I can see your deep concern, and you know how importantly I regard your opinions. Now that we're away from the scene, what conclusions do you . . .?

Now rewrite it as high and formal comedy?

A: Now, gentlemen, what are your thoughts about that little bastard . . .?

Now rewrite it so that the strength of C's *feeling* about the situation cows A and B into silence. This rewrite will become more extended.

The more you work with dialogue, the more you will appreciate the value of *listening* rather than just hearing. When characters begin to choose their own speech and become entities, it is as if they move under your hand, but this is the result of much listening to the flux of human interaction, as any professional dramatist or script-writer will tell you. As a test, you could try writing monologues for characters from different callings, telling your audience what it is like to be a lawyer, a fashion designer, a dentist, a plumber, a garbo, a farmer specializing in raising bulls. Write passages in which they talk about day to day *incidents* in their work, episodes they remember. See the face and the body language of the characters as you write. Have you listened enough to lawyers talking? Do they talk to each other differently from the way they talk to outsiders? How, where, do they socialize? What do they drink? How do they buy drinks, as against the way a plumber buys drinks? Plumbers working together on a new tank? A garbo? A teacher of English? How do they choose words, construct sentences?

Don't be deterred when you look back at a first draft of a play or script to find that you have been writing 'soap' dialogue, as one professional puts it. It can be polished when you rewrite. In the polishing you can balance the dialogue; balance wordiness against silence, for example. You can rearrange individual speeches to make them 'build' rather than trail away towards silence, unless that is the effect you wish to create. Consider this:

ELLIE: He doesn't load me with expectations. I'd gladly wash his wound every morning for the rest of my life. He leaves me freedom to move. You don't understand, do you!

This is a speech that could head downhill. Of the four sentences in it, one stands out as the image of Ellie's feeling, and yet it is buried in the middle of the piece, when all the other statements should be building towards its power. The speech ends weakly with a short question, whereas the ending of a speech should be its strongest point. What about this version?

ELLIE: You don't understand, do you! He doesn't load me with expectations. He leaves me freedom to move. I'd gladly wash his wound every morning for the rest of my life.

Write

Try amending these statements in the same way:
- In any case, that's my bike, of course.
- He's correct, isn't he?
- Now rack off, will you?

Most speeches have a relatively strong beginning, a softer middle, but a vital, deeply-felt and powerful end with a prose rhythm that doesn't fade away, but ends with a major beat. The final word should be able to be accentuated—'Isn't he *correct*?'

All this points again to the fact that you as a dramatic writer should see as much theatre, film and television, listen to as much radio drama, as you possibly can, seeking out chances to watch or work with directors, actors and workshop groups, in improvization classes, role-plays, even psycho-drama. Improvization is an immediate way to tap the subconscious. As Tyrone Guthrie, the English director once said: 'If a play has any depth at all, it comes largely from the author's subconscious. And the author is only aware of about 50 per cent of what he has put into the play'. Improvization is a way to *discover* ideas, words, strange situations. You could try it with a small group, setting yourself a theme and allotting each other characters distinguished by their different points of view. Make the topics or themes single-word or single-phrase subjects that touch people's fears, prejudices, sense of embarrassment, or guilt. Participants should then speak impromptu as their allotted characters, cutting in on each other, to see what cross-currents and tensions emerge.

Writing action

A play can hold an audience enthralled with passages of action spiced with brief exclamations and short dialogue. Samuel Beckett's 'Act Without Words 1' is an example, sub-titled 'A Mime for One Player'.

Write

• Write a sequence of action for two characters that humorously exposes character A's fear of the return of some figure of authority, so that he takes elaborate precautions to avoid discovery of some wrong-doing, only to find that when the authority-figure (character B) does enter, he is not the least interested in discovery and punishment, but commits the same misdemeanour himself and then, while character A is absent, begins his own precautions against discovery by a third party.
• Write a sequence of actions which repeatedly build to climaxes spelt out in each case by one explosive piece of dialogue. Then ring the changes on the situations and the outbursts of dialogue, playing it for humour.

Forms of drama

We have concentrated on four main forms of drama or performance, but the full list is longer than that:
• sound plays for radio
• plays for the stage
• television plays (television theatre)
• plays performed to be filmed (film theatre)
• singing plays for the stage (opera)
• filmed versions of singing plays (musicals)
• dance drama for the stage (ballet)
• filmed versions of dance drama
• original television scripts
• original film scripts
• novels or short stories (or myths or poems) adapted as film
• novels or short stories, etc., adapted as television drama

All of these originate in the minds of writers.

As a dramatist or script-writer, you might choose to write:

- half-hour or hour-long episodes of TV comedy and drama
- episodes of a TV drama series with common characters and theme, in which each episode is a separate story ('Softly softly', 'Seeing things', 'GP', 'The flying doctor', 'Callan', 'All creatures great and small')
- TV half-hour or hour-long documentaries
- TV short sketches, fillers, jokes, short passages of 'continuity' for quiz, interview or variety shows, etc.
- radio short sketches, fillers, comedy fillers, jokes, or linking segments of continuity
- radio documentaries and investigative reports
- TV documentaries and investigative reports
- 'corporate' audio and video material for staff training, selling products or services, or explaining the role or brief of a business or government department
- live drama for schools or educational playscripts for students
- educational videos for training or drama, educational material and audio-visual displays

Performance writing in Australia

From the beginnings of Aboriginal story and dance more than 50 000 years ago, through early white settler and convict theatre, to the Pioneer Players in Melbourne in the 1920s, the emergence of the Australian film industry on the world scene, its eclipse by imports in the 1930s, the revival of Australian drama in the 1950s and 1960s, and the advent of new and alternative theatre in the 1970s, 1980s and 1990s, together with the burgeoning of Australian film, the history of performance in Australia is very interesting. So too is the story of radio and television. But those stories cannot be told here.

If you would like to follow the post-war developments in performance and read examples of plays and scripts for their suggestion of ideas, the following list of some of the main figures in that development will provide a basis. Playwrights whose work you might look out for are: Ray Lawler, Richard Beynon, Peter Kenna, Alan Seymour, Michael Boddy, David Williamson, Barry Oakley, Patrick White, Jack Hibberd, John Romeril, Alex Buzo, Graeme Blundell, Bruce Spence, Bob Ellis, Alma de Groen, Betty Roland, Louis Nowra, Dorothy Hewett, Michael Gow, Steve J. Spears, Jack Davis, Stephen Sewell, Jennifer Compton, Jim McNeil, Kevin Gilbert, Barry Dickins, Janis Balodis, Ron Elisha, Sue Watkins, John O'Donoghue, Darrelyn Gunzberg, Hannie Rayson and others. Among scriptwriters you might follow the work of John Duigan, Paul Cox, David Williamson or Roger McDonald.

Nothing is new . . . but everything is fresh

The broad springs of drama have been used and re-used countless times by dramatists and scriptwriters—violence, pursuit of power, fortitude in the face of odds, failure, innocence set against experience, love, forces for good, the inevitable intrusion of evil, death, cruelty, sacrifice. Think of how Shakespeare touches these in his plays, as did the Greeks, as have the American playwrights, as did Chekhov. Think also of how modern Australian plays and scripts arise from the same elements—say David Williamson's *Emerald city*, Jack Hibberd's *A stretch of the imagination*, Dorothy Hewett's *The chapel perilous*, John Duigan's *The year my voice broke*, Douglas Stewart's *The fire on the snow*.

Although you are certain to re-employ these basic elements in human affairs in your own writing in one way or another, you will find nevertheless, at the level of detail and pertinence to a particular audience's experience, that you do indeed produce material that is fresh and has not been treated before. Think again of the range of human experience touched upon in the subject-matter of the plays and scripts of, say, Alex Buzo, Dorothy Hewett, David Williamson, Jack Hibberd, John Duigan. They include the story of a race-horse, the pain of growing through puberty in a country town, the male myths with which Australians surround themselves, the Gallipoli campaign, women's self-imprisonment in social convention, the power struggles and greed in an eminent Australian Rules football club, political and business corruption and the journalist's role in relation to it, and so on. Their products are universal and yet endemically Australian in reference.

The professionals speak

When you have written some material for stage, film, television or radio yourself, encountering the same challenges that all writers of drama encounter each time they sit down to create a new story, then the thoughts of the experts in the field become more pertinent and valuable.

You will be aware, through the works listed in the Bibliography, that there are many books on these subjects. You might also find useful four videos prepared by the Australian Film, Television and Radio School (AFTRS) consisting of interviews with experienced script editors and drama writers for all media. Here is a summary of some of the points made in the videos:

On character

Henrik Ibsen's workshop, translated by A. G. Chater, contains pages of Ibsen's planning, notes, sketches, drafts, and what he called fore-works and scenarios for his famous plays. They give a fascinating insight into how the Norwegian playwright conceived and built up his characters and their situation, and how he pondered the issues of his day (and ours) in dramatic terms. Toby Cole's *Playwrights on playwriting* contains similar material from other modern playwrights.

On writing comedy

The AFTRS video series contains interviews with such comedy writers as British script-writer Alan Plater; Carl Sauter, the American script-writer and editor; Sue Ingleton, performer and writer of much Australian comedy; and Geoffrey Atherdon, script-writer for the Australian programme, 'Mother and son'. They comment on the sources of comedy and the knowledge of human nature required to write it. Comedy writing in most cases is not one-liners and puns thick on the page.

As Alan Plater says, comedy lies in the gap between aspiration and achievement, in the dignity of failure—'I leap: I fall down'. He stresses that both comedy and tragedy involve the pain of life, but that tragedy in the end embraces the pain, while comedy looks away from it at the last moment. Both Alan Plater and Carl Sauter emphasize that comedy must arise from something real, generally something that lies deep in the human psyche. We create jokes out of things that make us anxious—birth, death, marriage, sex, war, work, threat, strangeness and the unknown, doctors, operations, men's and women's relations, ridicule and embarrassment. Real and silly is funny, says Carl Sauter, unreal and silly is terrible. Sue Ingleton's comedy often arises, she says, from what disturbs her; having made it into a laughable situation, she allows the resulting laughter to release tension, finding that a new attitude slips into the space in people's thinking vacated by the tension and concern over the subject. Comedy, she attests, has the power to change people's attitudes, provided it leaves room for hope.

On violence, pornography

When does comedy, horror, or violence that constructively reflects real life, tip over into excess? Alan Plater makes a distinction between comedy that engenders laughter that is 'clean' and offers redemption; comedy that is cruel in its implications, but allows growth; and laughter that 'stamps on life' and can lead only towards inhumanity and misanthropy. Frank Pierson, film critic and scriptwriter, makes a distinction between Alfred Hitchcock who used to frighten and shock his audiences but restored their happiness and sense of well-being at the end, and what he calls the more recent 'pornography of violence' in film that drenches the audience in blood and is destructive of values. Both writers, and many others, are concerned about the tendency to portray violence in all its details and for its own sake, although neither would be prepared to censor it. It is a question that exercises the minds of all who write for the visual media and frequently of those who write for print.

On 'nice' and 'nasty' people

It is easier, says Alan Plater, to write the character and actions of villains, than to create believable and interesting 'good' people as characters. You can ponder the point and try doing both.

On a balance of hope and fear

David Williamson speaks of the need for an intriguing question in writing for film and television, and he could have added other forms of writing, too. The aim of the writer, Williamson notes, is to raise hope that the protagonist will emerge from the dilemma, while leaving the audience tinged with the fear that he or she will not.

On pitfalls for new writers

David Williamson notes that two dangers face inexperienced writers of drama or scripts: they may become carried away with developing their characters and fail to advance the action of the play sufficiently; or they may have no deep interest in the *fate* of their characters.

On history and research

The story-lines of many Australian stage plays, television dramas, films and radio programmes have come from history: *Breaker Morant; Gallipoli;* Douglas Stewart's radio plays; *Phar Lap; Power without glory; Macquarie; The feet of Daniel Mannix; Flash Jim Vaux; Marvellous Melbourne; The Les Darcy show; Strikebound; 1915; Between the wars; The four-minute mile*, and others. For each of these, the writer decided that there was a story in what history offered, or a film in an adaptation of an historical novel or short story. If you are interested in writing about Australia's history, try to amass a library of Australian reference books and possibly tapes and videotapes against which you can check the historical period that interests you.

Tony Morphett, writer of many Australian drama scripts for television, speaks on the AFTRS videotape about his research methods, not only for historical detail, but for expertise about areas of life with which he is not familiar but which are integral to his dramatizations—Chinese literature, poetry, the *I Ching*, cooking philosophy! He crams his mind with material, then 'forgets' it and launches into his script.

David Williamson adds that it helps if the characters that history has thrown up are reasonably colourful and individual; if they are not, it may be an argument against attempting the script.

On technology, time and impatience

The pace and variety of television drama and film editing has increased markedly since the advent of Australian television in 1956. Nowadays the characters in the car announce their intention to go to the wharf and the next shot shows them looking down on the container terminal. In the 1950s and 1960s we might have followed their trip, arrival, car parking, introductions and their first steps up the ladder to their vantage point.

Technology has made the world speedier than it was, and this in turn has its effects on staging and production. A number of playwrights have concluded, for instance, that audience impatience with stage productions has increased because of the quick cut and slash of television and video. They find that two-act plays rather than three-act plays often satisfy an audience better in the 1990s.

Celebratory and event-based theatre

Jack Hibberd's play, *Dimboola*, later made into a film, holds the record for the longest-running Australian play (two years and one week!). Its success was largely due to the fact that it 'enfranchizes the audience in the event' as Hibberd puts it. The play concerns a country wedding. The audience attends a wedding breakfast and eats and interacts to some extent with the bridal party—the actors—during the reception. It is one outstanding Australian example of event-based or celebratory stage writing and production. *Dimboola* paved the way for the popularity of other cabaret-style or theatre restaurant performances at restaurant venues like Dirty Dick's and the Last Laugh in Melbourne.

The element held in common by this form of theatre and participatory theatre is that they involve the audience to a greater extent than traditional Aristotelian stage theatre and generally reduce and modify the role of the writer in creating the drama. Event-based theatre, simulation and role-play are often used with children's theatre groups, while much left-wing drama, frequently employing street theatre, is to be found in the Third World. It is sometimes known as 'socially active theatre' for its political and social-justice content and is discussed in *Theatre of the oppressed*, by the Brazilian playwright, Augusto Boal. Much of this theatre relies on group-developed drama rather than written scripts, perhaps using actors to develop a rough scenario in which they will take leading roles, while children or the untutored audience follow them and act as chorus, crowd or special group.

Participatory theatre in Australia has used all these elements, so that the audience is not only placed in the middle of the action as in Hibberd's *Dimboola*, but is given roles to play that arise partly from the planning of the scenario, partly from limited instruction, and partly from empathy with the mood of the performance.

Write

Write a page-long scenario for a participatory play, thinking of a regional or community story that could be dramatized, relying on historical research.

How will you have the actors address the audience in order for them to become workers, fighters of floods or storms, bereaved parents during wartime, or the crowd at a political meeting? How will the actors move among the audience? What properties will you develop to suggest floods, industrial processes, disaster scenes, etc.?

Dramatic practicalities

If you wish to write dramatic material for stage, film, television or radio, and to submit it to script editors, production companies, workshop groups, producers and others, the following information will help.

Making your own luck

Film and television drama is expensive to produce. Australia has a relatively small population, a correspondingly small viewing audience, a small investment base and a low level of advertising return. This means that opportunities for new and even for experienced writers are very limited in film, and only a little better in television and radio. The ABC is virtually the only producer of full length radio drama. There are chances for script-writers where dramatic story-telling skills are applied to sketches, fillers, advertising, documentaries, continuity pieces, researched reports and adaptations of stories, but these writing opportunities usually go to experienced writers, who may already be on staff or are experienced freelancers. The average yearly earnings of script-writers are not high.

If you are interested in entering this field of writing, therefore, you will probably have to 'make your own luck' by steeping yourself, perhaps for several years, in the industry, and doing production work while you watch, listen, and analyse the work of the professionals and steadily hone your own writing.

Professional bodies, professional assistance, publications

Just as the Australian Society of Authors (ASA), the Fellowship of Australian Writers (FAW), and the Australian Journalists' Association (AJA) look to the professional interests of writers for the print media, so the Australian Writers' Guild (AWG) is the major professional body for script-writers; film, television and radio editors, producers and directors; as well as production assistants of all sorts in the area of vision and sound.

The AWG supplies marketing information for the script-writer such as lists of production companies in stage, film, and television, and what their current needs are for material. It also provides legal, copyright and advisory services to its script-writer members.

The Australian Film Commission provides services to writers for film: it has a script assessment service, and makes funds available for worthy film and television scripts, treatments, draft development and production.

Nevertheless, new writers in these fields must be patient and realistic in their expectations. Just as in the print media, where few unsolicited manuscripts are accepted for publication unless they are by previously published writers, so probably fewer than 1 per cent of unsolicited film scripts ever reach production through the Australian Film Commission or the State Film Commissions.

The training grounds for script-writers in Australia include the Australian Film, Television and Radio School, Sydney; the National Institute for Dramatic Art (NIDA), Sydney; Melbourne's Swinburne Institute of Technology film production course; and several segments in film in various universities and colleges of advanced education.

Reading publications that deal with work in the visual media is a good way to become familiar with the milieu of film and television and to keep abreast of new developments and opportunities. The newsletter of the AWG, *Viewpoint*, and such journals as *Cinema papers*, *Film News*, *Film Views*, *Encore* and the more experimental *Cantrills' Filmnotes*, are valuable in this regard.

Script submission

It is important to study the markets for scripts before sending work to a producer, director or script editor. Look at the AWG marketing information and perhaps contact the production company you choose before submitting, to learn their particular interests and requirements.

It is vital that your play or script be correctly set out—always typewritten, set out with dialogue and directions in different type and on separate lines, with generous margins on all sides, dialogue indented, and following a format similar to the examples of scripts earlier in this part of the book or in a reputable book on script-writing. Note the differences in setting out between stage play, film script and radio script. It is generally advisable to preface a play script, film script or radio script with a short synopsis or statement, a list of characters and locations or sets. The script should be firmly stapled and bound in covers.

Impress an editor or producer with knowledgeable clarity, brevity and emphasis in wording. As the editor or producer sits down to look at your film treatment or proposal, he or she is silently asking you the expensive question: 'Why should I make this into a film?' There will be other scripts to read and yours won't get a second look unless it is clear and convincing in its story structure. Study books on the subject or seek a professional's advice about setting out and wording before you begin to type a final submission.

In writing stage directions, or in preparing script outlines and treatments, remember to keep to a minimum details of atmospherics, character's mood, camera directions and other instructions which intrude on the director's or producer's sphere of expertise. Allow those who work at making a production from your script the latitude they need to tell the story through action.

On the title page and at the conclusion of your script, it is advisable to write your name, address, telephone number, and the copyright symbol with the word 'copyright', then your name and the year it was written. Keep a copy of the script, and add necessary postage for return of the copy you send away, then wait for a response—it may take months. If your script is chosen for development, you will probably be paid a flat fee for the work.

If your radio script is chosen for production by the ABC a contract is organized when a satisfactory final version of the script is ready. The contract is in accordance with the ABC agreement with the Australian Writer's Guild and the Australian Society of Authors. Guidelines are available from the Director of Radio Drama and Features at the Australian Broadcasting Corporation.

Opportunities

Check the Saturday pages of newspapers like the *Australian*, the *Age*, and the *Sydney Morning Herald* for notices of opportunities to submit and workshop stage plays. Each year in May, for example, the National Playwrights' Conference is held in Canberra and advertises for scripts in the media some weeks earlier to select a number for workshopping; Anthill Theatre's Next Wave Festival for young playwrights operates similarly in Melbourne.

Agents

An agent specializing in scripts and visual writing, or a literary agent who handles playwrights and script-writers, will become useful to you when you have brought your scripts to marketable quality. Agents can place scripts with the most likely producer, negotiate contracts and fees and suggest and approach funding sources, but cannot edit or rewrite work if it is not of professional standard. An agent is equally valuable to you if a producer makes overtures to buy rights to your work of fiction, your play or your television script in order to make it into a film or television drama. In that case contractual arrangements can become quite complex and may involve negotiations interstate or overseas and are best handled by an agent and perhaps an experienced solicitor.

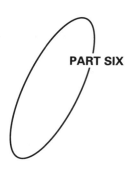

PART SIX

Advertising—persuasive stories

Advertiser's rubric:

If the client moans and sighs,

insert the name-block twice the size.

If the man is still refractory,

show a picture of his factory.

Only in the direst case

should you have to show his face. . .

Anonymous

Buy Brand X

Scene: Close-up of woman's face leaning over lover in midst of deeply passionate kiss. She overhears voice telling of special offers in a women's lingerie, fashion wear and track-suit sale. The kiss becomes more distracted, less passionate, until it seems to have escaped her mind altogether and she rises to quit her lover for the scene of the special offers while they last. When, where, and by whom the savings will be made available is reinforced by voice over at first hearing, by the maker's logo on the screen, and again by voice over as woman departs for the retail outlet. (Moderate humour, one-off television advertisement for women's apparel manufacturer, end-of-financial-year sale, thirty seconds; evening or midday show exposure.)

Scene: Heads and shoulders of young bush-walkers—two male, two female—carrying haversacks up rocky ridge in the high country, with backdrop of breath-taking view across deep valleys to mountain wilderness in distance. Clear winter weather? Sounds of joking voices against the silence as walkers slip haversacks from their backs and prepare to make camp and camp-fire. Women seen coming back to camp with billy of water for the fire. Bush-walker produces a purple block of Cadbury's Dairy Milk Chocolate to the joy of her companions, peels it open, takes a bite, while the voice over and print over emphasize the glass and a half of full-cream milk in every 200 grams. Everyone is in for a bite, with smiles of camaraderie and satisfaction at taste and sustenance. Voice over and print over reinforces milk-in-satisfying-chocolate message. (Straight thirty second television commercial for Cadbury Dairy Milk Chocolate; late afternoon, evening, weekend exposure, especially in Australian winter.)

Act 1: Nah, who needs a personal computer! We're maintaining our market position, no worries . . . We use an abacus and plenty of typewriter ribbon . . .

Act 2: Y's sales, efficiency, staff satisfaction, profits have rocketed 300 per cent since he installed his WizzBang K200 PC in the office.

Act 3: OK, OK—enough said. I've just taken delivery of a WizzBang K200 like Y's with the staff-satisfaction modem, the search-for-new-customer software and the multifactorial synthesizer . . . Hmmm . . . I'm getting to like this . . . Shirley, turn me up last year's production figures when you get a chance, will you? And our first six month's consumption of toilet paper . . .? (Three-act thirty second television or radio commercial. Evening or midday show exposure for television, or daytime, evening or weekend exposure for radio.)

We could go on; effective advertisements come in many different forms. We are beginning to enter the area of 'applied' writing, where story-telling skills already learned in poetry, prose fiction, drama and scripting are put to use for specific purposes.

In a book of this sort it is impossible to cover all the operating methods and convey the atmosphere of an advertising agency. Before you can write a professional television advertisement, you need to gain experience in copy-writing, as well as some background knowledge of the various parts of an agency and how they interact, and of what is possible in television production.

Ad agencies

Advertising agencies, whether they are 'large shops' which seldom handle campaigns costing less than $250 000 per year per client, or 'small shops' handling accounts worth much less, are usually made up of the following sections.

A media (or media analysis) section

This consists of people who are very knowledgeable about the print media (newspapers, magazines, brochures, posters and all the complexities of photography, typography, colour reproduction and printing that go with them); and about radio and its vast range of tone, presentation and taste, as well as its special demands and the audiences it brings to advertisements; and about the visual media of television and film and their peculiarities and audiences. 'Media people' also are walking encyclopaedias about how different audiences behave, live their lives and can be appealed to, as well as what time slots and seasonal variations will best reach a particular audience.

Accounts service section

People in this section provide the main contact with the client, interpret the client's needs, liaise with the client and his or her research and marketing section. They must also know a great deal about the client, his business, her product, etc. They convey the client's expectations to the agency and later convey what the agency produces to the client.

Creative section

This consists of working teams, each consisting of a copy-writer and an art director who provides the visual element to go with the words. This is where you as writer fit in, and your relationship with your art director is vital in making a team.

Production section

These people stand in their artistic and technical expertise between the creative section's idea and the medium in which the idea is to appear. They handle it, and usher it through all the processes necessary for its completion.

Planning and research section

Larger agencies may have such sections, to add to the research done by the client's marketing and research staff in determining who the likely buyers of the product are, and how they can best be reached. Research and planning sometimes intrude into the types of research expertise and surveying technique that the media section also employs.

There are other people in an advertising agency whose special skills are demanded by work that is destined for television, radio and print. There will be a typographer, for instance, who will advise on typefaces for headlines and body copy for print or television. There will be a studio director and paste-up artists, who work with production people to prepare finished artwork on print ads. There may well be an agency library and files of video footage showing TVCs produced by the agency in the past and dealing with clients with whom you will interact as copy-writer. Other specialized craftspeople may be in-house or hired from the outside world, such as strip cartoonists, stunt experts, and prop makers who make the items that you as copy-writer dream up—garden scenes, model towns, candles that undulate and writhe, armchairs that clasp their victims, or model, battery-powered rabbits that climb ladders.

Television commercials (TVCs)

The path to a television commercial (TVC) runs something like this.
- The client contacts the advertising agency, and the agency's account staff and creative director have discussions with the client to draw up an advertising brief.
- The brief becomes a guide to the agency and to you as the copy-writer, because it attempts to answer the vital questions upon which the nature of the ad depends:
  — Why is the advertisement necessary? Is it to overcome a problem with the product's success? Is it to exploit an opportunity to market the product?
  — What is the product? The agency's creative and accounts sections need to know the product in detail, its history, its modifications over the years, so that they can think about it, see its special 'magic' and characteristics.
  — At whom is the TVC directed? Which segment (or segments) of all the viewing public is being targeted and induced to act?
  — What is the single most important point to be impressed on viewers? How is it hoped they will behave as a result?
- The agency's creative team (you as copy-writer for the words; and your art director team-mate for pictures) works on the brief, trying out a range of ideas that might convey the basic message, then deciding on the best of these to put before the creative director. The idea is checked

against the brief, accepted for finer tuning if it matches it well, discarded if it does not. If it is discarded, you and your art director go back to work to develop other ideas arising out of the discussion.

• When a final idea is accepted, you and your art director develop it as a story-board that shows the main frames of the visuals to be shot for the TVC. These stills are sometimes videotaped and backed with a sound-track so that the client can get the 'feel' of the proposed TVC. You, as copy-writer, and your art director generally bow out of the sequence at about this stage.

• The account director, creative director and client meet to view and discuss the TVC. The client approves the TVC.

• The creative director engages a film production company and meets with its production team, director and producer to discuss how the TVC will be shot and produced against the predetermined budget.

• The director of the film production team auditions and commissions actors to play in the TVC or confers with prop makers and stunt people, while the producer finalizes the film crew, books time and studio space and checks filming locations.

• The TVC is shot and post-produced, approved by the client, and sent to the television network.

• Timings and frequency of showings of the TVC are finally scheduled, and the TVC begins to appear on the nation's televisions.

Creating an idea

Let's look at the general steps involved in generating an advertising idea for any product and then apply them to some specific campaigns.

• First, secure a sample of the product, and study it. Keep it on the desk in front of you, provided it is not a Centurion tank! Get to know it, how it feels, looks, smells, sounds, tastes. This will suggest words and stories, or the possibility of visuals or camera shots.

• Cast about for a way of linking the product and its desirability to a story that can be told visually and convincingly. Remember that your story must make only *one* basic point: that is all that the viewer will remember from your TVC.

• Think about the audience for your TVC, *that portion only* of the viewing audience who might be potential buyers. What might they think of the product already? Is there a resistance to overcome? What socio-economic group are they likely to come from? What is their likely life-style? What language and approach is likely to gain their attention and hold it? What *new* information can you tell them, linking it to the desirability of the product? What *new* way of looking at it can you suggest? Should your TVC appeal to the emotions? Is the use of the product connected in real life with a particular emotion or state of feeling?

• When you think you have a story, write a brief outline of 120–50 words, just as you might write a film treatment, or as the descriptions of ads at the beginning of this Part of the book are written. Write it in the present tense, so that it tells us what the visual story will be, what the dialogue or voice over will say in general terms, and where the emphasis on the product name and the product's special appeal will come. Remember that you may opt for a mini-play, a three-part drama, or for a structure with a tease opening, a twist, a follow-up and a denouement. You may opt for a steady and witty revelation, leading to the product and its advantages. Many approaches are possible, each based on drama of one sort or another. You may use humour—raising a laugh means your message has gained viewers' attention. Remember that of all the things you could explain or point out about this product, you are choosing to make just the *one* basic point.

• Now, before you proceed to set the drama out in more detail as a script, block it out on a scribble sheet, with rough drawings in frames to indicate the main camera scenes, with the words to be spoken as dialogue or read as voice over written in beneath. In a thirty second TVC you will not be able to afford any more than sixty words, and preferably fewer. When you know your 'rough' well enough to be able to 'see and hear' the TVC's content, read it through again, visualizing the shots, hearing the words as you read aloud. Then do another run through, this time with stop-watch in hand, to see if you are coming close to that magical and absolutely strict thirty seconds. Rewrite your message, cut your camera scenes, until you are not running over time.

Write

Now, better equipped with information, you can begin to write a television commercial (TVC). If you know someone who is a natural illustrator, they may stand in as your art director for the purposes of this exercise. If not, you will have to dream up the words and dramatic sequence and turn your own hand to sketching in the key scenes on a scribble sheet. The one following is a sample of a professional scribble sheet.

You have three possible campaigns (or 'accounts') from which to choose.

1 A client requires a campaign to publicize a range of home anti-theft devices (deadlocks, security screens, sensors, trip alarms, padlocks, special security bolts, sensor alarms, window screens, sensor lights, etc.), marketed by the Burgleoff company. After discussions with the client, it is decided to write two commercials, each of which is discrete if viewed alone, but which connect and refer to each other at certain points. Both are to be drama, one humorous, the other serious, each of thirty seconds. Write both the ads.

CLEMENGER CREATIVE WORK PLAN

"Stop me if you've heard this slogan!"
"If you haven't seen us, what's stopping you?"

Client:	Checkpoint	Date:	November 29, 1989
Product:	Checkpoint Brake Centres	Job No:	

1. Why are we advertising?

do they need shock treatment?)

Checkpoint Brake Centres suffer low awareness and hold only 6% market share, despite being a national chain. A major refurbishment and staff training programme is underway. A relaunch of Checkpoint will take place in early 1990.

Safety? That's it!

2. The product.

What's that?!?   Brakes!?   Experience?   STOPping!

Checkpoint Brake Centres, a national chain of 91 specialist brake centres servicing retail and trade customers.

point of purchase [STOP] shops

3. Who are we talking to?

Car owners/drivers, usually the "second" or family car. Strong female bias. Vehicle predominantly three years old plus.

stop them before they hit the street   school promotion   parachute

4. What must the advertising say?

Brakes must be checked on a regular basis at Checkpoint to ensure optimum safety.

family under 'chute.   No!

And why should the consumer believe it?

Most cars have "bad breaks", "bad" breaks cause accidents. Checkpoints conveniently located branches are staffed by trained, qualified experts working in professional environments. Checkpoint offer a range of initiatives and guarantees as a demonstration to their commitment to leadership in passenger safety/protection.

Doctors working on brakes?

5. What tone of voice?

urgent   to the point.   Glide parachute

Positive, stress benefits, not negatives. Sensible and business like, not flippant.

check point   yellow

6. What practical considerations?

Strength of branding and use of the logo device is obviously important. Consideration to developing a mnemonic device from colour scheme or logo.

man on building   Stopped by 'chute.   "If you haven't seen us, what's stopping you?"   falls   checkpoint

Figure 1: An example of a professional scribble sheet from Clemenger's advertising agency in Melbourne.

168

2 A client makes high quality art and photographic posters for interior walls of houses, offices, etc.—the French Impressionists, Andy Warhol, Australian colonial painters, Australian landscapes, Max Dupain's Sydney photography, wilderness and landscape scenes, 'educational' posters about world issues and past and forthcoming events. The client needs a campaign of three commercials, twenty seconds each, to convince people of the advantages of adding posters by 'Lustre' to their living and working environment. Write *one* of the ads.

3 Write a TVC for a product or service that you have always had a yen to promote—thirty seconds.

We can leave this exercise at this point, assuming the later amendments, the tightening, the polishing of the script and the final presentation. This is sufficient to give you some idea of what is involved in applying fiction or drama to advertising, and it will provide a useful base when you try some advertisements for the other media—radio and print.

Study the ads

Now that you have confronted some of the challenges of the copy-writer's job and before going on to other forms of advertising you should make your own study of advertising in newspapers and magazines, listen to advertising on radio, and watch television ads with an analytical eye.

Make your own list of ads in each of the three media that you find particularly memorable, and then in a separate column beside each note what strategy it employs to gain its effect.

Don't forget to examine advertising brochures and leaflets. They contain writing that does not involve copy-writing in the sense of the single and arresting advertisement for print, radio or television. This 'volume stuff' as it is called in the trade—print material in advertising brochures or catalogues—is often a training ground for new copy-writers as they progress towards an awareness and understanding of retailing, business, writing and agency techniques.

As you read, view, and listen you will realize that often the advertising you are analysing is a recycled version of an old standard. Here are some advertising truths, successful formulas and suggestions for further enquiry:

• Seek the uniqueness of the product. The brand's market niche may be very small and its buyers lured by the way it stands out from competitors.

• If journalism brings us basically bad news, advertising should bring us uniformly promising and gladdening news. It should in general not show us sad faces, unless they are funny or are part of a 'community service' campaign—highlighting the road toll, for example. In general (there will always be winning exceptions) close-ups of faces in print or television ads are not effective, unless they give a sense of intimacy (an animated face speaking long distance on the phone, for example) where the essence of the message is personality, intimacy, emotion.

• There are cultural differences in advertising. The French copy-writer, for instance, can generally use sophisticated sex and seduction themes much more readily in her or his work than any Australian copy-writer can get away with in addressing her or his more 'ocker' general audience.

• Different products need different ads. Advertising for a house—a big purchase—is generally soft sell and informative. Ads for essential packaged goods with well-known brand names but many competitors must often be hard sell and persuasive.

• Advertising does *not*, in general, aim to speak to everyone. Each ad speaks to a different segment of the viewing, listening or reading public. It is a matter of who in the household does the buying—of soap, cereals, instant coffee, shampoo, or beer. Some twenty-five per cent of adult men in the USA, for instance, were estimated to drink five or more glasses of beer per day in the 1970s. They accounted for eighty-five per cent of total consumption. So it was with that profile in mind that beer advertising was written.

• Some products are such an integral part of everyday life that there is nothing new to say about them to a potential buying audience—for example, dairy products, or petroleum products, or deodorants—unless there has been some special modification in the product or novel method of delivery. In these cases, the copy-writer replaces information with entertainment that links into the product in the end, leaving the audience feeling warmly about it; or perhaps considers the sort of people who use the product and the situations in which it is consumed; or maybe the copy-writer develops an imagined (and patently unprovable) symbol of the product's power or worth: 'Put a tiger in your tank,' we were exhorted on behalf of Esso in the 1960s. This catch-phrase was followed up by promotions through service stations, including a tiger's tail that could be draped from the car's petrol tank. Millions of drivers changed from other brands to Esso, aided and abetted by the urging of their children!

• Often the aim of a campaign is to identify the brand or service in the public's mind and then to remind them of its identity and value in each of the media. Sometimes this is done with a common headline. For the most important person in the world—you! Then several distinct ads, each with its own story, are developed to demonstrate the proposition in different ways, all coming back to that catch-cry.

• Radio ads often rely on humour, word-play, the sound of a particular voice and accent or the use of a particular comic personality, if the words and sentiments can be made to sit with that person's image in the public mind.

• In the right hands radio can be made to encourage the audience to 'see'—and radio ads are no exception. Listen to some of the three-part dramas, the wit, the up-to-date reference in the ads on capital city FM radio. Analyse how they work. Don't overlook how tellingly they use SFX (sound effects).

• Television, of course, is ideal for the 'demonstration' ad—something offering visual proof of how the product works, how comfortable it is, how speedy it is, etc. Since viewers are unlikely to switch off, television is more likely to gain and hold an audience than a newspaper or magazine. It is very apt for advertising cheap and commonplace items— foods, drinks, toiletries, pet foods—because there is not a great deal of information to give about these. More sophisticated and more costly items that change models yearly and introduce new features may be better advertised with fuller information in the body text of a print advertisement. Television ads can seldom afford body text: they are restricted to very few words in their thirty seconds.

• An important balance must be struck between picture and words in a TVC: if there are a lot of rapidly edited pictures, the words must be very few, since the viewer's attention is occupied with the visuals. If a lot of words and information is necessary, then the visual needs to be something that won't distract the viewer—possibly a single long shot of someone walking along a street, a car disappearing, a yacht sailing slowly from screen left to screen right.

• Remind yourself of your television audience. People more often than not watch TV together, and a TVC can exploit peer pressure. Son or daughter asks why don't *we* have one of those, wife or husband says I've been wanting one of those for ages—So-and-so-across-the-street's got one now.

• Television advertising makes good use of cute animals; cartoon animals and characters; humour—the same springs for laughter that Alan Plater stresses in the writing of comedy drama (accidents; noise; impending crashes; parodies of television itself, where the characters are taken into the world of the TVC and try to climb through the TV set into the world it presents; water and splashing; immersion; destruction; humorous disaster; people acting out of character; embarrassment etc.). Surrealism; space warps; distorted history; futuristic scenes, etc. can also be effective.

• Print ads, as distinct from TV ads, have for the copy-writer the lure of a sweet match between words (headline: body copy) and picture. Typefaces become a fascination for their suggestiveness, their authority, their beauty and there is real satisfaction in achieving crisp, economical copy.

Other tried techniques that you will notice employed in your reading, listening and viewing are:
• strip cartoons telling a story

- question approaches: how to be one step ahead of other car drivers? Why should you choose this electric razor rather than another?
- imagining the product's most fascinating use; its most unlikely application; how to show it to its best advantage
- before and after stories: 'before I used Burgleoff security bolts . . .'
- 'torture' tests of the product, involving stunts, elaborate setting up, trials of long life, strength, speed, etc.
- simple word play—putting words together in such an unexpected way that they change an audience's perceptions, make them read or think.
- contests—ingenious games of chance
- appeal to experts, connoisseurs
- inviting an audience to test themselves—'Are you up with the rest . . .?'
- appeal to facts—the copy-writer researches and emphasizes the product's superiority over competitors.

A considerable amount of advertising is directed at women, because in some key areas they do a lot of the buying. Consider the ten areas of selling on which the greatest amount was spent across all media in advertising in Australia just before the 1990–91 recession:

1   Foodstuffs
2   Motoring (cars, trucks, petrol, tyres, accessories)
3   Household equipment, furnishings, appliances
4   Travel and tours
5   Finance, loans, debentures, etc.
6   Building materials and industrial machinery
7   Magazines, newspapers, books
8   Men's and women's toiletries
9   Office equipment
10 Banks and banking

In the first, third, seventh and eighth areas of greatest spending women more often than men do the buying, while women do a considerable proportion of the buying in some others.

Advertising directed at men tends to be in the areas of motor cars, liquor, sport, home repair products and tools, finance, and building materials and industrial machinery.

The aware copy-writer

Considering the fine line between resounding success and mere adequate performance of any given ad in eliciting the desired buyer response, it comes as no surprise that copy-writers—and their art directors—must be instinctively lateral-thinking, creative, eclectic, witty and up-to-date people. They must feed off what life offers them in new ideas. Eventually they become, by second nature, people who are on the look-out for new experience, new ways of seeing things. They seek out the techniques of other arts, other artists, and follow drama, fiction, the media, the stage, film, music—all in search of ideas that they might employ years hence or tomorrow. As one copy-writer puts it: 'Reading Nabokov and watching the Three Stooges are equally important in my lexicon.'

The copy-writer and artistic director must also be aware of how society is changing, what people at all levels of society are thinking and how they see the world. Different classes think about things very differently! The copy-writer and art director must know how things are done, what is in the news, what is worrying people, where they find their latest satisfactions, how processes work in government at all levels, how people speak, what the current buzz-words and hip phrases are with the young, the aged, the upwardly mobile. Her words must strike the right note, his pictures must say something with which the audience can identify or to which they can aspire.

Write

1 Consider advertising for a moment as a way of thinking, a way of seeing and presenting reality, and try these exercises:
• Become critical of your society. Write a series of five pithy, two-line statements that accompany sketches or cartoons to make trenchant points about it—about its imbalance of wealth; about violence; about social injustice; about its anti-intellectualism; about its male dominance; about its environmental unconcern; about its marginalized minorities, etc.
• Watch TVCs without the sound to see how their messages are conveyed visually. Write a soundless TVC. It might rely on mime, on stark visual contrasts, on a series of signs and human responses to them.
2 Write a Dear X letter for a thirty second radio ad to the assumed market segment for:
• a car phone
• a pressure cooker
• a tennis shirt
3 Write a personality ad. Choose someone well known in Australian society and write a TVC around him or her. Then write a print ad.
4 Choose a product and write a before-and-after ad around it, making it humorous or surreal.
5 Devise an exaggerated 'torture-test' ad for a motoring product, a personal beauty product, a seagoing product.
6 Study the range of home-gymnasium equipment, discuss the items with the retailer, collect brochures and trade information about them and develop an advertising brief to promote them. Devise a press ad and a TVC for them.
7 Write a slice-of-life dialogue ad for oranges and citrus products to run for twenty seconds on radio.

Happy and rewarding advertising!

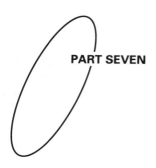

PART SEVEN

Introducing the media

The medium is an invitation. It has to be used.

Gabriel Garcia Marquez

Modern daily miracles

If you are interested in the telling of stories and have the opportunity, you might manage to see a large capital city daily newspaper produced any day of the week. Remember Monday morning's paper is produced on Sunday and the Sunday paper is sweated out of journalists on Saturday.

If you are doubly lucky you might be able to stand out of the way in the rush and watch the ABC or SBS evening television news go to air any week-night.

If you are trebly fortunate you might be invited to sit on the sidelines, sworn to silence and non-movement, to see and hear an evening radio current affairs and news background program going out to listeners across the nation.

In each case, you will come away realizing that you have witnessed a daily miracle of creativity, perception, wit, skilful writing, organization, adept storytelling, teamwork and judgement. In each case you will feel the inexorable turning of the world as day succeeds day, as new events wash over old, as people's lives are changed, as human drama is enacted.

You have written advertisements for some segments of the media in Part Six. What can you discover by taking a broader view of the outlets for which you might write in the 'applied' areas of advertising, journalism, public relations and the popular music industry?

The different media

It is a truism to point out that 'media' is the plural of 'medium', and yet the media are often treated as a singular. A medium, for a writer, is the means by which the writer communicates with an audience, with readers, listeners, or viewers.

The media come in a variety of forms, each offering writing opportunities and employment, despite the great competition for places and work.

The print media

In the print media a writer's story comes to its audience via words and images (photographs, line drawings, computerized graphics, reproduced paintings or sketches, cartoons, etc.) in the form of:
newspapers
magazines
brochures or pamphlets
books or booklets
handbills
annotated maps
posters

billboards
printed signs, neon signs, electronic signs, etc.

The electronic media

In television, radio, and film, a writer's story comes to its audience via words, moving images and sound, or via voice and sound, in the form of:
documentaries
advertisements
public service announcements
drama
comedy and sketches
news
current affairs
public relations material
video-clips
other promotional material, etc.

Story-telling in the media

We are now entering a multiplicity of fields of writing that, despite appearances, are firmly grounded in the story-telling skills you have developed so far. In fact, they frequently employ drama, scripting, fiction, fact, research, and even poetry.

The 'pure' and 'applied' come together tentatively in the mass media. Poetry and short fiction are peripheral—newspapers publish poems in their Saturday arts pages, and, rarely, publish winning short stories from competitions; popular magazines often publish one or more pieces of short fiction; ABC Radio National broadcasts poetry and book-readings; some radio stations have a literature programme; and book publishers bring out books of poetry, short fiction and novels as part of their lists. These products are for the few. The Australia Council's 1989 study of the arts in Australia shows that Australians spend only nine per cent of their leisure time reading, and forty per cent watching television. It is estimated that those with one hundred or more books in their homes make up the market for 'serious' books, and that only some 100 000 people out of Australia's population of seventeen million are in that category—bad news for writers of serious fiction, poetry, biography, autobiography and historical material!

Of course television dramas or mini-series are screened by ABC, SBS, and commercial channels; film scripts eventually reach their audiences in cinemas; novels are adapted as television or film; successful films even spawn paperback novels designed to catch the market's fleeting interest. Generally, situation comedies (sitcoms), TV 'soaps' or news broadcasts draw large audiences.

There is a close connection between the sense of what is a fascinating story for the script-writer or short-story writer, and a journalist's or editor's judgement that she should run *this* story first, and *that* story later, in magazine or newspaper. The news journalist or editor will call her judgement 'news sense', based on 'newsworthiness'. Newsworthiness is a complex mixture of what people want to hear or read or see, what will attract attention, and what responsible journalism dictates is important and in the public interest to write and publish at the time.

The media in profile

Writers need to be informed about the main features of the media in Australia, since these affect what material they can sell, the constraints under which they write, their employment opportunities, and their chances to make a reasonable income by freelance writing.

• The media are competitive, exciting and fast, and except for the ABC, SBS Television, and a few other instances, they are directly linked to profit, sales and advertising. They must be up to the minute, consonant with the community's thinking.

• Most forms of the media rely on advertising; that is why the best ratings for television and radio (the largest audience shares) and largest newspaper and magazine circulations, are bitterly fought for and jealously guarded. The Melbourne *Age* newspaper, for example, earns eighty-two per cent of its revenue from advertising and about fourteen per cent from circulation (sales). A paper with a smaller circulation can also work well for its advertisers if its readership is a select group, for example a rural newspaper can successfully advertise sheep drenches.

• Newspapers, television and radio are daily miracles. Their daily messages are produced at speed and consume ideas and writing at a great rate. They cannot afford to repeat themselves in the short term, so they have an appetite for new ideas, new images, new formats, new stories or new versions of old stories. Freelance writers must remind themselves that most work is done by in-house or staff writers who are professionals, who know the media's requirements to the last detail, and who can work fast and efficiently on different sorts of stories. Of all stories published in the *Age* and its ancillary publications, for example, some seventy per cent are produced in-house and thirty per cent are commissioned stories or stories submitted by freelance writers. Of *Age* feature stories, roughly forty per cent are commissioned, but very few unsolicited stories are used, and very few magazines publish more than a small proportion of unsolicited stories and articles.

• There are two main paths into the mass media for writers. The first is via a formal qualification in professional writing, communications, journalism, script-writing, creative writing or similar courses offered by tertiary institutions throughout the country. The other is through experience and practice as a freelance writer. Either method of entry emphasizes individual motivation. In the 1990s, newspapers take on four or five times as many writing graduates as they do school-leavers. Graduates commonly do a one-year cadetship, while school-leavers do three years of cadetship before receiving a 'grading' as a D or C Grade journalist.

• The media are fluid, both in the opportunities they offer to writers and in the readiness with which writers can move from one area of expertise to another. Successful writers in various parts of the media are skilful with words, creative and inventive in generating ideas and finding different ways of telling their stories. Therefore it is not uncommon for an able and motivated graduate from a tertiary writing course to begin her career in newspaper journalism, move to magazine journalism within three or four years, and possibly move again to television news reporting, and then sideways into television news production. It is much rarer, however, for someone to move from advertising to journalism, since journalism tends to be the primary training ground of people in the media.

• In-house employment in newspaper and electronic journalism is, however, generally a young person's career. Journalism is often a stepping-stone to other areas of work that come with mid-life career changes. Then the journalist might well move into public relations, advertising, marketing, stock-broking, financial consultancies or become a ministerial adviser in government.

• Serious and skilful writers are flexible; they will often find themselves willy-nilly involved in many different sorts of writing for the media over the length of their careers. Professor A. D. Hope, the elder statesman of Australian poetry, is an example. Hope has published several books of poetry; he has written scholarly essays and articles, journalistic feature articles, radio scripts, and papers for delivery at conferences, or submission to government bodies; he has been broadcaster and radio presenter, editor, literary judge, literary adviser, academic, and so on. Helen Garner, novelist and short-story writer, has also served as script-writer, editor, journalist, propagandist and activist. David Malouf, novelist, has also been at times poet, librettist, academic, essayist, feature writer, and autobiographer; Blanche D'Alpuget, novelist, has also been biographer, short-story writer, journalist and feature writer; Peter Carey, novelist, has also been short-story writer, advertising executive, copy-writer, and script-writer. So the story runs on.

• There are so many different markets and areas of specialization in the media that no writer can know them all in great depth. Nevertheless, some experience and knowledge of the terminology employed in the media makes it easier to find one's way about it and to understand it.

• There is a great range of standards in the media, and a great difference in the reliability, taste, and presentation of different sorts of journalism.

Different papers are pitched at different readerships, but that alone does not explain the difference in quality. Again there are honest and less honest advertisers, despite the strict codes of behaviour the industry imposes on its accredited members.

- Several agencies affect professional standards in the media. First, there is the law; then there are in-house checks or self-regulation, as well as professional accreditation and monitoring of standards across the industries involved. Each of these mechanisms is designed to maintain high standards.

- How might ownership of the media affect the accuracy and balance of what the media offers to the public in a democracy? What are the dangers of too few major companies owning the media in Australia or of too few book publishers publishing the majority of books in a society? What regulations have the power of law in relationship to ownership of Australian newspapers, radio and television stations, publishing empires and so on? What is the role of the Australian Broadcasting Tribunal in this area? Have you encountered instances of what you consider to be media bias in news and current affairs reporting? How would you describe it? How would you explain it?

- The Australian Journalists' Association (AJA) has developed its own code of ethics for gathering and presenting news, as have journalists in the USA and other countries. The Australian code is stronger in binding members across print media, radio and television than its American counterpart, and has the force of law. It recognizes that a basic principle in journalism is the right of the public to be given information, and makes allowance for special situations where the public interest 'may require activity (on the part of journalists) which would normally be regarded as unethical'.

The AJA Code of Ethics deals with such questions as:
— the public's right to know
— respecting the public's right to privacy where questioning and photography are likely
— the use of deceptive methods to gain information (the undisclosed tape recorder etc.)
— adherence to non-sexist, non-racist language and reporting
— the danger of the journalist's personal interests influencing his reporting
— the danger of the journalist being influenced in her reporting by gifts, considerations or advantages
— the journalist's obligation to be fair and accurate in reporting (that is, in avoiding bias)

- Journalists should also be aware of the dangers of 'stereotyping' in their reporting. Groups with less power in the community—Aborigines, women, migrants, homosexuals, punks, the unemployed, strikers, the elderly—sometimes feel they are overlooked, discriminated against or stereotyped by the media, while the moneyed in the community, especially white middle-class men, often gain media coverage, partly because advertisers wish to woo them, and partly because the status quo is self-perpetuating.

Write

Do some elementary media analysis of your own, to see what trends turn up in media coverage, placement, stereotyping, and types of stories. Start with the print media—capital city daily newspapers and their magazine supplements. Look at your nearest capital city daily, noting the general type of story it runs (local, international, political, editorial, human interest, sport, amusements, regular columnists, interpretative, educational, weather, cartoons, letters, arts, business, etc.). Why are these types of stories run where they are in the paper? Scan a week's issues to see if there is any major variation from the common pattern of placement. Note the special supplements run by the paper on specific days and list their content by subject-matter. Note the placement of advertisements—how is this geared to the type of news run on particular pages?

Now look carefully at a Saturday edition of the same paper. What sort of feature and arts magazine does it run? Write a list of its stories by subject-matter and genre—book review/political biography; feature article on theatre director; regular columnist/state of the national film industry; poem; etc. Again look at the nature of the advertising on each page. Where does it fall in the format? Does its positioning seem calculated to match the story content of the page?

Now look at the paper's Saturday colour magazine. Again do an analysis of its contents, noting regular features (columns; pages of pictures; informative round-ups for public information, etc.). Is there some advertising present in the guise of article or round-up? Make a separate list of the feature articles in the magazine, whether illustrated in colour or black and white or both, their wordage, and the type of situation, people and lifestyles they depict. Make a similar list for six past issues of the magazine and then tabulate similarities, so that trends in the stories that it runs can be seen. Then write a summary of the tone, common content and apparent value systems revealed in the content, and note any bias, stereotyping or discrimination that you can detect in coverage.

The media sometimes have to extract information, in the public interest, from people or organizations who strenuously avoid disclosing it or distort it so that it gives a good rather than bad impression. Journalists can now, under Freedom of Information legislation, check official or government documents and records, but they are sometimes constrained by Australia's quite severe defamation laws, which may prevent them publishing the full story for fear of legal action. Defamation can be a 'libel' (written or published words that defame a person or persons) or a 'slander' (spoken words which might be seen to defame a person, as in the case of libel, by exposing them to hatred, ridicule or contempt, or which might lower their image in the eyes of society). If something is in the public interest, then that may be a defence, but the truth of a claim is no defence in itself. You can still be sued for telling the truth. The journalist's job, is to report accurately and fairly and to avoid judging actions as far as possible.

Much of the media is now international in its content and methods of gathering news: satellites can beam television footage of the latest war across the globe, radio brings news from around the world as it happens, stories filed by journalists for the *New York Times* can be called up at the speed of light to the computer screens of Australian newspapers and sub-edited to fit into an Australian early-morning edition, while video-clips of news from overseas services can be quickly slotted into Australian television news.

Nothing is as stale as yesterday's news. A news outlet must present today's news at the same time as its competitors, or if possible, ahead of them. This puts pressure on writers to be accurate and fast in their writing. As the *Mini Age*, a model newspaper designed to introduce journalism cadets to the Melbourne *Age*, explains on its front page, Frederick Forsyth takes six months to produce one of his sixty thousand word novels, while the staff of the *Age* produce a paper over twice as long in some nineteen hours and they do it daily with new material that will not wait.

At the same time, a considerable part of a newspaper or to a lesser extent of radio or television news, or even of a monthly magazine, is routine work. It involves the publishing or broadcasting of the same type of material daily in a predictable place or time-slot—the weather map, court sittings, the shipping reports, an astrologer's report, the chatty column on page two, the race results, television or radio weather forecasts, cartoon corner, readers' letters, advice to the lovelorn, foreign news reports, entertainments, radio and television programmes, etc.

Even feature material is repeated, but over a longer time-span—the last article on off-shore oil rigs appeared three years ago, so the magazine can now afford another one, with a new angle; someone should write an anti-football article to liven up discussion and interest as the start of the AFL season approaches. Journalists and freelance writers keep a diary of important dates and coming events with such things in view.

Writing for the media is much more market-directed than writing fiction, poetry, plays, or television or radio drama scripts. In the latter, the readership or audience comes to the writer's product. But in advertising, journalism, public relations work, radio or television news and current affairs the writer must target the audience or readership, and adjust writing and tone to capture it.

Many students dream of becoming one of the svelte and famous news journalists and presenters they see regularly on television, but only half a dozen people in each decade become household names as media journalists. Others in the media—thousands of them—never go on camera, but work at bringing information, entertainment, and cultural stimulation to the community in jobs that largely go unacknowledged and yet are of great value. So the writer-in-training who wants to work in the media must have realistic ambitions, must want to tell stories, must like people and the whole of the flux of human life from its heights to its frightening depths, and must be prepared to learn.

Despite all the complexities, standard practices, partial restrictions and constant change and movement in the media, it does exhibit a great inventiveness and wit on the part of those who create its material.

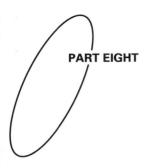

PART EIGHT

Journalism

A newspaper is a variety performance. It can be bought for a few coins, enjoyed at leisure, and carried about in a pocket or under the arm. Much that is great is published in newspapers yet the following day they become, as the old adage says, fish and chip wrappers. I have always warmed to that paradox.

Martin Flanagan

Writing as a journalist

Newspaper journalism, rather than magazine, radio, or television journalism, is generally regarded as the best training ground for the journalist. So let's begin with the hard news story written for a newspaper. From this point, technical terms used in describing media practice will be printed in bold.

You have already mastered a number of ways of telling stories and understand in general the way the media for which you are writing is organized. You are now ready for the no-nonsense race against time that is involved in much day-to-day journalism.

The hard news story

The **hard news story**, wherever it appears, has a simple aim—to bring to a mass audience the main points of a current event that is considered newsworthy.

The **hard news story** and its **intro** are written to a formula. As we unfold the formula, you should practise the skills involved. When you have mastered the elements of the **intro** and the **hard news story** that follows it, you can apply them by writing a news story from news 'fact sheets' (training substitutes for the information that might come to you by phone or through a computer terminal at work).

Here are the general requirements of a **hard news story**.

• The story must be concise.

• It must be written as far as possible using words familiar to a student who has reached Year Ten or thereabouts, but has not gone as far as Year Twelve.

• It must be published quickly before it becomes 'stale news'.

• The information must be written about in descending scale of importance, the first paragraph (the **intro** or **lead**) giving the most important points of the news, so that, even if nothing else were to follow, the public would nevertheless know the nature and importance of the event. Succeeding paragraphs give supporting information and further detail about the main report. This means that if space is short the report can be **cut** or **sub-edited** from the bottom up without losing meaning and value. Each paragraph should therefore be self-contained and linking passages should not be used between paragraphs.

• The **intro** should consist of about twenty-five words or fewer and should be a single sentence.

• The **intro** should be written in the **active voice** and *not* the **passive voice**.

Passive: A twenty-four-year-old man was questioned by police last night . . .

Active: Police last night questioned a twenty-four-year-old man . . .

Passive: The Men's Veteran's Singles Bowls Championship of New South Wales was won yesterday by a man who lost a leg in a tractor accident seventeen years ago.

Active: A man who lost a leg in a tractor accident seventeen years ago yesterday won the Men's Veteran's Singles Bowls Championship of New South Wales.

The last example also rearranges the content of the news so that the most important element comes first in the sentence: the man and his disability are of *first* interest, not the Championship.

• The **intro** should place the piece of information that is of the greatest interest (called **the news**) first in the sentence.

• The intro should present only the facts, since hard news **stories** do not always carry a **by-line** identifying the writer and are thereby deemed to be completely objective or neutral. Look at this example: 'Huge, white-capped seas prevented gallant Air and Sea Safety Service personnel from saving a careless fisherman from the Rip off Point Lonsdale yesterday afternoon, an Air Sea Safety spokesman said this morning . . .' The writing is too descriptive and at least 'white-capped', 'gallant' and 'careless' should go, since each of these has to be proved as fact. 'Huge' would be better rendered as 'rough' or 'very rough', and what about sexist language?

Write

Re-write the **intro** so that it puts the **news** first (has the reporter's emphasis on the rescuers taken attention away from the main news in the person of the drowned fisherman?) and does not exceed twenty-five words. Should part of it be relegated to the next paragraph of the news story? If so, which part should be moved? Can **source identification** (the Rescue Service spokesperson: note 'spokesperson'!) be left to a later paragraph?

News value

This brings us to the central issue of journalism: **news value**. A journalist may disagree with a sub-editor about which element has the greatest **news value** in a story. The argument is not likely to be acrimonious, but the sub-editor will probably prevail, he or she being able to take a more overall view of the news and having more experience in journalism.

Judgements about relative **news value** are the most crucial decisions that journalists make. There are no absolute rules to solve contentious cases. You as journalist must decide what will interest the greatest number of your readers. In fact, each paragraph that follows the **intro** is the result of another decision about **news value**; so are the decisions about which news stories will be **run** in any edition of the paper. It is not unusual for stories to be written but not **run** because they have been displaced by stories of higher **news value** on the day.

One way of testing **newsworthiness** is to imagine the most interesting headline (consistent with responsible reporting) for the information. You can then use the imaginary headline as the basis of the **intro**. In practice, the headline will be decided last, probably by a sub-editor.

• The **intro** should give readers answers to four logical and basic enquiries:

when did it happen?

who did what?

what happened?

where did the event take place?

An example:

who—a syndicate of restaurateurs

when—is (implying the present)

what—negotiating to buy the old salt factory

where—on the edge of Lugubrious Swamp

3 kilometres east of Jonestown

These, of course, are the questions journalists must ask when news gathering, whether they be on the scene or taking down information over the phone.

Write

Hone your news-writing skills by putting the following **intros** into acceptable form. Remember they should be no more than twenty-five words or so.

1 In the Uppity Magistrate's Court yesterday a man was convicted and gaoled for two years for burglary after stolen goods to the value of more than $80 000 were found in a caravan in his backyard.

(This is overweight by ten words, does not lead with **the news**, whether it be the man *or* his hoard and its situation, but has all the elements *who, what, where, when*.)

2 Ms Narcissus, a psychologist, said at a conference on male violence that as a result of a survey conducted by her of Brisbane hotel bouncers she concluded they were the gentlest of human beings.

(Is **the news** up front? Does it answer all the basic questions the reader might ask? Is it in the active voice throughout? What about word-count?)

3 Erected at a cost of $30 000, a fifteen metre anti-smoking sign will be illuminated for the first time tonight by an electrician who constructed it in the garden of his Deepdene home.

4 A survey commissioned by the Anti-Cosmetic Council released yester-

day shows that Australian men used more deodorants last year than Australian women.

5 Mrs Thatch, the Chairman of the Wongly Streetscape Committee, said last night that sunbathing on nature-strips by residents of the Shire would be officially forbidden.

6 A man charged with the killing of twenty cats in the Domain Gardens in February said in the Uppity Magistrate's Court that he loved all animals and was seeking a better life for them.

7 Forty ferry passengers were delayed halfway across Westernport Bay yesterday when an engineer's kitten refused to emerge from a half-closed airlock in the engine-room, causing the ferry's engines to be shut down.

(Apart from its other faults, does this **intro** indicate that the journalist has asked all the right questions on behalf of the interested reader?)

8 The Fulfilment Party will make a clean sweep of the next election because of the Government's complete failure to carry the State forward, the Federal leader of the Fulfilment Party, Ms Tryon, said today in Paltrey, South Australia.

(Ah, difficulties! This one raises the question of how the journalist should maintain a neutral position and avoid implying that Ms Tryon's remark is a statement of fact. It may turn out to be a fact, but for now it is Ms Tryon's opinion. Therefore, although it meets the other tests of a good **intro**, in this case there must be no doubt about whose words these are. The **intro** should begin with Ms Tryon's name—'Ms Tryon, the Federal leader of the Fulfilment Party, claimed in Paltrey, South Australia, last night that the Fulfilment Party would make a clean sweep . . .' The journalist's neutrality should not be left in doubt where controversial statements are being dealt with.)

As you will have gathered, journalism emphasizes conciseness and economy of language. Loose wording leads to trouble: wordiness cuts out other news. The following rules of thumb are a useful guide, and should be used where possible.

• Avoid clichés—'the towering inferno blazed against the night sky . . .'
• Delete all that is not strictly relevant and does not contribute directly to the story. Delete repetition, doubtful or libellous statements.
• Avoid adjectives and adjectival clauses, adverbs and adverbial clauses.
• Choose simple words rather than technical terminology, bureaucratic jargon and outdated words or phrases. Keep close to common speech.
• Avoid interpolative phrases that come between subject and verb—'The legislation, as yet undrafted, will be prepared for the next sitting . . .'
• Break down long sentences into shorter ones.

- Use a single word rather than a phrase—'because' in place of 'due to the fact that'.
- Begin sentences with their subjects, not with a supporting clause—'The rowers were showing the benefits of coaching, but were outclassed' rather than, 'Although they were outclassed, the rowers were showing the benefits of coaching . . .'
- Avoid negative phrases where positive ones are possible. 'It was feasible' rather than 'it was not unfeasible . . .'
- Type one paragraph per page, using only one side of the paper.

Longer stories

There are many different sorts of newspapers: morning and evening papers in capital cities, and dailies in provincial cities which carry a range of supplements on weekdays and which publish Saturday editions heavy with advertising and deeply-researched background reading on finance, the arts, tourism, food and wine, social issues, international affairs, new technology and employment. There are capital city evening papers designed for home-bound workers on the trains and trams and people sitting down after dinner to read in an armchair in front of the television. There are provincial city morning dailies, with more moderate Saturday editions. There are local smaller town newspapers appearing twice weekly, and suburban newspapers in the capital cities, appearing perhaps once or twice weekly. All of these newspapers carry advertising geared to their specialized area, publication rate and time, perceived readership, and their competition. Each of these factors influences the types of stories they run and how they handle them.

Imagine now that you are a journalist for a newspaper in Port Chalice, a provincial coastal city in Australia, large enough to support an evening daily in two editions. The paper, called the *Chalice City Mercury*, goes out to a population of over one and a half million people, spread through a series of radiating suburbs served by a train, bus and tram public transport system. The industrial and working-class suburbs of the city lie generally to the north of the Tract River, which flows through Port Chalice, while the wealthier, middle-class and white-collar suburbs follow the coastline to the south of the city, interesting to tourists on a national and international level for its rugged cliffs, interspersed with sweeping surf-beaches.

You come across a story that begins small and grows larger, changing in its **news value** as it unfolds and therefore requiring different treatments in the *Chalice City Mercury's* two editions. It becomes what journalists call a **running story**. Such stories, because they develop and take on greater drama, are valuable for evening papers with more than one edition and, of course, for evening hourly news bulletins on radio, and later for the evening television news and its late-night up-dates. The deadline for the first edition of the *Chalice City Mercury* is 12 noon; the papers go on sale on the streets at 2 pm. The second edition deadline is 2.30 pm, for sales on the streets from 4.15 pm and for home deliveries. It is January, the summer holiday season, and Port Chalice has been in the grip of a heatwave for the preceding three days.

From about 10 am on Wednesday, Clarke Dent, an outside reporter covering the beach resorts, begins to phone through information to you at your computer terminal. In fact, he dictates a narrative to you. You give his information the story label 'Car break'. Your notes read like this.

Car break 1

English family on holiday loses all money and credit cards in car break-in.

Family from Bournemouth, UK. Ted and Mary Greenhouse, both in their fifties; 2 teenage daughters, Meryl 15, and Hadley 18; Mrs Greenhouse senior, 72.

Minibus, bought specially for round-Australia trip, broken into while visitors in National Parks office, 400 m away in scrub, at Pure Point lookout and nature reserve on south coast, 30 mins drive from the city— $2000 cash, hidden behind rear seat, credit cards, wallet and handbags containing another $1000, and video camera stolen. Minibus locked, but windows partially down because of early heat. Time of break-in roughly 9.45 am.

Car break 2

Family only away from car for 10 mins. Ted Greenhouse: felt as though they had been watched leaving the car; felt someone had seen them stow money in storage well behind rear seat, since break-in quick and thieves had gone 'straight to it'.

Ted and Mary Greenhouse had sold small home in Bournemouth, paid out mortgage, and used balance to finance minibus trip overland to Australia. Sold original vehicle and bought another minibus for round-Australia trip. Had limited amount of money in travellers' cheques; remaining cash was to pay for accommodation round Australia.

Ted G.: This trip was everything for family. Knew it was last chance for Mum to come with us on driving and camping safari like this. Knew was the best time for the girls to have the experience. Hadley already working and Meryl preparing for serious years of secondary education. Family on the road nearly eight months now, through France, Portugal, Spain, Italy, Middle East and India. From Calcutta took ship to Perth and started round Australia clockwise from there.

Knew we were taking a risk storing so much cash in the bus, but we weren't geared into Aust. banking system. Never liked using 'the plastic' (credit cards), even though we had some, and were so constantly on the move. Thought we would always be able to keep an eye on the money. Travelled all that way overland, been held up at border points, had to make convoy with other travellers in Middle East for safety from bandits. Through all that and 6000 km driving in Aust. never had trouble like this. Don't know what we do now. Suppose we get what we can for the bus and ask family in Britain to send remainder of air fare home.

Mary G.: We have housebreakings in Bournemouth, but not so many car-breakings. Have warm days in Bournemouth summer, but nothing like this heat. Day after day, wearing us down. Now we're hot, exhausted, penniless, in a strange country. Nowhere to stay, no money for fuel. It makes you feel very vulnerable.

Mrs G. Senior is a remarkably fit 72-year old. Always wanted to come to Aust., British Army nurse in Singapore, before and during WW2. Treated Aust. soldiers at Fall of Singapore, later in Japanese prison camp in Burma, where some Aust. artillerymen imprisoned.

Mrs G. Senior: I love Australians. Very friendly people. Remember the humour of those gunners, even though they were skeletons in the prison camp. Half didn't last out the war. Japanese worked them to death. Loved being in Aust., meeting Australians. Now feel as though I've been slapped in the face. Have lost all our resources after going so well. Really nothing to do with Aust., of course, but has turned the trip sour.

Greenhouses had planned to drive to Perth, where they landed five months ago, before returning to UK.

Car break 3

Evidence of Enrico Pertucci, 42, who runs drink and hamburger caravan on boundary of National Park at Pure Point look-out. Saw Greenhouse bus arrive (Union Jack on aerial) and family walk off through scrub to go to National Parks display.

Pertucci: Lot of people moving about early in summer weather, especially during heatwave; it gets so hot in middle of day and afternoon. Cars shuttling in and out of Pure Point car-park all day.

Saw 3 people—2 men, one dark, one sandy-haired, in twenties and blonde woman early twenties—sitting drinking in 1970s dark red Valiant sedan near Greenhouse bus. They later walked past Greenhouse minibus, but Pertucci lost sight of them behind tourist coach. Valiant had one door sprayed grey; 3 people from Valiant drinking from stubbies as they walked down the car-park.

Pertucci: You note these things if you're serving the public here all day. You're on the look-out for trouble-makers, drinkers, wild drivers, car-loads of toughs. You keep an eye on them if you can. One of the blokes was carrying an old sports bag over his shoulder.

Constable J. Jackson of Sally Bay police, 15 km south of Pure Point, on scene after travellers phoned police on behalf of Greenhouses.

Constable J.: Common problem in summer. Gangs from northern

suburbs well organized and equipped to 'do over' coastal car-parks. Daylight saving gives them long day to operate. Just come from scene of another breaking (at approx. 10.10 am) at Witch's Cauldron look-out. Range Rover broken into. Video camera, credit cards and cash stolen. Car door jemmied. Young Albury couple owners. Couple saw red old-model Valiant parked at side of tourist access road when they drove out to highway to report to police. Valiant not found. Constable J. investigating.

This is as much information as you have by mid-morning. If this is to be a story for the first edition of the *Chalice City Mercury* then you have to write it from these dictated notes. The time is approaching 10.40 am and the deadline for the first edition is noon, so you must begin putting it together for the sub-editors.

First, some questions. What sort of story should you write? Where is **the news** in it? Is a car-breaking of itself a significant enough event to be treated as a **hard news story** in a city of more than a million people? Your editor and the sub-editors will have some opinions about that. Does **the news** in this story lie somewhere else? Many of your readers will be on holiday themselves and reading the *Chalice City Mercury* in their easy chairs or on the beaches. Is the story of the Greenhouse family something readers will identify with? Has the story some public service elements to it—dangers of leaving cars unattended with windows down and containing valuables, especially during the holiday season, etc?

Human interest stories

You decide that the story is unlikely to work as a **hard news story** and opt for a **human interest (HI)** piece that centres round the Greenhouse family and their now tenuous position as a result of the robbery.

Since you are writing this as a **human interest** story you can, if you want, break away from the standard **intro** we have been practising as a **lead** to a **hard news story**. Look back over the narrative notes dictated over the phone and consider the tone of the information from and about the Greenhouse family. Should you open with one of the direct speech statements by Ted or Mary Greenhouse, and then follow it with a sentence akin to a **hard news intro** that puts the direct quotation in context? Is Mrs Greenhouse Senior more interesting as an opening, given her life story and her interest in Australians? Look through several copies of capital city daily newspapers to see what sort of **human interest stories** they run and the variety of ways they open. They are likely to occur on page 1, and then page 3 and perhaps in the later pages of the paper beyond the international and national news and the editorial and feature pages. They are often set across four or more columns and don't run as deep down the page as hard news items. They frequently carry a photograph.

In a **human interest story** you need to develop one main angle (secondary angles may also be developed). Such stories are generally not structured in strict descending order of **newsworthiness** as **hard news stories** are. They may not lend themselves to sub-editing from the bottom up. You might end with another direct quotation that returns to the angle of the story or that asks a rhetorical question and leaves the reader thinking. What possible 'angles' are there to this story? The irony of the Greenhouses' situation? So near and yet so far? All that effort and initiative—and for this? Australians devalued? A cautionary tale?

Write

Write the story in the 320 words the editor has asked for. 'Give me 20 centimetres on Car Break', she says, meaning 20 cm depth of a 12 pica newspaper column, the rough equivalent of 320 words, 'and I'll see if we can get a pic of the Greenhouses. I can give it a bit of space on page 3. It looks as though it'll be a light news day.' The word limit means that you must condense, summarize, or perhaps ignore altogether some of the information that has come in. If art involves selection then so does journalism!

Allow yourself one hour to finish the piece. Newspaper editions wait for no one. You could also add your suggestion for a five-word headline, although the sub-editor will ultimately decide that. Don't forget the elements of the formula we discussed in writing **intros** and basic news reports. Don't forget, one paragraph only per page.

The running story

It is now 12.12 pm in the early afternoon of the day of the theft of the Greenhouse family's savings and valuables. You have filed your story for the first edition of the *Chalice City Mercury*. Clark Dent is on the line with further information from the south coast resorts. You compile further facts sheets. This is now a very different story: this, in journalistic parlance, is a **new lead**.

Replace car break 1

Police constable shot dead at Pure Point on the south coast late this morning. Time of shooting approx. 11.25 am in front car-park at Pure Point look-out.

Assailants thought to be 3 people—2 men and a woman—driving a dark red Valiant and suspected of being involved in car-breakings, including that of Greenhouse family's minibus, at Pure Point and the Witch's Cauldron earlier in the morning.

Killed was Constable Jervis Jackson, (age unknown: in his 20s), of Sally Bay Police Station. Constable J. had been following up the earlier car breakings in the area; had suggested local groups that might help Greenhouse family.

Information of Mr Enrico Bertucci (correction, Bertucci, *not* Pertucci) who was working drink and hamburger caravan alone at 11 am at Pure Point car-park (just outside boundary of National Park). His son had driven to Downwater for supplies of soft drink.

Constable J. took details from Greenhouse family, and later talked to other police cars by radio for 5 mins. Came to caravan for cool drink. Said he was going to 'do the rounds' and check Platter Beach. Left at about 10.45 am.

11.20 am—red Valiant returned, driving fast, parked halfway along the car-park. Constable J. in police car followed them in. Not using siren (3 or 4 other cars in car-park, owners absent at National Parks office and display). 2 men got out of Valiant and began to walk towards the back car-park. Constable J. challenged them. They seemed to wait for him.

Mr Bertucci (60 m away) heard first shot, but didn't see it. Saw darker of the 2 men fire a second shot at Constable J. who was leaning for support on bonnet of parked car. Constable J. fell to ground.

Mr Bertucci: They didn't seem in a hurry to get away. They just moved in slow motion. I couldn't believe it. The other man (sandy hair) called out something like, 'Go down, Pig! Go Down Pig! as they walked away from Constable J. 'writhing on the ground'.

Darker man turned back, walked up to Const. J., leaned down, extended arm, shot Const. J. in side of head, then walked away to car. Other sandy-headed man already running to Valiant. Blonde woman (early 20s) in Valiant. They drove fast past hamburger caravan and out towards highway.

Bertucci ran to Const. J.—'seemed to be dead: *had* to be dead'. Ran 400 m to National Parks office, phoned police, ambulance. Dr Rockland, visiting Nat. Parks display, returned to Const. J., pronounced dead 11.30 am. More to come.

You can't wait for the 'more to come'. You have to write this story now, knowing that more detail will change it, but not its basic news. It is already nearly 12.45 pm. The editor would like further information on Constable J. both from the police and from the Sally Bay community. This will almost certainly make a separate background story to the shooting, but someone else in the office may have to write it.

Write

Write your **hard news story**, checking it as you go, and again when it is completed, against the requirements of the formula for **intros**. You can check later on how many words you'll be allowed. The task is to get as much down in descending order of news value as you can, and let editorial decisions cut the piece to size. This is now a front-page story that will spill over to page 3. You have just over an hour to write and file it for the second edition.

There is no argument about what your **intro** will contain, but think about how you will preserve news value in the rest of the story, while not missing the graphic detail in Bertucci's information. A photographer is racing to Pure Point and will probably get pictures of the scene and Bertucci and his hamburger caravan. Bertucci is no hero, but is, presumably, a reliable witness. His reactions to the shooting are the most immediate you have and reflect the impact violence has on the ordinary person.

If you were the editor, or Clark Dent, the journalist on the spot, what other 'angles' would you be pursuing? What information might you ask Dent to pursue when he next rings in? Consider who is involved— Bertucci; other tourists; the Greenhouses and their impressions of Constable J.; the police, who will be descending in force on the area in the hope of apprehending the killers; the Sally Bay community who knew Constable J. well in his one-person police station; etc.

If you were writing this story for radio or television, you would go through the same basic news decisions, writing of **intros** and follow-up, and arrangement of material in descending order of news value. The story might also change as it develops, in much the same way as it does in print, being broadcast in different forms in successive bulletins.

Electronic news

The electronic media process and bring to the public the same types of news items, the same stories, that appear in newspapers, but the writing of news for sound in radio and for sound and pictures in television has to be different. Print news writes for the eye, radio and television news write for the ear.

• A listener or viewer must get all the news in the first attempt; they cannot reread as they can in a newspaper.

• The news-reader dictates the pace of the news on electronic media, not the audience's varying ability to comprehend.

• Radio news stories must be briefer and therefore more concise than those for newspapers. The news broadcast may be fifteen minutes long at key times of the day, but is often only five minutes long on the hour. At a news-reader's pace of some sixteen to eighteen lines of copy per minute, a five-line story will take fifteen to twenty seconds of air time. Six or seven five-line items are all that can be handled in a two minute news broadcast. If items run to more than ten lines of copy then very few can be fitted in. Much radio news is written in items of no more than six lines, with simple, easily understood wording and no complex or technical terminology.

• Valuable as it is to read newspaper and magazine copy aloud to test its flow, it is *vital* to read copy aloud as a trial for radio or television.

• In comparison with a newspaper lead, the **intro** for a radio story is often only the first few words, given that the whole story is only five lines long.

• In radio stories the source is often quoted in the first words: 'Weather experts around the world say . . .', thus the listener is alerted to what is likely to follow and absorbs it more easily.

• News-readers rarely read direct quotes in radio news, although there may be a short **grab** from the *actual* speaker of the words recorded on a reporter's tape recorder. Direct quotes are more common in television news, where they may be accompanied visually by print-over points. Television, like radio, also uses **grabs** from a TV camera's microphone or a reporter's tape recorder.

• Negatives must be written to be clearly *heard*: 'is *not*' rather than 'isn't'; 'isn't' and 'aren't' can be misheard as affirmatives.

• Names merit particular care, the writer providing a phonetic pronunciation key in brackets after names that are difficult to pronounce.

• Radio and television news changes in importance hourly: an item may be scaled down from five lines to two as the day progresses, or be dropped from broadcasts altogether after one or two airings as other stronger items replace it.

• Punctuation and numbers are handled differently in writing for the news-reader for ease of reading, and for emphasis and clarity: '20 dollars' for ease of reading, rather than $20; 'John Bloggs, who is 33, left. . .', rather than the newspaper version of 'John Bloggs, 33, left. . .'.

• Quite long identification detail may come before the name of the item's subject in electronic news writing: 'Former State Aboriginal Affairs Director, Janice Jackson . . .' but long job descriptions and titles generally follow the name.

• Ages often precede names: '42-year-old Samuel Wilberforce. . .' Titles are often written out in full for electronic news: 'Brigadier General Thomas Quack'.

• Radio and television reports sometimes mix tenses in a way that is considered unacceptable in newspapers—'The spokesperson for the Ministry *said* that the anti-corrosion pellets *are* new to the Australian market', rather than 'The spokesperson for the Ministry *said* that the anti-corrosion pellets *were* new to the Australian Market'.

Following is some radio news copy as it has gone to air. The copy exemplifies the economy and clarity of wording emphasized above.

19
2 2cc

```
3AW- hudson  -exadels-Wed Jun 26 12:02 Ct:19  Du:0.12Tot: 0.35:fleming.1200
=============================================================================
```
O/NITE

```
    JANE FLEMMING is confident she'll still make it to the

    BARCELONA OLYMPIC GAMES, despite suffering a broken bone in her

    foot.


    The champion AUSTRALIAN athlete has ruled out any hope of

    competing in the TOKYO world championships in AUGUST, after

    injuring her foot last week in EUROPE.


    But FLEMMING says BARCELONA is still firmly on her agenda.


    CART: 19

    DUR: 0.12

    OUTCUE:one then
```

Figure 2: A piece of radio news copy from Radio 3AW in Melbourne.

Television news

A television evening news bulletin is a modern daily miracle! It is complicated to prepare because of the split-second timing necessary to match words and pictures, to say nothing of the quick processing and editing of news footage that reaches studios in the two hours before a bulletin. Television news must be up to the minute. A reporter's item on a flood is often edited together from the flood pictures taken in the field and flown in earlier in the afternoon, together with file footage of a previous flood and statements about flood control. Then the news-reader's voice-over words are written and the whole is edited on to tape before it is broadcast. If a story is late but important it may be completed with only a couple of minutes to spare before the bulletin goes to air.

A television news script is therefore arranged with the visuals on the left side of the layout and the accompanying words on the right for clarity.

Write

You can, within reason and with discretion, 'make' your own **hard news stories**.

1 Seek permission to attend a Council Meeting in your district and report its decisions for a local paper.

2 Report a sports contest, but remember that if it is not your sport you may have to do a considerable amount of homework beforehand about teams and their performance, individuals and opponents.

While you are at the contest, keep an eye out for a 'good news' human interest piece that you could write and file to help a local or metropolitan daily columnist.

3 Attend a magistrate's or more elevated court and report the cases. Use daily newspaper court reports as models.

4 Write a 'round-up' piece that is of interest to readers of a metropolitan or local paper—an entertainment guide for the coming three days; a survey of organic food outlets; a survey of the changing nature of book-shops in the city centre and inner suburbs.

5 Attend an official opening—of a bridge, a building, a gallery, a res-taurant—and report it.

6 Attend a conference or convention or public meeting and report it.

7 Attend a public demonstration; report it as a **hard news story** and then as a **colour piece** (an article, generally carrying a writer's by-line, which concentrates on the human drama and atmosphere of the event).

8 Make arrangements to secure the text of a political or public speech and write a report of it, suiting its length to the length of the speech and its relative news value, but writing at least nine hundred words.

Writing features

The British newspaper magnate, Lord Northcliffe, once observed: 'It is hard news that catches readers. Features hold them.'

We speak of **features** or feature articles in newspapers. We also often call them **human interest stories**. They generally appear in the middle pages of the paper (the **feature pages**), they can be short or quite long, they carry a **by-line** (the journalist's name) and often a description of the journalist's position on the newspaper—'Chief Environmental Correspondent'.

Magazines have an insatiable appetite for feature articles, and run them with illustrations, photographs by in-house photographers, by the author of the feature or by a commissioned photographer.

Radio features are generally half-hour programmes dealing with a variety of subjects similar to those in magazine or newspaper features, but in the case of radio, features rely heavily on a narrator's voice and on other voices and sounds recorded in interview or in the field.

Television documentaries are the equivalent of features on radio or in print. They are generally half-hour episodes of a series, or a one-off.

Some features are best described as **news features**. One example is the basic news story, later treated as a feature because of its fascination, its humour, its pathos, or irony. It is a **human interest story**, capitalizing on the fact that readers are always interested in what happens to other people.

Another type is the piece written for one of the special supplements that appear in the capital city dailies on certain days every week—a story on life-style, housing, decorating, gardening, entertaining, child-raising, the environment.

A further type is the very short, intriguing paragraph (**par**) or **pars** that the columnist writes for a daily column from stories phoned in by readers or suggested by colleagues—the man whose car developed a mind of its own when left out of gear in the hilly suburb of Blank; the tattooist who got the message embarrassingly wrong; the ex-juvenile offender who protects an elderly man from racist thugs on a commuter train while other travellers bury their noses in newspapers; or a strange court case and ruling.

Yet another type is the specialist background article about finance, politics or public affairs in the features, business, or current affairs sections of a newspaper or magazine. Other pieces, of two thousand words or so, appear in magazines with a specialist readership—on diving in Piccaninny Ponds; on the Bathurst motor circuit; on the Greening of Australia.

Features in print lend themselves to the new or freelance writer, provided they are adept at assessing markets and in cultivating a working relationship with particular editors.

Features demand research and research skills. They often require interviews and therefore demand interviewing skills. Sometimes specialist knowledge of markets is required, and canny assessment of the level of expertise of the readership, its age and experience. Features often require visual illustration, therefore, the writer who can take photographs for publication has an advantage.

Most of these points apply also to the making of radio, television and film features or documentaries. You will realize that it is much more difficult for the freelance or new writer to write for radio, television or film documentaries, and visuals are, of course, the responsibility of experts in these media.

The writing of features requires a special sensibility for both story and readership, a fascination with what human beings do and with the constant succession of events in a society. It also requires certain skills in the way information is revealed and in sentence and paragraph structure and rhythm. As we discovered in the writing of prose fiction and poetry, there is no single golden rule that guarantees success, but there are better rather than worse ways to work and write.

Some writers have a nose for the sort of story that will become a feature story. Again, like most short stories in fiction, each feature has one basic angle or point of fascination. The ability to sniff out a story's possibilities comes from constant curiosity and practice in observation. Ernest Hemingway, journalist, short-story writer and novelist, said: 'If a writer stops observing he is finished.'

Here's an example. Living and writing on the western coast of Victoria, I trod down some remarkable fishermen's cut into a sixty-metre cliff. Then, nose for a feature story already quivering, I heard that one of the men who had dug those steps almost sixty years before was still living in the Western District. Would he talk about the making of the Deany Steps? What, from his vantage point of ninety-three years, could he say about his own life on the coast? I needed no further convincing.

There was the physical beauty and awe of the coast; the story of two men working on the cliffs with pick and shovel and wheelbarrow, the sub-plot of a life begun there in 1891, a life that had seen shipwreck, forest clearing, war, country sport, hardship, joy in simple pleasures. I rang the editor of a magazine with a market-niche for these elements of Australian social history. Yes, she would like to consider the article, length perhaps two thousand five hundred words, and yes, photographs would be very important. I took notebook, camera, tape recorder; I researched the story, interviewed my subject and others, checked facts, took photographs, wrote the story, submitted it with numerous photographs. It was accepted, published, paid for.

Sometimes a story, researched and published as an academic article, can be told in other ways for a more general readership; sometimes a general feature article written for a magazine is so fascinating it lures one on to deeper research.

Write

Make a list of the subjects that you are eager to research and write about. Do you have access to research materials and contacts? Can you 'place' the feature with an editor? In many cases feature writing has direct links to public relations. Many organizations can provide you with information and photographs which will make interesting reading if you write the story to suit a particular market.

The mechanics of a feature

There is no one recipe for a feature, but broadly it depends on:

- an interesting opening that draws the reader into the subject-matter and atmosphere of the story
- a following passage that provides some more specific information, and an indication of the point-of-view of the story, so that the reader knows its basic subject and is interested in where it will tend
- a series of alternations of story, atmosphere, anecdote and direct-speech quotation on the one hand and facts and statistics on the other,

until the story's main points have been made; this is part of the rhythm of the telling—the point of attention changes from sub-topic to sub-topic, all the while serving the story's overall point

• an ending that is in keeping with the direction and main points of the story, that perhaps leaves someone's words ringing in the reader's ears or a question hanging in the air.

Openings

Feature openings repay careful writing and rewriting, since the story's attraction depends on creating in the reader a favourable first impression.

Here is an opening to an article-cum-book chapter about Joseph Furphy, the nineteenth century Australian novelist, author of *Such is life*. Note how repetition, quotations and detail are used, how it allows us to hear voices, how it builds towards Furphy's name through detail that begins to picture him and his habits, attitudes, passions. Everything moves towards the pinnacle of the final sentence, which is to become the main theme of the article. Think of the research that lies behind the detail in the words.

He was a man with green fingers, as we say—he grew moss roses, tree ferns, fuschias. He worked in his garden by moonlight after a day's farm work at Corop. A man not given to hoarding either money or time. An hospitable man—'He was not content to give a meal to the tramp at the door', his son recalled. 'He would invite him in and waste a whole Sunday in talking to him or anyone.' A big man—'. . . his bronzed face, his tall, strongly-built figure and the leisurely intonation of his voice were not the salients of the city dweller.' Norman Lindsay wrote of him. A man self-educated, and with a passion for reading and knowledge—half bushman and half bookworm' is how he described himself. 'A lean, shrewd, proud, modest, kindly man', said A. G. Stephens of the *Bulletin*. A man who had been goldminer, labourer, travelling demonstrator of farm machinery, foundry hand, farmer, bullock-driver. A father of two sons and a daughter—and of three children who did not survive infancy. A dour student and lover of his own country. Miles Franklin, his friend and correspondent, tells us that in moments of frustration he would mutter, 'Never mind: I still have Australia.' A man who never lost the fondness for the Bible and for Shakespeare that his mother had instilled in him, who travelled the Riverina as a bullock-driver with a small edition of Shakespeare's plays in his pocket. A man for whom the Sermon on the Mount was a pointer towards socialism. This was Joseph Furphy, the author of *Such is life*, one of the most important Australian novels yet written.

This opening is pitched at an audience of serious readers first as a journal article for a literary magazine and then as a chapter for a book on Australia's major writers. It is a bit long for a glossy magazine article or a newspaper feature.

Here is an opening for an article in a glossy magazine that concentrates on Australian subject matter with a travel, geography and history bias. Note the differences in paragraphing, the simpler sentence structure and vocabulary.

It's worth hearing a Grampians man curling his tongue round a tale of the early days.

'Tough? Too right they were tough,' says Hubie Hines, forest foreman, stopping work on the stump, leaning on his shovel. 'We put most of the first roads in with only a Trewhalla Jack and winches to handle the trees.'

Below him in the gully a bulldozer bellows its strain into the bush, trees flailing down in front of it. Its driver is anonymous in cap and protective earmuffs. By this afternoon the forestry men will be blasting out the last stumps and rocks. This is the Mount Thackeray road inching forward along the Victoria Range.

'Old man Jensen,' says Hubie. 'Have you heard of him? This was when the Grampians were hardly roaded at all. Jensen was a Grampians pioneer, you might say. Lived at the southern end of the Victoria Valley.

'One day he decided he'd walk up the valley and pay a visit to the forestry blokes at the Lodge. Took his fourteen-year-old grandson with him. They started early. Warm day. Didn't reach the Lodge till late in the afternoon, and blow me down if the boy didn't collapse on the floor. Started retching. Old man Jensen scratched his head; just couldn't work it out.'

' "Got me beat," he said. "The beggar hasn't had anything to eat since six this morning. He can't have anything to bring up. What's wrong with him?" '

'Of course,' says Hubie, 'They'd only been walking all day, that's all. Come right up from Mirranatwa Gap. More than fifteen miles, no lunch, no rest. The kid was exhausted!' . . .

Or there was the city newspaper reporter at the Grampians bushfire, eagerly questioning the firefighters and taking notes. He'd never seen a crown fire before. Suddenly he stopped, listened.

'Hey, where's the train?' he asked. 'I can hear a train.'

'That's no train, mate,' said a laconic firefighter. 'That's the fire coming.' That was the last they saw of the reporter.

There's some of the essence of the Grampians in those stories. They're old and tough. That's part of their interest, even of their beauty. Whatever way you approach them, they're as dramatic today as when the explorer

Major Mitchell discovered them for Europeans in 1836.

The article then goes on to establish where the Grampians (Gariwerd) are in Victoria, since the magazine for which it was written has an Australia-wide readership not necessarily familiar with individual regions. The opening and the following detail of geographical location both serve to combine with the lead photograph of the ranges taken from a high vantage point that shows their configuration in valleys and mountain spines. It is placed beside the opening and beneath the story's title. Then come details of the mountains' geological age. At that point the story changes gear to put the reader in the position of a tourist, explaining what walks and drives the ranges offer, focussing eventually on the history of nearby pastoral stations, early contact between settlers and Aborigines, and the role of recreational forestry in making peak and valley, Aboriginal cave sites, waterfalls and wildlife accessible to visitors. The story concludes with emphasis on the wilderness remaining in the Grampians, the story of the Grampians' puma, the dangers of the terrain for the unwary, and goes out with a local naturalist's voice celebrating the mountains. The direct quotation describes the lonely beauty of peregrine falcons and eagles as they soar on the thermals generated by the precipices of Mount William and then plummet towards the plains below.

The article carried four photographs, chosen from some twenty colour transparencies and fifteen black and white glossy prints. It involved interviews with seven people, as well as telephone calls to check facts and gain further information from official sources.

Write

Write a feature article of your own. Give some thought first to subjects which you can research and write about with enthusiasm, and about which you have *some* knowledge. Make sure you can reach 'contacts' who have more extensive information.

There are other ways to structure a feature, of course, apart from the ones covered here. For advanced variants, look at some of the writing of New Journalists such as Tom Wolfe, Hunter S. Thompson, and Truman Capote. Study the style and organization of the sorts of stories that appear in, say, the *Age Good weekend*, the *Australian magazine*, *National geographic*, *Geo: Australasia's geographical magazine*, or *Rolling stone* among many others.

Now, having decided on a subject, go to the library or a tolerant newsagent's and spend a half-hour browsing among the magazines on the racks. Find a magazine that might be receptive to the article you intend to write. Look at the length, the style, the illustration of its stories. Who is the editor? What rates of payment are stated on the magazine's title or imprint page? What advice is there, if any, about submission of manuscripts? Skim through some recent back issues of the magazine at a library to learn more about the range of work it publishes and to make sure that neither your subject, nor something akin to it, has been dealt with recently.

On this first occasion, research and write the article as if for this magazine and submit it, taking care to follow the steps for submission of manuscripts suggested in Part Three of this book. Ask for any comments the editor has time to offer. If these comments are encouraging, write another feature for another market, again studying the new outlet as before. This time, before you write the article, send a query letter to the editor to whom you hope to submit it.

Make your query letter brief and to the point—no more than a page—but include enough information for the editor to make an interim judgement about whether your article would fit the tone and direction of the magazine or newspaper and whether they might like to consider your work for publication. Clearly indicate whether you are planning to offer illustrations also, and of what type. Give an idea of the article's planned length, its central idea, its projected title, a little of the factual detail and anecdote you will include that make it different from run-of-the-mill articles on that or similar subjects. State when you will be able to submit it, and explain your own background, publications experience and qualifications to write it. Enclose a stamped, self-addressed envelope.

Commissions

When you can show a folio of published work in reputable magazines or newspapers, editors might begin to commission stories from you. If so, make sure you know the brief exactly—length of article? to appear when? payment? to be illustrated how? in any particular style? with any particular emphasis? what expenses offered, if any? what rights required by the commissioning editor? etc.

The more flexible you can be, within reason, the more commissions you are likely to get, provided you can meet deadlines and stick to a brief. If you submit late, or write too much, you are likely to gain a poor reputation editorially, because the editor, with expensive typesetting and printing deadlines to meet, may not be able to afford the time to reduce an over-long article, especially when it is not written to be edited from the bottom up.

Although flexibility in handling different subjects is desirable in the feature writer, it is sensible to develop two or three specializations in the subject areas in which you commonly write. Freelance writers, who aim to produce two or three features each week, develop such specializations so that editors know their expertise and can commission them, and so that one specialization can be played off against another for variety of work and interest for the writer.

Write

1 Print: Look back at the suggestions for making your own **hard news stories** and use them to practise writing features. Make sure that you write at least one feature based on a personality interview, and one on a controversial issue where opinions differ markedly among the interested parties.

2 Radio: Try writing a script for a recorded voice piece for radio and 'produce' it in simple form on tape.

• First, practise speaking and reading into the microphone of the tape recorder that you intend to use. Practise conveying information as if you are having a conversation with the listener—not too fast, not too deliberate. Write brief pieces of script and practise speaking them. Replay your pieces and listen to how they *sound*, rather than how they read. Mark your script for places where emphasis is needed, where longer than the normal pauses are important.

• Choose a specific place that you can write about with some knowledge and which will be interesting to your listening radio audience. Go there and research it thoroughly, perhaps setting up chances for brief interviews on a second visit.

• Write a narrator's script timed to take six minutes of a ten-minute broadcast voice piece, the remainder to be taken up with sounds and brief interview excerpts. Make your script structure quite definite in its order, so that its main questions, its main topics and subdivisions determine what sounds you record and when you record them, the questions you ask in interviews and when you ask them, and the order in which you do your interviews. The order in which the material goes on to the tape is the order of the finished feature, since this is an amateur mock-up to give you some idea of what is involved in producing a sound feature. A professional would be able to change the order of segments by editing, but in this exercise, you *cannot* edit—unless, of course, you are experienced in radio production work and have access to the necessary equipment. The same provisos apply to the use of television and video below.

• Using your knowledge of how life proceeds at the place you have researched, set out the *order* of segments in your script. For example:

  • sound of bird noises in gully
  • narrator's voice reading script opening, speaking of this as precious environment, giving facts of surviving bellbird numbers and area of habitat, and concluding with the statement that this small habitat is threatened by the advance of heavy traffic.
  • sounds of constant traffic on uphill pinch against sounds of bellbirds

- The answer only of a local environmentalist/bird photographer to your question (unrecorded) about this threat, followed by a further couple of questions and answers.

and so on . . .

Build into your questioning statements that identify your interviewee and her particular area of expertise; plan to draw out the personal reactions and anecdotes that you established in your research visit.

- When you have done some dry runs, reading your narration into the microphone, perhaps interpolating some sounds and practice questions, then go to the site and alert the people whose voices and expert opinions you are seeking. Explain the order of the script and what you are going to ask them in general terms. You will need to check the sites of the actuality sounds you need (bellbird calls; heavy traffic) to be sure there are no unforeseen factors that will make it difficult to record them within the next few hours.

- Make the tape in the order you planned, moving from site to site, person to person, rewinding and listening after each segment to check that you have got what you want, and repeating if you haven't.

- Listen to your brief radio production.

3 Television: You can do a similar mock production on videotape by following basically the same steps, remembering that in this case your script outline must take account of visuals first.

What will you choose to shoot? For how long? Will it carry your scripted narrator's voice over it as you shoot? If so then you need to rehearse without shooting, or arrange a practice shoot of each segment which you can later record over.

Will you have an interviewee walking with you as you shoot this segment? Rehearse movement, camera angle, zooming, climax, points at which questions will be asked.

Don't be too ambitious in what you attempt. Keep the main point of the feature simple. Aim to produce only eight minutes on tape. Ensure that your subject and the locations you choose will allow you to concentrate, and that your interviewees can spare the time to do rough rehearsals. Again, for the purposes of this exercise, in contradistinction to making a professional production, you *cannot* edit.

A dragooned script assistant or camera-operator can be invaluable here to help you check detail, and to take shots that include you as interviewer or narrator. See if you can organize someone to work with you.

You will be surprised at what can be produced with reasonable simplicity on video, providing it is carefully planned and scripted with attention to its order. You will find the video-camera microphone is remarkably sensitive and flexible, and that the video camera allows you to shoot in a great range of lighting conditions.

Research

Before you can write your piece, you must establish what questions must be answered in full or in part, then you need your own efficient method of finding out those answers. How you record your findings is important, and also how you reveal them, directly or indirectly, in what you write. All this depends on the urgency of the writing task, the sophistication of the market, and the availability of resources.

The 'personal computers' sitting on our shoulders will hold and recall an incredible range of information, but they cannot know everything. What they should know is where and how to find information.

Sources of information

Your information may be in the form of a *primary source*, that is, an original memo, letter, statement, photograph or diary; or it may be a *secondary source*, that is, material reported after the event, or edited or summarized from the primary sources. Thus a soldier's account in his diary is a primary source, while the military historian's book is a secondary source.

As general writer or journalist you should keep a list of sources of information in a suitable notebook, and make a list of possible *forms* of information—speeches, articles, reports, statistics, interview tapes and so on. Note in the following list of sources how technology affects the availability of, and speed of access to, information. Computer technology is changing so rapidly that any list of information sources will be obsolete by the time it is published.

• **Libraries**: Libraries vary greatly in their size, purpose and specialization. The National Library, Canberra, holds manuscripts, interview tapes, collections of photographs, correspondence, historical documents, artefacts and other nationally significant items, but your local library cannot be expected to match that. Nevertheless, remind yourself that collectively libraries will hold the following and much more—books, magazines, back issues, reports, newspapers, photographs, works of art, gazetteers, almanacs, government statistics, atlases, bibliographies, encyclopaedias, dictionaries, manuscript collections, interview transcripts, audio and video interview tapes, and *Who's who* collections in special areas of interest. The list could go on.

The information systems in one library can often give information about holdings in other libraries. Don't forget specialized libraries (law, medicine, etc.) at universities and other institutions. With computerized catalogue information, practise thinking of key words that will throw up a range of possibilities on the screen. These seed their own lines of enquiry which will ultimately bring you to the sources you need.

• **Australian Public Affairs Information Service (APAIS)**: This monthly publication, held by most major libraries, lists all reputable articles published in Australian periodicals and is a valuable source of information that can be accessed by subject and author. APAIS and several other databases can be accessed electronically via AUSTROM (CD-Rom-Read Only Memory) in libraries.

• **Court records**: Access to these varies from jurisdiction to jurisdiction. In some States the clerk of courts will have records of trials and convictions, while law reports, published quarterly, carry some trial proceedings and judgements.

• **Parliamentary and local government records**: Hansard carries federal and state parliamentary proceedings and debates. Council minutes carry the details of local government decisions, but most councils also record their proceedings and will allow access to their tapes for a legitimate purpose.

• **Government reports**: These are commissioned by local, state and federal levels of government, or organized internally as enquiries by government departments or instrumentalities. They enquire into a great variety of subjects—the environment, literacy problems, assimilation of migrant groups, the future of the motor industry, housing shortage, funding for the arts, and so on.

• **Databases or databanks**: Prepared and updated by private information agencies, corporate organizations, governments or libraries, these are whole libraries of constantly updated information available through computer terminals. More and more large newspaper offices are connecting to these through terminals in their libraries, so that reporters can access disparate pieces of information with great speed—from the number of casualties (dead and seriously injured) in car accidents in Australia in the last ten years, to the titles and dates of production of all of Patrick White's plays, to a list of press photographs of the Saturn probe available through press agencies.

• **Newspaper archives and libraries**: These hold past issues of the newspaper, selected speeches, photographs, basic biographical information on public figures, surveys, annual reports, magazine press clippings, bibliographies on various subjects, etc.

• **Public relations hand-outs**: Companies and organizations commonly distribute material about themselves and their activities for the public's information, and these can be useful sources of information, statistics, diagrams and illustrations.

• **Corporate, organizational or private libraries, archives and records**: Unions, special research groups, lobby and interest groups, businesses and product-directed organizations (the Wool Board, for example) run their own libraries and archives.

• **The Australian Government Publishing Service catalogue**: This shows the many books, occasional papers, reports and other materials available through Commonwealth Government Bookshops.

- **Sound and film archives**: These are private, library, organizational or government collections of recordings, films, video material, radio broadcasts, photographs and transparencies. You need to plan ahead to gain authorization to consult them.
- **Telephone books**, street and residential directories, maps, plans, statistical digests and summaries, census reports, business and media directories: all are readily available sources that in turn lead to more specific information.

'Precision journalism' is the name given to a growing practice made possible by the more and more sophisticated computerization of information. In precision journalism journalists adopt the objective and quantitative sampling and surveying techniques perfected by social scientists (psychologists, sociologists, economists, and others) and run and analyze their own surveys, using the resources of their colleagues as research teams and their own computers to analyze the data. The objects of their research are often similar to the information sought by the research arm of advertising and public relations firms—people's behaviour and views, and reader and public opinion. The technique can also be useful in reporting an election, or backgrounding social problems, crime, spending patterns, attitudes to government, the political importance of environmental issues and so on.

Agesearch, a professional fee-for-service research unit, is part of the information service of the Melbourne *Age*. Another unit under the same umbrella is The Age Education Unit. In combination with the *Age* library, these units can provide information for *Age* journalists, outside clients, educationists, the general public, and writers. They supply material from books, archives, news clippings, magazines, other newspapers and wire services, as well as research material from one thousand electronic databanks world-wide that are accessed by the *Age*, and which take in areas as diverse as pharmaceuticals, medicine, politics, energy and pollution, science and mathematics, history and sociology.

Access by 'modem' is becoming increasingly common. Personal computers often carry a 'modem' as an extra or even as a standard feature. A 'modem' is a piece of hardware that can make a link, via the normal telephone, to distant computerized library catalogues or information databanks. Information from these can then be called up on your screen at home and printed out, providing you have the accompanying dedicated software. There is usually a fee charged for the service.

Assessing sources

Not all information is equally reliable. You should give some thought to why the person or group provided the information you are considering—was it a government agency, a private individual, a member of a lobby or interest group? The answer to these questions might well give you reason to check the information from another source.

You should also be alert to the tone of the information and how it is presented and acknowledged. If the wording is loose here and there and obvious chances to attribute information to a source are passed over, you should suspect the reliability of the whole and must do some counter-checking.

Reading technique—suit it to your purpose

Another element in your research is reading efficiency. In the name of balance and accuracy, you will need to get into the habit of reading more than one book on your subject.

- Learn to read at different speeds for different purposes. There is no one ideal reading speed. Approach reading preferably with a question to which you seek an answer, and move from the general to the particular. You can learn a lot about a book or information source by flicking through its pages observantly. That might be sufficient to tell you that it is not the type of source that suits your depth of enquiry—your time would have been wasted if you had begun to read it laboriously page by page.
- Look at tables of contents, chapter headings, and bibliographies at the end of the book—all will give you a quick indication of the book's nature and reliability and its usefulness to you. If it has no table of contents or index it may be difficult to find what you want.
- Read the book's preface or introduction to find out what the author intends to emphasize and how the book or booklet is organized.
- Use the table of contents, perhaps in conjunction with the index, to turn straight to the pages that seem relevant to your research and then read in more detail.

Recording

Researchers working on a long project (biography, thesis, history, how-to-do manual, analysis of a big event) sometimes keep a system of cards, arranged alphabetically, each card devoted to a different person or subject that arises in the research. As each card is filled with notes, another bearing the same subject-name is started. This system puts a premium on tidy writing and precise organization. You can establish and use a database on your computer in much the same way.

Other researchers, myself included, keep a numbered series of larger notebooks, containing notes well spaced out so that they can be annotated or added to, and with liberal margins allowed for the same reason. I sometimes have secondary notebooks labelled 'Extra notes' which contain additional information on subjects found in the earlier notebooks. Each of these can be made part of the system by indexing each basic subject inside the front cover of each notebook and providing cross-references to 'Extra notes'.

The reporter or journalist may often have to work from a more portable notebook at great speed, and maybe supplement her normal notes with shorthand jottings or information whispered into a tape recorder. The feature journalist might be able to afford a more organized note-taking system. Some writers work on separate, numbered sheets contained in a folder or loose-leaf system. Those files can then be stored in a filing system.

If you are writing on a word processor you will probably develop a system that allows you to store much of your research information on disc—summaries of research; bibliographical additions; lists of contacts; ideas for further writing stimulated by research.

Working effectively

The continual brain work involved in research and writing at typewriter or word processor can be very intensive and debilitating. Experienced writers, like closeted scholars, know how to pace themselves, how to avoid wearing themselves out or becoming jaded. If you find yourself overdoing it, consult a book on study technique or relaxation. In the meantime, the following hints might help you with your research and writing.

• Have a plan of action, a notion of what you might achieve in your next stint at the word processor or in your research reading. Don't worry if you cannot see immediately where it is best to go next. Allow time for thinking about the most economical use of your time. Don't be afraid of inactivity: do something domestic while you are thinking out your next research or writing move.

• Have a plan of action, yes, *but not an unrealistic one.* Set yourself realistic goals.

• Plan your work sessions around two-hour stints at the most. Within that time, roughly every forty-five minutes, you must get up from the desk and the screen and walk about, do some exercises, or dig a row in the garden for five minutes.

• Not all research and writing time is joyous. Sometimes it's lonely, boring, repetitive. Promise yourself at the outset of such a session that you will reward yourself at its end by doing something you enjoy and that makes for a physical and mental contrast with your research and writing—play a record, go for a walk, hit a tennis ball, ride the bike, punch a bag, plant the lavender.

Photography

The possibility of your feature articles being accepted for publication in newspapers and magazines is considerably enhanced if you supply a package of illustrations of *quality* with your manuscript, illustrations for these general markets generally consisting of black and white or colour photographs.

Not all writers have innate skill in 'seeing' photographic possibilities, composing pictures, and achieving dramatic impact by skilful use of lenses, depth of field and type of film, just as not all writers have equal skill in sensing the possibilities of feature stories in what they see, hear and read. Nevertheless, if you equip yourself with a camera you can do a great deal to enhance your photographic ability through reading and practice, and perhaps by doing a basic photography course. Practice, known as 'shooting film', is vital.

Space does not permit a full analysis here of photographic technique as it applies to illustrating human interest and other features. But some pointers will help you find your way in a field that relies largely on self-development and enquiry.

You need an SLR (Single Lens Reflex) camera. It need not be a Nikon, unless you are regularly shooting up to five hundred shots a day, but it needs to be solid and reliable, with bayonet mount and perhaps two lenses, one reasonably wide-angle, the other perhaps a zoom that ranges from, say, 70 mm to 210 mm in telephoto. You are then equipped to photograph buildings, industrial processes, landscapes, seascapes, street scenes, and gatherings of people, and to take portraits without getting too close to subjects who might be ill at ease in the presence of a camera.

You may decide to buy two identical camera 'bodies' to which you can bayonet-mount either of the lenses, one body carrying colour slide film (since colour reproduction in magazines relies on good colour transparencies) and the other black and white film.

Learn to compose pictures so that there is nothing unwanted in them, so that they tell one main story, so that they have strong lines of com-position, and their main elements are balanced. Photography is about walking and climbing—walking into the subject until there is nothing extraneous in the viewfinder; climbing to gain an unusual or overall view. Learn also what effects can be achieved by using different lenses and film of different speeds.

Learn to 'bracket' your shots (take several of the same subject to allow for movement, facial change, unexpected outside intrusion) so that you have several from which an editor can choose.

Learn, if you can, to load your own film into cassettes from bulk rolls, and to do your own dark-room processing. It's cheaper.

Keep a running record in a manageable notebook of the shots you take, the date, the names of the people in them and their positions, place-names and other detail that might later provide part of your manuscript or caption material.

Study magazines and newspapers to see what sorts of pictures they publish. Look at photographic books and magazines for skilled photographic work and fresh ideas. If necessary, enrol in a course to improve your skills.

Interviewing

Interviewing is talking to people for a purpose. You might do it to publish the interview verbatim as an article in itself, to publish it in an edited version, or to gain information for a feature in which you will quote from the interview as well as use facts and anecdotes gleaned from the interviewee. You might interview in order to report a piece of **hard news** or in order to write a lengthy feature. Here we will concentrate on the more thorough-going interview necessary to write a feature, while making comparisons with the more catch-as-catch-can interviews by phone, in pubs, at accident or incident scenes, that unearth the material for more urgent **hard news** stories.

There are several stages to the interviewing process, as well as points to be kept in mind while the interview is in progress and after it is completed.

Setting up the interview

Aim to make an appointment with your subject if possible, giving them some preparation time, deciding a suitable venue and time between you, and giving some idea of the ground you want to cover and the use to which the information will be put. Such preparation may not always be possible, especially for **hard news** work, and you should learn how to approach subjects unannounced. This includes dealing with the 'minders' of busy and important people, as well as unwilling or uncomfortable subjects. There is no abiding rule for success: you need to be flexible and show equanimity, while making it clear that you want to talk at least for some time in a place where it is possible to concentrate, listen, tape or take notes.

The subject or interviewee

Your interviewee may have one of several reactions to you—amongst them trepidation, anger or defensiveness if he has something to hide; joy and openness if she has just won the prestigious science prize; relaxation if he is being invited to talk on a familiar subject and if he knows your interview will advance or publicize him.

The most desirable atmosphere in an interview is one of mutual trust and respect. Many achieve this, but many do not, for various reasons: some subjects have been grossly misreported in the past; some are defensive because the interview is likely to cover material that the subject does not want unearthed. There are sloppy, inexperienced and malign journalists, just as there are dishonest interviewees. You should be aware of this broader context when you interview. You should also remember that people's memories sometimes play them false and may mislead you, or that some people have memory for some sorts of information but not for others, despite what they think and say. The most erudite person may find it difficult to tell you the dates of the Second World War, for example. Therefore keep alert for evidence of such weakness and check your 'facts' elsewhere.

Recording interviews

Opinions vary about the advisability of note-taking, tape recording, shorthand, reliance on memory, or combinations of these methods, in registering what transpires in an interview. Furious note-taking or taping of the subject's words can be inhibiting. Replaying tapes when writing the article can be time-consuming, and yet some features rely on exact quotation from the subject, in which case a tape is the only sure check. The nature and urgency of the work may determine which method is best. For a series of biographical profiles of writers, I used a tape recorder as back-stop, while taking skeletal notes that allowed me to maintain rapport and eye contact with the subjects. I filled them out later and then numbered them according to the tape counter, so that I could find verbatim statements with relative ease.

Preparing for the interview

Research your subject's achievements, work, pastimes, place in the power structure, opinions, life chronology, living places, friends and colleagues, plans, etc. Glean what you can of their character from others. Prepare a list of questions or notes on the ground you want to cover.

Questioning

Several suggestions come from the accumulated experience of journalists and other writers, as well as from other professional interviewers.
• You may have to set the subject at ease before the interview with a general chat about current events, weather, family, where he or she has come from, etc.
• Let the subject know, if appropriate, how you are going to cover the ground—in chronological sequence, topic by topic, starting from the present and moving back to the past, etc.
• In pursuing a topic, move from the general to the particular, allowing one question to seed another of greater detail. Try to elicit as much *detail* as possible from the subject and *hard evidence* to back up any general assertions.
• Allow the subject's knowledge to come first. Don't argue. Don't ask

loaded, leading or judgemental questions ('How do you explain your organization's hopeless record?').

• Don't make everything a question initially. Make a point of your own ('It seems to me that . . .') and elaborate it so that the interviewee knows exactly what you mean. Then ask for comment or opinion ('Am I right in thinking that . . . or is it rather that . . .?').

• Don't speak, grunt assent, or murmur agreement with the interviewee's answers if you are interviewing for radio or television. Nod and keep eye contact, but train yourself not to say, 'Yes . . . yes . . . mmm' on air.

• Your written feature needs facts; anecdotes and atmospheric detail; and direct quotations. Make sure your questioning provides them.

• Cover the sacred questions: How? When? Where? Why? What? Who?

• Leave contentious or 'tough' questions until well into the interview when rapport has been established and the subject is relaxed.

• As you interview, remember the ways in which your feature needs to entertain and inform, who your market or audience is, and what you see as the overriding theme of the article.

• Keep control of the broad direction of the interview while allowing your subject to talk as freely as you can. As far as possible listen without interrupting.

• Listen for what is said at deeper levels than surface meaning. Monitor body language.

• Listen for what the subject does not want to say as well as what they do want to say.

• Calculate whether a second interview at another time would be advantageous.

You now have insights into the wide range of skills involved in journalistic writing, and of the limitations dictated by time and space restrictions and by advertising revenue and the requirements of specific audiences or readerships.

PART NINE

Public relations

The price of justice is eternal publicity.

Enoch Arnold Bennett

Public relations work

You are a writer. In this field you will deploy words, have definite stories to tell, will determine *how* your stories should be told and how they will relate to each other. Your organization needs your skills. It may well expect you to produce, help produce, or participate in:

- speeches
- brochures
- films
- articles
- statistics
- diagrams
- launches (of a new product, idea, campaign, activity)
- maps
- campaigns and campaign strategies
- annual reports
- videos
- news releases
- photographs with captions
- transparencies with commentary
- exhibitions
- displays
- conferences and meetings
- special events and stunts
- newsletters
- surveys
- personal appearances (on stage, screen, radio, conference floor, or at board meeting table, dinner, etc.)
- handbills, direct mailing
- phone-ins
- school project kits . . . and so the list goes on.

If you are trained in journalism or advertising you are well equipped to attempt public relations work. How then, does public relations (PR for short) differ from journalism and advertising? The answer is that at many points it does not differ at all. Its skills are often those of journalism and advertising, but there are subtle differences of *purpose* between the three. Journalism is basically about news and bringing it accurately and reliably to the general community. Advertising makes people aware of a company's products or services and persuades them to buy these rather than similar products or services provided by someone else. PR is sometimes about both of these, but it is generally more concerned with influencing people's image of a company, organization or institution, and with encouraging them to think well of it and its activities in the broadest sense.

There is another basic difference between *advertising* and *PR:*—advertising is a planned and sharply focussed campaign and is paid for, with the client approving in detail what the advertising will say and having the power of veto over content, and where, how and with what frequency the advertising material will appear.

Public relations, as its name implies, is designed to bring information to the notice of the public, to gain *publicity* in other words. Such publicity cannot be planned in the same way as advertising, and is not paid for in the same way by a client. Instead, PR relies on feeding a heartening message about its subject to the media, who are always seeking information that they can bring to the public and for which they do not have to pay. PR often employs techniques used in both advertising and journalism to feed the message to the media. PR practitioners must understand the media and be on very good terms with them.

PR frequently communicates with several 'publics', both within and without the organization or institution. For example, when the Reserve Bank and the Federal Government implemented the change to decimal currency in 1966 there were two PR campaigns: one to inform the general public, and the other to inform bank employees and financial institutions about the changes they would face.

There are several good handbooks that will give you useful detail about PR: Candy Tymson and Bill Sherman, *The Australian public relations manual,* and Jerry Hendrix, *Public relations cases,* for example.

Let's look at two imaginary PR cases. The Girl Guides Association decides it should be better known in the 1990s for the work it does and the training in initiative and enterprise it gives to girls. Lacking a PR section of its own, it engages a PR consultancy firm to do the job of spreading its heartening message in the media. The result is a *consultancy* job, rather than an *in-house* job. If a large corporate entity like Westpac decides to let Australians know about its community relations activities (such as support for helicopter rescue during the summer and its sponsorship of the Surf Lifesaving Association) it can draw on its in-house community relations section (part of its overall PR department) to do the job, with perhaps some consultancy assistance in areas where very refined skills are required.

Following is a diagram of the skills and activities required of a public relations practitioner. You will gather from the model that writers working in public relations have demands made upon them that involve many disciplines and areas of life.

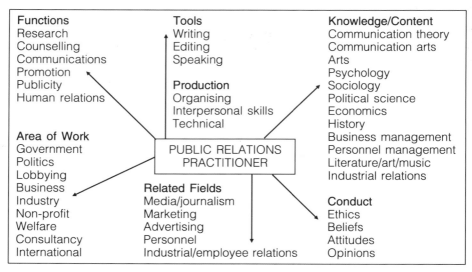

A model of the public relations practitioner

Write

Think of each of the organizations listed below and make brief notes about its image and activities. Then analyse more closely on paper what you see and hear about *two* of these organizations in print, on television, on radio, and in what segments of those media it gains publicity (news? current affairs? documentary? feature? public service announcement? etc.). Then draw up in note form what you imagine the public relations strategies of these two organizations might be.

The National Heart Foundation	The Sydney Zoological Gardens
Qantas	AMP
CSR	The Salvation Army
Melbourne's Olympics 1996 Bid	The Australia Council

PR practitioners consider their work under three main heads, which will remind you of those used in preparing an advertising brief:

1 What is the detailed profile of the main activity of the client, organization or institution?

2 What 'problem' or change of direction is the organization or institution attempting to solve or effect in its PR strategy?

3 What are its main 'audiences' or 'publics'? Who should think well of it?

The four stages most commonly worked through in a PR campaign are:

1 Research into the present image, changes in image, crisis in image, etc. How do people think of the organizations or institutions now? How will they think of them when the impending crisis—if that is the problem—breaks? What might be the most desirable way for them to be thought of?

2 Establishment of objectives of the campaign to rectify problems in the current image. What do the organizations or institutions want to effect in the way of change? Whose thinking do they want to influence?

3 Planning, budgeting for, and executing the objectives. How will the objectives be achieved—in print, in specially arranged occasions, in direct mailing, in sponsorship, on television, radio, via a conference, etc? What 'tone' will be adopted—serious, humorous? How much will it cost to achieve these ends in different ways? Which is the most cost-effective mixture of media to use? Who will write and produce the print and electronic media releases? How will the special events be arranged and by whom? Will consultancy be used?

4 Evaluating the success of the campaign. What does the survey of opinion taken before the campaign indicate? What changes are there in the post-campaign survey or sales figures or number of subscriptions or number of enquiries? Have encouraging responses from the community increased? If not, does surveying show why not? Should the campaign be taken further? Should it be followed up by one with different emphases?

You will already have become aware that PR penetrates every avenue of life. It deals with:

- business and industrial enterprises, large and small, labour and capital
- international affairs, lobbying of overseas governments and officials, separate interest groups, etc.
- social justice organizations, community welfare, non-profit organizations and charities
- health care, hospitals, emergencies, disasters
- universities, schools, colleges, training centres, kindergartens, parent organizations
- governments—local, state, federal, and international
- employees of all sorts.

In dealing with these entities, PR performs a variety of functions, including:

- encouraging social responsibility (seat-belts; anti-smoking)
- advising about human behaviour and reactions
- predicting the future
- researching changes in public thinking, imaging, attitudes
- establishing and maintaining good relations and understanding between groups ('publics') with different interests
- conflict management, both before and after the event
- creating and promoting a corporate or institutional identity

- promoting international understanding and goodwill
- maintaining and increasing profitability
- promoting good management—labour relations
- attracting quality employees, and holding them
- promoting products and services
- establishing communication and sharing of information between different industrial or institutional entities
- promoting good relations between public and government bodies and the private sector
- influencing decision-making at organizational or government or international level
- raising funds, securing sponsorships, and so on.

Write

We are now going to mock up a PR campaign so that you can try your hand at some of the writing and thinking involved and get some idea of the work in a campaign. The writing you do will be selective, since it is difficult to create the feeling of a complete campaign.

You are engaged as a PR consultant to do the writing for a campaign aimed at gaining $3 million from public donations and corporate and government contributions for building extensions to create a new children's ward at the local hospital.

At meetings between you and the hospital committee it has been decided that:

- the campaign will run intensively for four weeks
- the campaign will have a memorable logo and slogan throughout
- newspaper, radio and television will be used
- direct approaches will be made via letter and personal lobbying to corporate and government sources of funds
- media releases will be written at an average of one every three days for print and electronic media
- message posters will be produced for display in shops and offices in the district
- a major special-day event accenting the hospital, its service to the community and its new needs will be mounted—the nature of the event is unspecified as yet
- eight-minute television and radio documentaries on the hospital, its history, personalities, present status and future will be made
- public appeal letters will be sent to every household, with donations tied to sponsored competition prizes
- three different twenty-second TVCs and five different ten-second radio ads, echoing logo and slogan, will be made and broadcast.

Phew! If you can do it, make this imaginary exercise more real by adopting your nearest hospital, or one where you have a contact on the staff, and research it as if it were about to appeal for funds for a new children's ward. This will probably mean interviews, gaining copies of hospital annual reports, details of its history, specializations, staff, and so on. If you can do this without making yourself a nuisance to busy people, pursue it.

An alternative is to base your writing brief on some other institution or organization that you are close to, or a member of, and adapt this exercise as a fund-raising campaign on its behalf. Whichever way you choose, try to have an actual community-based model that you can refer to and envisage as you prepare the campaign. If there is a need in the institution you choose as a model, this might become a real campaign!

Do your research. Learn as much about the hospital or institution as you can by talking to those connected with it, reading, interviewing, delving into history, reading records, amassing statistics, perhaps taking photographs, sitting in, and observing.

Now, you become the PR officer. List all the people you will need to contact, from the Minister for Health and Community Services down to Belinda Citizen and her husband, Mark. Then list all the people whose skills you will need to enlist—photographer, poster artist, etc. Then list your media contacts—newspaper editor, television channel executive or producer, radio station manager and people further afield. Now you are getting a feel for the net of contacts that a PR officer develops, nurtures and guards jealously.

Down to the nitty-gritty. Think first of a slogan of around six words. This slogan is important—it will become a household word. It must suggest memorably the importance of the appeal and what it will do for the community; or sow a favourable image of the hospital or institution in the community, corporate and government minds. Now list suggestions for a logo that an artist or designer can draw and that will carry the pithy typographical slogan. These will become part of your letterhead, posters, television ads, radio ads, newspaper ads and media releases. Take your thoughts to an artist or designer friend or colleague if you have one (or alternatively, to someone whose judgement you trust) and let them work on several alternatives for a logo—then meet to decide on one.

You are now armed with enough knowledge of the hospital or institution and the spread of people you must reach to begin thinking and writing.

First draft a three-page letter to the Premier and the Minister for Health and Community Services (or equivalent) explaining the hospital's background and current needs, and giving specific reasons why a new children's ward is vital at this stage. Remind the government of the hospital's achievements and service, and ask for a matching grant for the $1.5 million that the campaign hopes to raise through corporate and other sources in the campaign. Give a full summary of what is intended in the campaign, and invite the government to respond with suggestions.

This letter will of course be only a general and initial approach—even though economical and to the point—and will be accompanied by a set of general interim plans and artist's drawings on which the hospital committee will liaise with you and the architects who later hope to be contracted to draw up specific plans when it is clear that funds are available. You may at a later stage be asked to frame a detailed submission of needs and plans in detail.

In the normal course of events you should also write a letter to your local parliamentary member(s) explaining your approach, asking them to make representations to Cabinet on behalf of the project and inviting suggestions. Don't spend time on that letter at the moment, but remember that your local members should be progressively informed of developments and kept on your mailing and invitation list for the campaign's duration.

Write a draft letter that might be sent to businesses and interested institutions, again explaining the hospital's achievements and needs, detailing the plans for the new ward in general terms and the purposes it might serve, stating where you can figures of how many children will benefit and the nature of the complaints the ward is expected to help alleviate.

This letter should be shorter than that to government—perhaps one page. It will not be followed or accompanied by a formal submission as was that to government. It should build on current and historical links between the hospital, the community and the business enterprise being approached wherever possible. Your draft letter needs to be able to be quickly modified to address particular businesses that might be approached as sponsors. These businesses or organizations will probably expect to gain 'naming rights', as they are termed. In return for a donation of $X000, the company or institution might have its name attached to the visitor's lounge of the new ward, for instance, or to a piece of medical machinery, or a particular specialist area.

You will guess that the PR practitioner and the hospital committee need to know the local business and welfare community intimately. The time you spend studying local businesses will save you from wasting your time on those who are most unlikely to help.

Direct mailing is an important way of spreading information and gaining interest and contributions.

Write a letter that will go to every household in the district. It will be pitched at the layperson, but will build on local knowledge, on little-known details about the hospital, on your readers' natural need for assurance that necessary health care is available when emergencies arise, and their sense of helping themselves and the community by contributing to the hospital's fund-raising campaign.

Striking the best tone for the readership of your letter is very important. It must inform without complicating issues or being patronizing, must not be too familiar and yet not austere and distant—it may require some economical story-telling. It should be one page only, and may be in brochure or letter form. It might be accompanied by a special appeal envelope, carrying logo and slogan, in which donations can be deposited or mailed. It will probably carry a tear-off segment for mailing or depositing with a donation that is identified with the giver and which may make them eligible for a prize or tax deductions.

Your letter might carry on its reverse side, but not on the back of the tear-off section, a diary of the other events that are forthcoming in the campaign. These need to be mentioned in a way that gives a clear invitation to the community to participate.

Next, write a news release for newspaper, radio and television. Bear in mind that this is not advertising: the media can use your information in whatever way they see fit. You are relying on their professionalism and integrity, and on the fact that all three will manage to set aside space or time for community service announcements when they are appropriate.

This news release will announce the hospital's campaign. It may carry an embargo date, but only in unusual circumstances. Normally a release carries the typed instructions, 'Use at will' or 'Immediate release'. If an embargo (something of a nuisance to editors and producers) is necessary so that its release coincides with other elements of the campaign, it might carry an instruction, 'EMBARGO: not for release before 7 pm 27 May 1994'.

This is a first news release, to be followed by others as the campaign progresses. It is written in a way similar to a hard news story, with a twenty-five word intro and in descending order of news value, so that it can simply be edited from the bottom up if it has to be shortened. It could carry a quickly informative headline of perhaps six words or less, but that is not mandatory. It should not be longer than one hundred and fifty words.

A few minutes thought will give you the essentials of your news release. Its main aim is to alert the public to the approaching campaign and give them some idea of its nature, urgency, what part they as citizens are expected to play and what is in it for them. The hospital's name should come through clearly early in the release, and statements about the details of the campaign should be sourced to some key figure in the campaign—probably the hospital chairperson or chief executive. It can use quoted comments, especially if they are striking.

Don't forget to use one side of the paper only. Head the piece 'News release', and use double-spaced typing for its contents. Allow wide margins, date the release, indicate where the copy ends and leave details of contact names and telephone numbers at the end of the release. Staple its pages together, and if you are offering photographs for the press, make sure they are black and white glossy prints of good contrast. Write captions, contact names and phone numbers on labels and stick on the back of each photograph. Package the prints with cardboard stiffeners when posting them or delivering them, and send enough to allow the editor a choice.

Now you will write a colour or human interest article on the hospital and its campaign for the most appropriate newspaper. This is the first of perhaps two or three colour pieces to be used during the campaign. It requires research and good photographs, including historical shots if any are available. It should stress the hospital's service to the community in cases of illness and emergency, and it needs direct and memorable quotes from official voices and perhaps community voices. There should be one main 'angle' that is not hackneyed, obvious or already well known to the community—if possible an accurate and arresting concept. It should run to one thousand words and should be written as a feature and not as hard news. A range of photographic prints relevant to the story is even more important for this than for the news release.

The rest of the campaign will include colour material similar to that used for the newspaper article but pitched at television or radio. You are likely to become the contact point here for other journalists in those media, supplying them with information which they can use when they tape radio interviews or put together some television footage about the hospital, the involvement of government and business, historical 'angles' and the general community feeling generated by hospital services. The later campaign might include colour or human interest pieces for other smaller local papers and even trade journals or business newsletters. Part of your writing job is to foresee possibilities of reaching publics through avenues which, like these, already exist.

PR technology

The technology available for the transmission of information, is becoming more sophisticated every day. It affects you and your working methods as a writer. It is used in PR, advertising and journalism and where the three overlap.

- **The Fax (Facsimile)**: This can put the news release on paper and into the hands of someone in an office in a distant city very quickly, as can a teleprinter, but the fax can also transmit copies of existing documents, diagrams, charts and photographs very quickly.
- **Electronic mail**: This is the name given to a method, already widely used, of typing a news release or other piece of information directly

into the computer of another organization at a distance, so that it can then be called up on screen by a journalist, editor, or radio or television producer for editing whenever she or he chooses. Electronic mail uses a mixture of leased lines and telephone modem links to do this.

- **Teleconferencing**: In this case a television closed-circuit link-up is used to allow participants in widely distant locations to sit down to talk or receive information. Thus travelling time and costs are saved, and the same message can be conveyed to several large audiences at the one time—to exchange ideas, to telecast an annual general meeting, to convey the details of a new product, new policy, new campaign.
- **Electronic access to databank information**: This is possible through processes that are generally called videotex facilities. These are easily accessed via a telephone modem connected to a personal computer or word processor and carry up-to-date information on stock exchange reports, current prices, economic surveys, corporate reports, airline timetables, media directories and other information valuable to writers working on reports, public relations releases, speeches and other jobs. There are international equivalents available via the Overseas Telecommunications Commission so that users can share links to overseas databanks, as we mentioned in discussing the modern newspaper reporters' room and 'precision journalism' in Part Eight.
- **Laser printing technology**: High quality printing can now be done directly from the keyboard of a computer, by-passing the need for professional typesetting, by using the latest laser printers and the software that accompanies them. The advantages of this in saving money and time in PR work and in some aspects of journalism are obvious.

Write

Consider how you would go about writing material for rather different campaigns in PR from that above. Draft a structure in note form for the following campaigns, writing some of the material for the media if you wish.

1 You are engaged to mount a campaign in the capital cities to promote the image and ideas of the Oceanic Society, an organization committed to saving the oceans from pollution, so that they remain a resource for fishing and for recreation. Devise a campaign.

2 Devise a new, Australia-wide campaign for the Anti-Cancer Council. Look at their past campaigns, study their tone and weight, do some research, perhaps write some material for radio, print and television.

3 Almost all PR, advertising and journalistic practitioners at some time confront a conflict of values. You are asked to devise a pro-smoking campaign, taking in all knowledge of smoking's dangers and the limitations and disclaimers now imposed by government. Do you refuse? If you attempt it, what arguments can you mount? Is it to be 'hard-sell'

material or is a broader cultural approach likely to be more successful? Who are your 'publics'?

What does research show about which 'publics' are anti-smoking, which are pro, which are ambivalent? What arguments do you have to combat? What does your conscience say about this assignment?

4 A 'crisis campaign', sometimes called an 'issues' campaign, involves developments that become 'issues' for governments, corporate bodies and institutions. Such 'issues' are problematic and may erupt in a 'crisis' that threatens and undermines the public image of the government or body or institution. Crisis PR attempts to foresee such crises and to have a plan of action in place to circumvent the crisis or to minimize its effects if it occurs. This is not a cynical exercise: to be prepared, to work on the 'issue' and erase it if possible, or to have an effective plan ready to act in a crisis often makes for greater human understanding of what is happening and lessens human suffering and worry arising from it. For example, imagine that a new biological threat is added to logging as a serious problem in Australia's south-eastern forests near the border be-tween Victoria and New South Wales, and it becomes clear to the governments of the two states that for fifty years at least, timber-milling must be reduced to a quarter of its present levels in that region. This means the closure of no fewer than thirty mills with resultant unemploy-ment. This requires a PR crisis campaign that needs to be mounted before the closures and which must continue for at least two years after, ex-plaining to various publics why the decision is necessary, suggesting action that can alleviate the plight of workers and coinciding with coun-selling and welfare strategies that must follow the closures.

Your first step might well be to extrapolate from the number of mills to be closed to estimate how many workers will suffer and how many in ancillary industries will follow—timber retailing, building, machinery operators, paper manufacturers, etc. Then you might work out what publics your campaign must address (and there will be publics other than those directly affected), how you must use the media and other avenues to reach them and what that will cost. Make a list of the most apt methods you might use in the campaign.

5 You are a writer in an internal PR team devoted to organizing and publicizing the open day of a university, CAE or secondary educational institution. Do some of the planning for such a campaign, part of it fund-raising, using as a model an actual institution with which you have contact. Write some of the print and radio news releases and colour pieces your research and planning indicates will be necessary.

6 Imagine you are asked to inaugurate a newsletter for an organization or institution with which you are in contact. The more widespread its operations, employees and permeation of the community the better. An important part of your role as writer in this context is to understand

how the newsletter might best operate:
- What should it achieve?
- Who should it reach?
- What format should it adopt (page shape and dimensions)?
- How frequent? Colour? Black and white?
- What sort of articles should it carry? Where will they come from? What regular features will it carry? Sources of pictures? Sources of information?
- How can feedback be arranged?
- What title will draw readers to it? Spend some time on naming, until you find a title that seems to 'work' from a number of points of view, is informative, pithy and inviting.

In writing for the newsletter the same principles apply as for general journalism—good headlines that draw the reader's eye, accurate intros, interesting openings, use of contrast, effective marrying of word and picture. Work out a list of contacts who can feed in information from all sections of the organization and who could sit on an editorial committee to make suggestions about content and direction. Think about opportunities for building in reader participation and contributions—articles, statistics, photographic competitions, short staff pars, news items about achievements, new processes, staff changes, etc.

7 You could refer again to the list of avenues open to PR work with which we started this Part of the book. They include mounting an audio-visual presentation, arranging and preparing a news conference, mounting a display or exhibition, organizing a special event or a conference, changing a corporate image and identity and so on. To explore these practices and to gain more experience in writing for them, consult the specialist handbooks listed in the Bibliography.

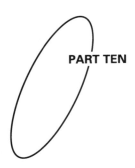

PART TEN

Song-writing

If you can get the words, the Almighty sends you the tune . . .

English farm labourer song-writer

Words and music

Music is an integral part of the media, not only in its own right in concert performance, on record, on tape, or on video-clip, but also in the supportive role it plays in radio, stage production, television and film.

Popular music, rock, jazz, and the various mixtures of these, can draw an international audience with an ease that is denied some other arts. In the 1990s Australia can count on international renown for its rock groups, its bands, its musicians, song-writers and singers, and much of the music they perform is in the form of songs—that is, a persuasive combination of words and music. Words and music are a very moving mixture.

Songs are stories. They have been called 'three-minute films', since most popular songs run to about three minutes and must tell a convincing and intriguing story in that time. Even so, few people pause to think that the song-writer is the linchpin of that process.

In this brief section, we will try to discover how songs are written. Here we approach only the writing that goes to make a good song lyric, leaving chord progressions, phrasing and melody largely to one side, although not forgetting their intimate relationship with the words. It goes without saying that if you can strum a guitar or play the piano yourself, or can work with someone who has a good musical sense, your lyric-writing workshop will be much more effective in relating words to musical tone and mood.

Songs you know

Since you can't begin to think about writing lyrics without also thinking of music and its variety, try writing down something of the range of songs that have moved you over the years.

Everyone will have her or his distinctive list. The same song will remind different people of different singers' renditions. Some songs are popular, some are traditional or mock-traditional, some are ballads. Each person is drawn to different singers, different groups, different bands, but you will probably be surprised how many songs you begin to call up, and for how many you know most of the words! That is a testimony to how persuasive they are and to the skill that has gone into their writing.

Think of singers, groups, performers; you will realize that each has a particular territory into which most of their songs fall, though the variety of moods in that territory is vast.

Think now of those in the musical world who are renowned for being *writers* of songs, whatever they may also do as performers—George and Ira Gershwin, Paul McCartney, Billy Joel, Christie McVie, Phil Collins,

Irving Berlin, Eric Bogle, Cole Porter, Lerner and Lowe, Rogers and Hammerstein, Sting, Peter Garrett, Harold Arlen, Peter Gabriel, Bob Dylan, Randy Newman, Mark Knofler and a host of others. All of these people are consummate story-tellers.

Now, with music and words in your head, you can think about writing a song lyric, but first, a portrait.

Gary is an Australian song-writer. His songs are sung in discos, on television, on radio:

I am self-taught. Sometimes I'll get to the piano or guitar first, strum away on chord progressions, listen, try things. Then, something starts to gell, a tune, a rhythm in what I'm playing. Then I mess with words, to see what will fit the metre of the tune, the mood of the tune. By that stage the tune has established a mood—it might be romance, it might be something slow and sad, it might be a ballad with a strong story, it might be something light, celebratory, happy. From that point it's a matter of trying chords, writing words, phrases. Then both the shape and the mood of the song get clearer at each step.

As he talks, Gary reveals the same antennae extended to pick up what is happening about him as we have found in writers of poetry, prose fiction, drama, and scripts, the same curiosity and fascination with life's stranger-than-fiction turns and twists that the good journalist and advertising copywriter has. Gary continues:

More often than not, at the first stage of unearthing a song, I'll be reading the paper and something will grab me, or I'll be feeding on experience of some sort, or I'll be in an art gallery and the paintings or sculpture put thoughts into my head, or I'll have seen a film that starts a train of thought. Then I write a poem of sorts, usually with a four-line stanza, I play with words and ideas, eventually find a central idea, find a story that has stages to it. Then I work from the lyric towards the music that will reflect the story and its tone. But I'm all the time comparing, too, seeing how other people are doing it, looking at video-clips, analysing new songs to see how they're made up, looking at the verse, at the bridge, at the chorus and its high point. It's a learning process. It's also very satisfying.

Song structures

It is generally easier to fit a melody to words that have been written first, than to write words to fit music. This is the way we are about to operate, since we haven't a piano or guitar handy: words and story first.

We will write song lyrics of two common types. The first will consist of the pattern: verse, chorus, verse, chorus. The second will consist of a pattern that is perhaps more common in popular song: verse, verse, verse, bridge, verse. There are possible variations on this basic structure that allow for verse, verse, bridge, instrument break, verse, chorus, ending. We will come to that later. First, there's some thinking to do.

Several elements must come together in a song lyric. This is *not* poetry writing, although lyric-writing has some things in common with it— rhyme, rhythm and some similarities in word-use and economy. Lyric writing allows for major possibilities that are not available to poetry, and imposes major limitations that do not restrict poetry.

Write

1 Cast about in your experience, current interests, recently heard anec- dotes, newspaper reading, radio listening, television watching, for a story that has something to say to the ordinary person. It must be something that will make a brief, 'three-minute-film' that anyone will understand and be moved by, that will match their experience to some extent, that will ring bells of sadness, familiarity, concern, satisfaction, happiness, love, dread, uncertainty or loss. It might carry the sense of coming through a difficult period into a time of hope. These are some of the universal human happenings that make for good lyric material. Write your story down in one economical paragraph.

2 Try at once to give your story a title. A title is vital, since the lyric must be written 'to it' as songwriters say. The title should be interesting and memorable: the phrase or line that contains it will be heard again and again throughout the body of the song and should encapsulate the story. It must have something that 'grabs' the listener. For that reason it is often called 'the hook'. This word or phrase and the way it recurs and links with the instrumentation can make or break a song. It will probably carry the strongest musical phrase in the song and should therefore sound convincing when it is sung.

Your title may be one word ('Yesterday'; 'Summertime'; 'Laura'), a phrase ('Let's get physical'; 'My old flame'; 'Bess, you is my woman now') or multiple short and related phrases, but generally not more than two ('Don't worry, be happy'; 'For you, for me, for evermore').

Do some interim practice. Write half a dozen single-word titles that might lead to songs, then half a dozen phrases that are memorable enough to be titles and that will stand being sung several times. They can be figures of speech, clichés, or words gleaned from books, magazines or newspapers. You must sense a story behind each.

Study books about the song-writers of Tin Pan Alley or about in- dividual song-writers—Ira Gershwin, Bob Dylan, Irving Berlin. Analyse their song titles to see how they gain their strength and how they carry the key musical phrases in their songs.

3 Now, with your story in mind and a title to focus it, decide on a rhyme scheme. Let's make it first a four-line stanza using an ABAB rhyme scheme, as in Ira Gershwin's 'I got rhythm':

Days can be sunny, (A)
With never a sigh: (B)
Don't need what money (A)   *verse*
Can buy. (B)

After a few verses, perhaps with a build-up to a chorus, you can try a refrain or chorus, as Gershwin does:

I got rhythm,
I got music,   *chorus*
I got my man—
Who could ask for anything more?

And then you can repeat the chorus with variations, each repeating and underlining the title and the song's main concept:

I got daisies
In green pastures,   *variation on chorus*
I got my man—
Who could ask for anything more?

Old Man Trouble,
I don't mind him
You won't find him
'Round my door.

When you build to a finale, you underline the final line (but, in Gershwin's case, not the title!) by repetition:

I got starlight,
I got sweet dreams,
I got my man   *finale chorus*
Who could ask for anything more—
Who could ask for anything more?

Gershwin is breaking the convention here. His title is not the repeated refrain, or 'hook', of his lyric. He explains in his book *Lyrics on several occasions*, that although the line, 'Who could ask for anything more' should logically be the title, he decided that the first line of the chorus—'I got rhythm'—sounded 'more arresting and provocative' and chose to use it as title.

Use Gershwin's model to write two or three verses with an ABAB rhyme scheme. Write varying choruses where the rhyme is ABCD, in other words where there are no lines with matching rhyme within any chorus quatrain. Make sure that the title or 'hook' line and its sentence construction is repeated. Start from a story and its title in each case.

Song lyrics

Now let's look at the other elements of the song lyric that you can see exemplified in Gershwin's lyric and that you will note in the work of other song-writers as you listen and read record or CD sleeves.

The language of song lyrics is generally of a *conversational* tone, using phrases and words in common parlance, even wilfully employing common or clichéd phrases for their tongue-in-cheek familiarity—'green pastures', 'sweet dreams', 'what money can buy', 'never a sigh'.

This points to the ultimate test of a song: it must communicate with the millions of people who hear radio, watch television, attend concerts, listen to CDs, tapes and records. That is why song lyrics do not use the intense and refined language we come to expect from much poetry. The song lyric can get away with, often positively relies on, the use of generalized words and phrases that can be highly emotive, yet can allow for the individual listener's interpretation: love, happiness, kiss, hope, loneliness, smiles, tears, cries, crying, fears. Such words are generally death to poetry! Even while good song lyrics employ such opaque and general words and phrases, lyrics often strike a chord of emotion in listeners because they arise from song-writers' genuine observations of human nature and universal emotions.

There are several structure patterns to the stories of 'three-minute films'. One of the most common is the one we have seen in the short story, the play, film-script and the short television commercial. It is the three-part structure that:

1 develops a conflict or question that begs to be resolved or answered
2 expands, explains or develops further that conflict or question
3 resolves the conflicts, answers the question, *or* injects a new element or surprise in the ending.

The subject can be one of the ever-popular 'love' themes. In these, the lyric's verses and refrain state the breaking-up of a relationship and what it means to the person whose thoughts and point-of-view make the song's message; or verses and refrain celebrate the happiness of a love that has been found and that is going to last. Perhaps verses and refrain describe a potential love that can never be, or finally, they might become the pleas of what Ira Gershwin calls 'the importunate male' who is trying to persuade or seduce the resistant female. Sometimes, too, verses and refrain might exhort the listener to look on the bright side, suggesting a plan of action in romantic matters.

In general, the more descriptive the lines of a lyric, the better the listener can identify with them, provided the description is not too dense or overdone. So imagery, as in poetry, becomes important. The songs of Bob Dylan and Tracy Chapman, to name only two writers, are good examples. The genius of the successful song-writer is to tap the mood of the time in settings, locales, imagery, comparisons, and detailed description. With that aim in mind, many song-writers write a complete prose story, with full background for their characters or for the narrator of the lyric, then, as they rewrite, descriptive phrases and metaphors and similes flow from the prose version into the verses and refrain.

Words and phrases that attach to the senses—touch, hearing, sight, smell, taste—are productive in song lyrics, because they make mental states and emotions more immediately communicable to the listener.

Song lyrics can stand romantic exaggeration and hyperbole in a way that poetry in general can not. In a lyric a lover can promise to sail a million miles to his love, to wait until the sea runs dry, to weep a sea of tears.

Carrying the story forward in brief pictures is often important in songs, each sentence supplying a new piece of information or context.

The words chosen to end lines become doubly important in a lyric—they connect with words in previous lines in logic and in rhyme, and must carry conviction, rather than merely making a rhyme. Again, they are often dwelt on by a singer, and need to be chosen so that they can be sung with ease and resonance. More often than not they require an open vowel sound ('been good to me . . .'; 'Smoke gets in your eyes').

Alliteration and assonance (repetition of consonant or vowel sounds—'Ye Banks and Braes'; 'Tea for two'; 'Hickory Dickory Dock') are also useful in the lyric. There are examples in both nursery rhymes and children's songs and in adult popular songs.

The bridge

The bridge usually breaks the pattern of line length, rhythm, and chord structure that has been set up in the verses and which the listener has become accustomed to in the song. Therefore the bridge is often the emotional high point of the song, a point where the phrasing of the music also changes. It is the stage in the song where the song's point is made clear to the listener. Billy Joel's 'Baby grand', a personal song (like many of his songs it arises out of his own experience), is a good case in point. In 'Baby grand' the rhyming pattern, you will note, is more complex than the simple ABAB, and each verse carries a sort of mini-chorus in its last two lines that repeats and emphasizes the title with variations:

Baby grand
Late at night
when it's dark and cold
I reach out
for someone to hold. When I'm blue,   *verse*
when I'm lonely
she comes through
she's the only one who can.
My baby grand
is all I need.

In my time
I've wandered everywhere
around this world
she would always be there   *verse*
any day
any hour.
All it takes
is the power in my hands.
This baby grand's
been good to me.

They say no-one's gonna play this on the radio.
They said the melancholy blues were dead and gone.
But songs like these   *bridge*
played in minor keys
keep those memories holding on.

I've come far
from the life I strayed in.
I've got scars from those dives I've played in.
Now I'm home   *verse*
and I'm weary.
In my bones
every dreary one-night stand
but baby grand
came home with me.

Ever since this gig began
my baby grand's   *final repeat of chorus line and title*
been good to me.

Write

Now try writing a lyric whose verse and chorus is in the form of verse,
verse, verse, bridge, verse.

Start with a story-line and think it through. Then develop a memorable title line. Now you are ready to write the verses that build the story. Note how one central idea runs through the detail of Billy Joel's song. Try to emulate that. Note, too, that Billy Joel gets extra emotional juice from his lines by planting convincing rhymes within the line, in addition to those that fall at the line endings in his verses.

When you reach the bridge of your song let your ear and your 'emotional logic' determine how the rhythm and sentiments of the preceding verses will change and how the bridge will extend the main point. Study Billy Joel's bridge and those of other song-writers.

Now, say over, hum over the song to this point and determine how it should end. Will it finish in a final verse modelled exactly on the earlier verses? Will it have an extra repetition of the title line? Will it carry an extra couplet to emphasize the title and central idea in a finale, as in Billy Joel's song? Write your finale.

You may already have heard Billy Joel's 'Baby grand'. If you haven't, you will be impressed by the added power given to these carefully judged words when you hear them sung with instrumental backing, musical phrasing and subtlety of pace. The length of line and the speed with which it is delivered musically can vary greatly within each verse. Three words in one line can be drawn out rhythmically to equal seven or eight words in the preceding line. Slowing down and dwelling on words can have great emotional impact in musical terms.

Further suggestions

• Learn from other song-writers. Listen to songs, follow up the printed lyrics whenever you can get them. Study their structure, remembering the elements we have discussed: central idea or story; title and title line; opening; key words; lines of strong emotion and their placement; rhyme schemes; verse form and bridge; 'singability'; logical progression; effectiveness of finale, etc.

• Emulate the song forms of the famous song-writers, using your own words and experience and story within the forms they adopt.

• Since lyric-writing is about words and their power, have a thesaurus with you as you work—it will suggest shades of meaning. A good rhyming dictionary will also be useful.

• Keep a journal of sorts where you note ideas for song stories and individual lines and phrases as the world brings its stories to you.

• Be aware of other types of music that require the word-skills of writers. Investigate new and experimental forms of music and performance art and poetry. One example is 'industrial music' which often consists of recorded sounds from real life (industrial processes, traffic, birds, footsteps, the call of a paper boy, etc.) with a voice-over that gains its force by repetition over the background sounds.

Epilogue

In *Writer* you will have found reflected some of the various faces of writing—not all. The formal literary or journalistic essay, the academic article and those short meditative pieces written for editorial pages are not included in *Writer*. Nevertheless, with what you have learned in reading this book and responding to its suggestions you are equipped to attempt such pieces and to develop skill in them. Again, this book does not involve work towards the scholarly and footnoted essay or assignment, nor the book review intended for academic journals, magazines or newspapers. Nor does it treat the business, government or committee report. But your writing experience and the knowledge that you can refer to other books devoted to these forms, reassures you that you can attempt such pieces.

You can leave this book confident that you are now considerably more professionally informed as an artist and writer than when you began it. You have become familiar with writing's broad range and are adaptable enough in your skills to take on new projects—some commissioned, some ideas of your own. *Writer* sets you on a trail of interest that will afford you many more insights as you engage with the day-to-day work of writing. And you should not lose sight of the fact that it is that day-to-day world of the practising and specialised writer that will be your ultimate and best training-ground. That is where you will develop your expertise and make contact with colleagues who will remain life-long colleagues in what Hal Porter called 'the freemasonry of writing'.

The close of a book of this nature seems to demand an awareness of the bountifulness of creation. It provides a vantage-point from which to see the writing you have practised as part of a larger human ingenuity.

There are two statements by writers steeped in the wisdom of the calling that occur to me again and again. The first is the voice of the American poet, Marianne Moore: 'Do the poet and scientist not work analogously? Both are willing to waste effort. To be hard on himself is one of the main strengths of each. Each is attentive to clues, each must narrow the choice, must strive for precision'.

Then comes the voice of the story writer John Sherwood Anderson, uttering words that might be the emblematic statement of this book and your own future writing career: 'After all there is the fact of life. Its story wants telling and singing. That's what I want—the tale and the song of it'.

Bibliography

General—writing and writers

Abel, Elizabeth, *Writing and sexual difference*, University of Chicago Press, Chicago, 1982.

Abrams, M. H., *A glossary of literary terms*, 4th edn, New York, Holt, Rinehart and Winston, 1981.

Allen, Walter, *Writers on writing*, Phoenix, London, 1948.

Anderson, Don, *Enchanted apartments; Sad motels*, McPhee Gribble Ringwood, 1989.

Australia Council, The, *Books, who reads them?*, North Sydney, 1990, available from David Thorpe, PO Box 146, Port Melbourne, 3207, $29.95 posted.

Australian Booksellers Association, The, *Australian bookseller and publisher*, D. W. Thorpe, Melbourne, (monthly).

Australian Government Publishing Service, *Communicating in writing*, Brian Palfrey, Canberra, 1975.

Australian Government Publishing Service, *Style manual for authors, editors and printers*, AGPS, Canberra, 1988.

Baker, Candida, *Yacker, Yacker 2*, and *Yacker 3*, Picador, Sydney, 1986, 1987, 1989.

Barthes, Roland, *Image–music–text*, Collins/Fontana, London, 1977.

Bates, Dianne, *The new writer's survival guide*, Penguin, Ringwood, 1989.

Bell, Diane and Shreiner, Shelley, *This is my story*, Centre for Australian Studies, Deakin University, Geelong, 1991.

Bertagnolli, Olivia, *Creativity and the writing process*, J. Wiley and Sons, New York, 1982.

Bird, Carmel, *Dear writer*, McPhee Gribble, Ringwood, 1988.

Bolt, David, *An author's handbook*, Piatkus, London, 1986.

Borges, Jorge Luis, *Labyrinths* (Donald A. Yates and James E. Irby, eds), Penguin, Harmondsworth, 1981.

Bromby, Robin, *Writing for profit in Australia*, Simon and Schuster/Cromarty Press, Sydney, 1987.

Burack, A. S., *The writer's handbook*, The Writer Inc., Boston, 1978.

Burgin, Richard, *Conversations with Jorge Luis Borges*, Discus Books, distributed by Avon Books, division of the Hearst Corporation, New York, 1970.

Camus, Albert, *Carnets 1935–1942* and *Carnets 1942–1951*, Knopf, New York, 1963 and 1966.

Cusick, Anne, *Choices: What am I doing with my life?*, Simon and Schuster, Brookvale, NSW, 1990.

Daiute, Colette, *Writing and computers*, Addison Wesley Publishing Co., Reading, Mass., 1985.

di Giovanni, Norman Thomas, Halpern, Daniel, McShane, Frank (eds), *Borges on writing*, Allen Lane, London 1974.

Disher, Garry, *Writing professionally*, Allen and Unwin, Sydney, 1989.

Duerden, Dennis and Pierterse, Cosmo, *African writers talking: A collection of interviews*, Heinemann Educational, London, 1972.

Dugan, Michael and Hamilton, J. S., *Bookmark*, Australian Library Promotions Council, Melbourne, (yearly).

Dumbrell, Laurel, *Becoming a writer*, Unwin Paperbacks, Sydney, 1986.

Duras, Marguerite, *Practicalities: Marguerite Duras speaks to Jerome Beaujour*, (translated from the French by Barbara Bray), Collins, London, 1990.

Elbow, Peter, *Writing without teachers*, Oxford University Press, London, 1973.

Ellison, Jennifer (ed.), *Rooms of their own*, Penguin, Ringwood, 1986.

Fadiman, Clifton, *Reading I've liked*, Hamish Hamilton, London, 1946.

Fairfax, John, *Creative writing—Word games and exercises to help you get started*, Elm Tree Books, London, 1989.

Gass, William, *The world within the word*, Nonpareil Books, Boston, 1979.

Gilbert, Pam, *Contemporary Australian women writers*, Pandora, Sydney, 1988.

Golvan, Colin, *Words and law: A practical guide for all those whose business is writing*, Penguin, Ringwood, 1989.

Gorky, Maxim, *My universities*, (translated from the Russian by Margaret Wettlin), Progress, Moscow, 1989.

Green, Stephanie, *Publish: The ACT Arts Council writers' handbook*, Arts Council of Australia Inc., Braddon, ACT, 1989.

Guiffe, Guilia, *A writing life: Interviews with Australian women writers*, Allen and Unwin, Sydney, 1990.

Hall, Donald (ed.), *The modern stylists—Writing on the art of writing*, Free Press, New York, 1968.

Hart, Horace, *Hart's rules for compositors and readers at the University Press*, The Clarendon Press, London, 1983.

Heller, Louis et al., *The private lives of English words*, Routledge and Kegan Paul, London, 1984.

Jacobus, M. (ed.), *Women writing and writing about women*, Croom Helm and Barnes and Noble Books, Totawa, New Jersey, 1979.

Kenyon, Olga, *Women writers talk: Interviews with 10 women writers*, Allen and Unwin, Sydney, 1989.

Kernan, Alvin, *The death of literature*, Yale University Press, New Haven, 1990.

Kinross-Smith, Graeme, *Mankind's spies—How writers work*, Cassell Collier Macmillan, Melbourne, 1972.

Kinross-Smith, Graeme, *Australia's writers: An illustrated guide to their lives and their work*, Thomas Nelson, Melbourne, 1980.

Kavanagh, Paul, and Kuch, Peter, *Conversations: Interviews with Australian writers*, Imprint, Angus and Robertson, Sydney, 1991.

Knott, William C., *The craft of fiction*, Reston, Reston Virginia, 1977.

Lloyd, Pamela, *How writers write*, Methuen, North Ryde, 1987.

Mamet, David, *Writing in restaurants*, Viking, New York, 1986.

Maugham, W. Somerset, *Points of view*, Greenwood Press, New York, 1958.

——, *A writer's notebook*, Readers Union, William Heinemann, London, 1951.

McGregor, Craig, Beal, David, Moore, David, Williamson, Harry (eds), *In the making*, Thomas Nelson, Melbourne, 1969.

Miller, Henry, *My life and times*, Playboy Press, Chicago, 1971.

Moore, Robert E., *So you want to be a writer*, Boyd and Fraser, San Francisco, 1974.

Newquist, Roy (ed.), *Counterpoint*, Rand McNally, New York, 1964.

Nieuwenhuizen, Agnes, *No kidding: Top writers for young people talk about their work*, Sun Books, South Melbourne, 1991.

Odgers, Sally, *Storytrack—A practical guide to writing for children in Australia and New Zealand*, Kangaroo Press, Kenthurst (NSW), 1989.

Paris Review interviews, Series One to Seven (various editors), Secker and Warburg/Viking Penguin, New York, 1957–91.

Pasternak, Boris, *Letters to Georgian friends*, Secker and Warburg, London, 1968.

Peters, Pam (ed.), *The pocket Macquarie writer's guide*, Jacaranda, Milton, Queensland, 1990.

Phelps, Robert and Deane, Peter, *The literary life*, Chatto and Windus, London, 1969.

Phillips, Larry W., *Ernest Hemingway on writing*, Scribner, New York, 1984.

Price, Greg, *Latin America: The writer's journey*, Hamish Hamilton, London, 1991.

Provost, Gary, *Make every word count: A guide to writing that works for Fiction and non-fiction*, Writer's Digest Books, Cincinnati, Ohio, 1980.

Purchase, Shirley (ed.), *The Australian writers' and editors' guide*, Oxford University Press, Melbourne, 1991.

Quinn, John (ed.), *Portrait of the artist as a young girl*, Methuen, London, 1987.

Raban, Jonathan, *For love and money: Writing, reading, travelling*, Collins Harvill, London, 1987.

Ruas, Charles, *Conversations with American writers*, Knopf, New York, 1985.

Spender, Dale, *Two centuries of Australian women writers*, Pandora, London, 1988.

Stein, Gertrude, *How to write*, Dover Publications, New York, 1975.

Strauss, Dagmar, *Facing writers: Australia's leading writers talk with Dagmar Strauss*, Australian Broadcasting Corporation, ABC Enterprises, Crow's Nest, 1990.

Strunk, William and White, E. B., *The elements of style*, Macmillan, New York, 1979.

Stultz, Russell, *Writing and publishing on your micro-computer*, Woodware Publications, Plano, Texas, 1984.

Tanaka, Yukiko, *To live and to write—Selections by Japanese women writers*, The Seal Press, Seattle, 1987.

Turner, Barry (ed.), *The writer's handbook 1991*, Macmillan, London, 1991.

Tate, Claudia (ed.), *Black women writers at work*, Oldcastle, Harpenden, 1985.

Victorian Writers' Centre, *The handbook for Victorian writers*, Victorian Writers' Centre, East Melbourne, 1991.

Wells, Gordon, *The successful author's handbook*, Macmillan, London, 1989.

Welty, Eudora, *One writer's beginnings*, Faber and Faber, London, 1983.

White, Stephen, *The written word and associated digressions concerned with the writer as craftsman*, Harper and Row, New York, 1984.

Winokur, John (ed.), *Writers on writing*, Running Press, Philadelphia, 1987.

Woolf, Virginia, *A room of one's own*, Chatto and Windus, Hogarth Press, London, 1984.

Wright, John K., *The writing machine*, McPhee Gribble, Ringwood, 1990.

Writers and artists yearbook, A. & C. Black, London, 1984 (yearly).

Poetry

'Art of Poetry, The', series of interviews with various poets in *The Paris review*, Paris and New York.

Basho, *The narrow road to the deep north and other travel sketches*, (translated from the Japanese by Nobuyuki Yuasa), Penguin, Harmondsworth, 1966.

Duwell, Martin, *A possible contemporary poetry: Interviews with thirteen poets from the New Australian Poetry*, University of Queensland Press, Brisbane, 1982.

Edson, Russell, 'Portrait of the writer as a fat man: Some subjective ideas or notions on the care and feeding of prose poems' in Friebert and Young (eds), *A field guide to contemporary poetry and poetics*, Longman, New York, 1980.

Fussell, Paul, *Poetic metre and poetic form*, McGraw Hill, New York, 1979.

Gibbons, R. (ed.), *The poet's work: 29 masters of 20th century poetry on the origins and practice of their work*, Houghton Mifflin, Boston, 1979.

Hall, Donald, *The pleasures of poetry*, Harper and Row, New York, 1971.

Hollander, John, *Rhyme's reason: A guide to English verse*, Yale University Press, New Haven and London, 1981.

Hughes, Ted, *Poetry in the making*, Faber and Faber, London, 1967.

Matthiessen, Peter, *Nine-headed Dragon River: Zen journals 1969–1985*, Random House, Boston, 1986.

McAuley, James, *A primer of English versification*, Sydney University Press, Sydney, 1976.

Packard, William (ed.), *The poet's dictionary*, Harper and Row, New York, 1989.

Preminger, Alex (ed.), *Princeton encyclopaedia of poetry and poetics*, Princeton University Press, Princeton, New Jersey, 1986.

—— (ed.), *Princeton handbook of poetic terms*, Princeton University Press, Princeton, New Jersey, 1986.

Richman, Robert (ed.), *The direction of poetry—An anthology of rhymed and metred verse written in the English language since 1975*, Houghton Mifflin, Boston, 1988.

Roberts, Philip Davies, *How poetry works*, Pelican, Harmondsworth, 1987.

Scully, James (ed.), *Modern poets on modern poetry*, Fontana, London and Glasgow, 1973.

Skelton, Robin, *The practice of poetry*, Heinemann Educational, London, 1971.

Spender, Stephen, *The making of a poem*, W. W. Norton, New York, 1962.

Stillman, Frances, *The poet's manual and rhyming dictionary*, Thames and Hudson, London, 1966.

Valery, Paul, *The art of poetry*, (translated from the French by Denise Folliot), Vintage Books, New York, 1958.

Fiction

Aiken, Joan, *The way to write for children*, Elm Tree Books, London, 1988.

Alderman, B. and Owen Reader, S. (eds), *The inside story: Creating children's books*, Children's Book Council of Australia, A.C.T. Branch, Canberra, 1987.

Allott, Miriam, *Novelists on the novel*, Routledge and Kegan Paul, London, 1959.

Bail, Murray, *Longhand—A writer's notebook*, Penguin, Ringwood, 1989.

Beachcroft, T. O., *The modest art: A survey of the short story in English*, Oxford University Press, London, 1968.

Benstock, Bernard (ed.), *Art in crime writing: Essays on detective fiction*, St Martin's Press, New York, 1983.

Braine, John, *Writing a novel*, Eyre Methuen, London, 1974.

Carver, Raymond, *Fires*, Picador, London, 1986.

Disher, Garry, *Writing fiction: An introduction to the craft*, Penguin, Ringwood, 1983.

Doubtfire, Dianne, *The craft of novel writing*, Hodder and Stoughton, Sevenoaks, 1983.

Duras, Marguerite, *Practicalities: Marguerite Duras speaks to Jerome Beaujour*, Collins, London, 1990.

Evans, Christopher, *Writing science fiction*, A. and C. Black, London, 1988.

Fadiman, Clifton (ed.), *The world of the short story*, Picador, London, 1986.

Frankau, Pamela, *Pen to paper: A novelist's notebook*, Heinemann, London, 1961.

Gardner, John, *On becoming a novelist*, Harper and Row, New York, 1983.

Gass, William H., *Fiction and the figures of life*, Nonpareil, Boston, 1978.

Grenville, Kate, *The writing book—A workbook for fiction writers*, Allen and Unwin, Sydney, 1990.

Handke, Peter, *The left-handed woman*, Farrar, Straus and Giroux, New York, 1978.

——, *The weight of the world*, (translated from the German by Ralph Manheim), Farrar, Straus and Giroux, New York, 1984.

Hildick, W., *Thirteen types of narrative*, Macmillan, London, 1968.

Jute, Andre, *Writing a thriller*, Black, London, 1986.

Keating, H. R. F., *Writing crime fiction*, A. and C. Black, London, 1986.

Kenyon, Olga (ed.), *Women writers talk*, Carroll and Graf, New York, 1989.

Kundera, Milan, *The art of the novel*, Faber and Faber, London, 1987.

Lloyd, Pamela, *How writers write*, Methuen, North Ryde, 1987.

Maugham, W. Somerset, *The summing up*, International Collectors' Library American Headquarters, New York, 1938.

——, *A writer's notebook*, William Heinemann, London, 1951.

——, *Points of view*, Heinemann, London, 1958.

Mirrielees, E. R., *Story writing*, The Writer Inc., Boston, 1947.

Nin, Anaïs, *The novel of the future*, Peter Owen, London, 1969.

O'Faolain, Sean, *The short story*, Collins, London, 1948.

Palmer, Vance, Foreword to *Coast to coast 1944*, Angus and Robertson, Sydney, 1944.

Sansom, William, *Birth of a story*, Chatto and Windus, London, 1972.

Saunders, Jean, *The craft of writing romance: A practical guide*, Allison and Busby, London, 1986.

Steinbeck, John, *Journal of a novel: The East of Eden letters*, Heinemann, London, 1970.

——, *Working days—The journals of the Grapes of wrath* (ed. Robert de Mott), Viking, New York, 1989.

——, *The harvest gypsies: On the road to the Grapes of wrath*, (Intro. Charles Wollenberg), Heyday Books, Berkeley, 1988.

Stevick, Philip (ed.), *Anti-story: An anthology of experimental fiction*, The Free Press and Collier Macmillan Ltd, New York and London, 1971.

Stone, Wilfred, Packer, Nancy Huddleston and Hoopes, Robert, *The short story: An introducton*, McGraw Hill, New York, 1976.

Wallace, Irving, *The writing of one novel*, Sphere Books, London, 1987.

White, Patrick, 'The Prodigal Son' in Heseltine, H. and Tick, S., *The writer in the modern world*, Cheshire, Melbourne, 1962.

Zinsser, William, *Worlds of childhood: The art and craft of writing for children*, Houghton Mifflin, Boston, 1990.

Biography, autobiography, life histories, memoirs, journals

Baker, Russell, *Inverting the truth: The art and craft of memoir*, Houghton Mifflin, Boston, 1987.

Bertaux, Daniel, *Biography and society*, Sage USA, Beverley Hills, 1983.

Blodgett, Harriet, *Centuries of female days*, Rutgers University Press, New Brunswick, 1988.

Burnett, John, Vincent, David and Mayall, David, *The autobiography of the British working class: An annotated critical bibliography*, Harvester, Brighton, Sussex, 1984–89.

Clifford, James, *From puzzles to portraits: Problems of a literary biographer*, University of Carolina Press, Chapel Hill, 1970.

Colmer, John and Dorothy (eds), *The Penguin book of Australian autobiography*, Penguin, Ringwood, 1987.

Daniel, Lois, *How to write your own life story—A step by step guide for the non-professional writer*, Chicago Review Press, Chicago, 1985.

Edel, Leon, *Telling lives: Principia biographia*, W. W. Norton, New York, 1985.

Field, Joanna (Marianne Milner), *A life of one's own*, Virago, London, 1986.

Felt, Thomas E., *Researching, writing and publishing local history*, American Association for State and Local History, Nashville, Tennessee, 1983.

Gilbert, Kevin, *Living Black*, Penguin, Ringwood, 1977.

Vine Hall, Nick J., *Tracing your family history in Australia*, Rigby, Adelaide, 1985.

Halpern, Daniel (ed.), *Antaeus—Journals, notebooks and diaries*, Collins Harvill, London, 1989.

Heilbrun, Carolyn, *Writing a woman's life*, The Women's Press, London, 1989.

Hood, Lynley, *Who is Sylvia: The diary of a biography*, John McIndoe, Dunedin, 1990.

Lejeune, Philippe, *On autobiography*, (trans. Katherine Leary), University of Minnesota Press, Minneapolis, 1989.

Mairs, Nancy, *Remembering the bone house—An erotics of place and space*, Perennial Library, Harper and Row, New York, 1989.

Mallon, David, *A book of one's own; People and their diaries*, Pandora (William Collins) and Ticknor and Fields, New York, 1984.

Porte, Joel, *Emerson in his journals*, Belknap Press of Harvard University Press, Cambridge, Mass., 1982.

Siebenschuh, William R., *Fictional techniques and factual works*, University of Georgia Press, Athens, Georgia, 1983.

Smith, Sidonie, *The poetics of women's autobiography: Marginality and the fictions of self-representation*, Indiana University Press, Bloomington, 1987.

Spengemann, William C., *The forms of autobiography*, Yale University Press, New Haven, 1980.

Rainer, Tricia, *The new diary: How to use a journal for self-guidance and expanded creativity*, J. P. Tarcher and St Martin's Press, New York, 1978.

Updike, John, *Self-consciousness—Memoirs*, Alfred A. Knopf, New York, 1989.

Playwriting and scripting

Armer, Alan A., *Writing the screenplay: TV and film*, Wadsworth Publishing Co., Belmont, California, 1988.

Australian Broadcasting Tribunal, *Broadcasting in Australia 1989*, ABT, PO Box 1308, North Sydney, 1989.

——, *TV 2000: Choices and challenges*, 1989.

——, *The child audience*, 1980.

Ash, William, *The way to write radio drama*, Elm Tree, London, 1985.

Australian Film, Television and Radio School videos: 'Writing for film'; 'Writing for comedy'; 'Writing for television'; 'Writing for radio'; Distribution Unit, Australian Film, Television and Radio School, PO Box 126, North Ryde, NSW 2113.

Baker, G. P., *Dramatic technique*, Da Capo Press, New York, 1976.

Bentley, Eric, *The life of the drama*, Atheneum, New York, 1964.

Blum, Richard, *Television writing: From concept to contract*, Hastings House, New York, 1980.

Brady, J., *The craft of the screenwriter*, Simon and Schuster, New York, 1981.

Brandt, George (ed.), *British television drama*, Cambridge University Press, Cambridge, New York, 1981.

Bronfeld, Stewart, *Writing for film and TV*, Simon and Schuster, New York, 1986.

Catron, Louis, *Writing, producing and selling your play*, Prentice-Hall, New York, 1984.

Cole, Toby (ed.), *Playwrights on playwriting: The meaning and making of modern drama from Ibsen to Ionesco*, Hill and Wang, New York, 1961.

Crisell, Andrew, *Understanding radio*, Methuen, London, 1986.

Dimond, Peter, *Writing documentary script and narration*, Australian Film, Television and Radio School, Open Program and Resources, North Ryde, 1980.

Dmytryk, Edward, *Screen writing*, Focal Press, Boston, 1985.

Egri, Lajos, *The art of dramatic writing: Its basis in the creative inter-pretation of human motives*, Simon and Schuster, New York, 1960.

Field, S., *Screenplay: The foundation of screenwriting*, Delta, New York, 1979.

Giustini, Rolando, *The film script: A writer's guide*, Prentice-Hall, Englewood Cliffs, 1980.

Goldman, W., *Adventures in the screen trade*, Warner, New York, 1982.

Gooch, Steve, *Writing a play*, A. & C. Black, London, 1988.

Heath, S., *Questions of cinema*, Macmillan, London, 1981.

Kerr, Walter, *How not to write a play*, Simon and Schuster, New York, 1955.

Lowndes, Ginny, *Writing for television*, George Allen and Unwin, Sydney, 1988.

MacGraw, Judy, *The magician's art*, Science Press, Marrickville, NSW, 1988.

Miller, William C., *Screenwriting for narrative film and television*, Hastings House, New York, 1980.

Moran, Albert (ed.), *Australian television drama series, 1956–1981*, Australian Film, Television and Radio School, North Ryde, 1989.

Pike, Frank, *The playwright's handbook*, New American Library, New York, 1985.

Richards, Keith, *Writing radio drama*, Currency Press, Sydney, 1991.

Rodger, Ian, *Radio drama*, Macmillan, London, 1982.

Root, W., *Writing the script*, Holt, Rinehart and Winston, New York, 1979.

Schwarz, L., *The craft of writing TV comedy*, Allison and Busby, London, 1988.

Seger, L., *Making a good script great*, Dodd, Mead, New York, 1987.

Self, David, *Television drama: An introduction*, Macmillan, London, 1984.

Smiley, Sam, *Playwriting: The structure of action*, Prentice-Hall, Englewood Cliffs, 1971.

Truffaut, Francois, *The films of my life*, Penguin, Harmondsworth, 1982.

Viewpoint, the bulletin of the Australian Writers Guild Ltd, monthly, A.W.G., 60 Kellet Street, King's Cross, NSW 2011.

Walter, Richard, *Screenwriting: The art, craft and business of film–TV*, New American Library, New York, 1988.

Willis, Edgar E. and D'Arienzo, Camille, *Writing scripts for television, radio and film*, Holt Rinehart and Winston, New York, 1981.

Women working in film, Television and video—1991 national directory, Women in Film and TV (WIFT), Broadway, NSW, 1988.

Writers directory: Writers for radio, screen, stage and television, Australian Writers' Guild, King's Cross, 1984. (There is also a wide range of contracts, guidelines, publications, broadsheets and pamphlets concerning all aspects of scriptwriting for radio, film and television available from the Australian Writers' Guild Ltd, 60 Kellett St, King's Cross, NSW 2011).

Advertising

Australian Government Publishing Service, *Advertising and selling: A business guide to consumer protection under the Trade Practices Act*, Trade Practices Commission, 1981.

Baker, Michael J. (ed.), *Macmillan dictionary of marketing and advertising*, Macmillan, London, 1984.

Barnes, Shenagh and Blakeney, Michael, *Advertising regulation*, Law Book Co., Sydney, 1982.

Berkman, Harold and Gilson, Christopher, *Consumer behaviour: Concepts and strategies*, Kent Publishing Co., Boston, 1986.

Bolen, William H., *Advertising*, Wiley, New York, 1984.

Corke, Alison, *Advertising and public relations*, Pan, London, 1986.

Crompton, Alastair, *The craft of copywriting*, Business Books, Communica Europa, 1979.

Douglas, Torin, *The complete guide to advertising*, Macmillan, London, 1984.

Dunn, S. Watson, *Advertising: Its role in modern marketing*, Dryden Press, Hinsdale, Illinois, 1974.

Dyer, Gillian, *Advertising as communication*, Methuen, London, 1982.

Fowles, Kenneth A., *Understanding advertising*, University of New South Wales Press, Kensington, 1975.

Hewat, Tim (ed.), *Advertising in Australia—The force that feeds the marketplace*, Ure Smith, Sydney, 1975.

Lodish, Leonard M., *The advertising and promotion challenge: Vaguely right or precisely wrong*, Oxford University Press, New York, 1986.

Mason, Jim, *Advertising without tears*, McCulloch Publishing, Carlton, Victoria, 1990.

Quinn, Pat, *The secrets of successful copywriting*, Heinemann, London, 1986.

Wearne, Neil, *The truth about advertising: Effective methods of communicating without waste or indulgence*, Information Australia, Melbourne, 1985.

The media

Armstrong, Mark, Blakeney, Michael and Watterson, Ray, *Media law in Australia*, Oxford University Press, Melbourne, 1990.

Tulloch, John and Turner, Graeme (eds.), *Australian television: Programs, pleasures and politics*, Allen and Unwin, Sydney, 1989.

Windschuttle, Keith, *The media: A new analysis of the press, television, radio and advertising in Australia*, Penguin, Ringwood, 1984.

Journalism

Avieson, John, *Applied journalism in Australia*, Deakin University, Geelong, Victoria, 1989.

Boyd, Andrew, *Broadcast journalism*, Heinemann Professional, London, 1988.

Clements, Ian, *Experience of radio*, Deakin University, Geelong, 1983.

Demers, David, *Precision journalism: A practical guide*, Sage Publications, Beverley Hills, 1987.

Grantano, Len, *Newspaper feature writing*, Deakin University Press, Geelong, 1991.

Hall, Mark, *Broadcast journalism: An introduction to news writing*, Hastings House, New York, 1971.

Hemingway, Ernest, *Dateline: The complete Toronto Star dispatches 1920–1924*, Scribners, New York, 1985.

Henningham, John (ed.), *Issues in Australian journalism*, Longman Cheshire, Melbourne, 1990.

Hosley, David H., *Hard news: Women in broadcast journalism*, Greenwood Press, New York, 1987.

Hough, George A. 3rd, *News writing*, 4th edn, Houghton Mifflin, Boston, 1988.

Jervis, Bob, *News sense* and *More news sense*, Advertiser Newspapers, Adelaide, 1985.

Mayer, Henry (ed.), *Media information Australia*, Media Research Exchange, Sydney, 1976 (periodical).

Mencher, Melvin, *Basic news writing*, WCB (William C. Brown), Dubuque, Iowa, 1989.

Usher, Rod (text), *Their best shots: 21 years of the Nikon awards*, Macmillan, South Melbourne, 1990.

Walker, Sally, *The law of journalism in Australia*, Law Book Co., Sydney, 1989.

Public relations

Hendrix, Jerry A., *Public relations cases*, Wadsworth Publishing Co., California, 1988.

Jefkins, Frank, *Public relations techniques*, Heinemann Professional, London, 1988.

Moore, H. Frazier, *Public relations: Principles, cases and problems*, R. D. Irwin, Homewood, Illinois, 1981.

Tymson, Candy, *How to do public relations*, Millenium, Newtown, NSW, 1988.

Tymson, Candy, and Sherman, Bill, *The Australian public relations manual*, Millenium, Newtown, NSW, 1987 (revised and updated 1990).

Song writing

Australian sound and recording yearbook, 420 Elizabeth St, Surry Hills, NSW 2010.

Australian music industry directory, 3 Ross St, Chippendale, NSW 2008.

Gershwin, Ira, *Lyrics on several occasions*, Elm Tree Books, Hamish Hamilton, London, 1959.

Jones, LeRoi, *Blues people—The Negro experience in White America and the music that developed from it*, William Morrow and Company Paperback Editions, New York, 1963.

Radic, Therese, *Songs of Australian working life*, Greenhouse, Melbourne, 1989.

Ray, Glenn and Leary, David, *Successful songwriting and marketing*, A Greater Songs Publication, Brisbane, 1989.

Rolling stone interviews, The 1980s, various, by the editors of *Rolling stone*, St Martin's Press/Rolling Stone Press, New York, 1989.

Shepherd, John, *Tin pan alley*, Routledge and Kegan Paul, London, 1982.

Song placement guide, PO Box 189, Pacific Palisades, California 90272–0189, USA.

Audio-visual resources

Australian Broadcasting Corporation, 'The practicalities of writing', 1990, from 'Practicalities' (presenter Amanda Armstrong), ABC Radio National Audiotapes, PO Box 4444, Crow's Nest, NSW 2065.

Australian Broadcasting Corporation, 'Making the news' (videotape).

Australian Film, Television and Radio School videos:

    Writing for film, 52 mins, David Williamson

    Writing for comedy, 54 mins, Sue Ingleton

Writing for television, 48 mins, Carl Sauter
Writing for radio, 44 mins, Alan Plater
(Available from Distribution Unit, AFTRS, PO Box 126, North Ryde, NSW 2113.)

Tipping, Richard Kelly (Director), 'Roland Robinson: The land as voice', (video), Artwrite Pictures, Darlinghurst, 1987.

——, 'Randolph Stow: A country of islands', Artwrite Pictures, Darlinghurst, 1987.

——, 'David Malouf: An imaginary life', Artwrite Pictures, with assistance of the Australia Council, Darlinghurst, 1987.

——, 'Les Murray: The vernacular republic', AFI Distributors, 1984.

Wilcox, Christina (Director) and Yowie Films, 'The nights belong to the novelist' (A Study of Elizabeth Jolley, novelist), 48 mins.

Women's Film Fund, the Creative Development Branch of the Australian Film Commission, the Australian Literature Board and Archival Film Program of the Australian Council, 'Rapunzel in Suburbia' (a film directed by Patricia L'Huede, being a study of Dorothy Hewett, playwright, poet and novelist), 1984.

Index